THE CIVILIZATION OF THE AMERICAN INDIAN SERIES

(Complete list on pages 311–13)

PUEBLO GODS

AND MYTHS

By HAMILTON A. TYLER

UNIVERSITY OF OKLAHOMA PRESS *Norman*

Library of Congress Catalog Card Number: 64–11317

Copyright 1964 by the University of Oklahoma Press, Publishing Division of the University. Composed and printed at Norman, Oklahoma, U.S.A., by the University of Oklahoma Press. First edition.

For Mary and Brenda
who shared experiences and waited patiently
for these explanations

THE PUEBLO WORLD

Ahul, a Sun kachina

IN THIS BOOK I have aimed to present a composite picture of all the Pueblo gods and many lesser supernaturals. Yet there is no pan-Pueblo pantheon. To that difficulty one must add the fact that myths relating to these gods are as variable as they are viable, even among a single generation of tellers within one town. Any attempt to bring the available material into focus leads inevitably to syncretism—the reconciliation of contradictory beliefs—and the view I present will be to some extent distorted through selection. As a counterbalance I have used the Pueblo's own words as often as possible, and whenever the material was available I have traced changing attitudes toward deities.

Since comparisons are often useful in orienting the reader, I have made frequent reference to Greek religion in the hope that it is well known to a large number of people to whom Pueblo religion is a closed book. I have not sought comparisons at every turn, which could be done, but have rather taken only those which come readily to mind; there is no thesis involved in the process.

Two other attitudes drawn from Greek culture are important in the shape of this book. In Greek drama there was a place above the stage where the gods appeared and spoke directly to the audience. Whenever their words were available I have used this device and let the gods speak for themselves. The Greeks also had a word, *theologos*, which has come down to us in a modified form. To them it did imply knowledge and study, but it was also applied in a general way to "one who discourses of the gods." I would accept that epithet as the best description of my role.

For any reader, and particularly for those who have been raised in a Pueblo culture, I offer a consolation which may quiet objections to some of the particular views offered. Classic mythologies and religions come to us not fresh, but sifted through writers of various ages and intents, while the Pueblo gods and their stories come to the public almost new. At the very least, the following chapters offer to every reader the chance to become his own Ovid and to rewrite the themes of the gods in his own poetry.

Since *Pueblo Gods and Myths* is my theme on the subject, I will tell how it came into being. I am not an anthropologist by training; whether that is a fact to be rued or a handicap which may be used to some advantage I cannot tell. By way of apology, I hope that the fresh view, even the sudden view, and more empathy than would be allowed in the science, may in another way compensate for variations in standard techniques.

Some years ago chance brought my family to New Mexico. Our knowledge of Indians was only slightly beyond that which popular culture provides. We were led afield by an interest in topography, plant life, and whatever else was once included under the heading of "natural history." Landscape, which includes the human element in a study of vegetation and contour, soon arrested us. There were ruins everywhere. The buildings, even in desolation, had a simplicity and grace which both challenged the immediate countryside and at the same time were a part of it. There was harmony. Since I had been engaged in landscaping, I was keenly aware of the qualities involved in integrating vegetation, structure, and site. The role of people had been of less interest; in our culture they come and go— they rent, buy, and sell, but in any event they move. One reason they do move so often is that they have had little part in the actual construction of their dwellings and surroundings.

Pueblo ruins modified that view with a personal appeal. The construction is so simple one feels that with the help of friends, relatives, and even children, a similar work of beauty might be accomplished. The buildings are composed of adobe or sandstone blocks, of a size which anyone could grasp easily in either hand, and a mortar of the dun earth to bind the blocks together. Such complete simplicity is not an ideal in itself, but it does draw one powerfully. The human element is immediate and one can grasp that too, in a way which cannot be duplicated in response to the works of artist-engineers in our own culture, even when the art is good.

When looking at these vacated monuments of collective endeavor, a second thought occurs. Pueblo Bonito's great structure is not a desolated temple, nor the tomb of a dead king; it was a safe dwelling place for the whole population of a fair sized town. Pueblo religion, then, must have been expressed not in material construction, but in mental constructs which would be available to all who wished to live within them. The ancients were gone, but their descendants were still very much alive. We determined to find out how mankind joined in the integration of landscape, structure, and human life.

Some of the Pueblo villages appeared quite prosperous, others very poor, but even there the Indians seemed to have achieved a kind of elegant frugality which is not really the same thing as poverty. To the outsider this elegance is most notable in the ritual dances. One cold, bright winter day my family and I attended a dance at Santo Domingo. It was a weekday, out of tourist season, and we were the only spectators. A few old faces peered from windows; all others, down to very small children, were participants.

We sat for several hours, absorbing drumbeats, listening to the shuffle of moccasined feet, smelling the odor of piñon and juniper smoke, and watching the monotonous dancing of scores of people. In such a setting reflection is inevitable, even though the first thoughts are commonplace. An infant begins to lose part of its costume and a clown deftly puts things right without disturbing that line of dancers. How is it possible that these people are still here? What do they mean by this dancing?

A more insistent thought formed and followed through changes of lines and kiva groups. What we are seeing is not a performance, since no one else is here and it would go on without us, as similar dances doubtless have gone on for centuries. The rite must have, then, interior meanings for the performers which are sufficient and strong enough to keep this complexity of ritual alive within a few miles of the centers of a vastly different culture.

I asked myself, "Why do the Pueblos still dance? For whom do they dance? What do they mean by their dancing?" I asked friends the same questions.

"For rain," they said.

The first books I read agreed and added material on times and places. Rain is not a wrong answer, perhaps, but it is a very limited one. My first premise was that people do not worship rain, they invoke it. If no human audience is required, there must be supernatural powers to whom the dancing is addressed, and these divinities were unknown to me.

I began to study more learned books and found to my surprise that most students were not greatly interested in the gods. The most comprehensive of Pueblo scholars noticed, in the middle of one paper, that she had neglected the pantheon altogether, because: "In a religion as highly ritualized as is Pueblo religion, the Spirits tend to become negligible, for the observer, if not for the believer." In such a case I want to leave the ranks of the observers and join those of the believers, at least until I comprehend what they mean.

The invisibility of deities is not an answer; they are not negligible merely because we cannot see them, but only because we are blind. I wanted to see. When one cannot find the book he needs, the next best alternative is to write it himself.

Who are the Pueblos? I assume that the Pueblo Indians are known to most people, by name at least, but a few facts may be of use to place them solidly on their ground. The Pueblos and their ancestors are closely bound to the Plateau region of the southwestern part of the United States. That area contains about 130,000 square miles, but much of it, which is now in the state of Utah, was not of great importance to the Pueblos or their antecedents, although there are Basketmaker burials as far to the northwest as Baker, Nevada. In southwestern Colorado the famous ruins in Mesa Verde are a most important link with the past, but the Pueblo present is confined to New Mexico and Arizona. The Plateau is high country, with an average elevation of about 6,500 feet. At the present time the valley of the Río Grande forms the eastern edge of Pueblo country and the Acoma reservation marks its southern extent, although related cul-

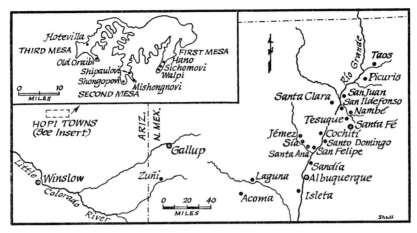

The Pueblo Territory

tures once spread somewhat east and considerably south of the area presently occupied.

The present western limit of the Pueblo world is in the poorly defined Hopi reservation, northeast of Flagstaff, in Navaho County, Arizona. At no time was the population dense in any of the area. There were small towns and clusters of even smaller villages. The name "Pueblo" was used by the Spanish to designate all of the Indians who lived in similar permanent towns. While we still follow that classification there are differing groups of Pueblos, which I shall call tribes. They speak widely differing languages and, as we shall see, worshiped distinct gods. In economy and ceremony the tribes were quite similar to one another.

In the year 1540 a warrior named Castañeda accompanied Coronado in his fruitless quest and later wrote down his opinion of Zuñi religion:

> There are no regular Caciques as in New Spain. Neither are there any councils of old men. They have priests who preach; these are aged men who ascend to the highest terrace of the village and deliver a sermon at sunrise. The people sit around and listen in profound silence. These old men give them advice in regard to their manner of living, which they think it their duty to observe; for there is no drunkenness among them, no unnatural vice; they do not eat human flesh; there are no thieves; on the contrary, they are very laborious.

At that time the Spaniards defeated the Zuñis, but more than four centuries have since passed and the miniscule republic is still intact. Another adventurer in the same sally added a note on what the Zuñis worshiped.

> They perform rites and sacrifices to certain idols; but what they most worship is water, to which they offer painted sticks and plumes, or bunches of yellow flowers; and this they do commonly at springs. They also offer turquoises, which are, however, poor in quality.[1]

The orderly culture described by Castañeda was but one branch of the Pueblos. Taken together, Pueblo culture has a rather specific date of origin, which is placed in the year A.D. 800. I find that kind of dating highly suspect, but it is handy enough. Behind the Puebloan were a number of earlier cultures. An agricultural society whose members raised corn in the Mogollon area has been given a date somewhere around 2000 B.C.[2] Whatever the date of its origin, the Puebloan, or Anasazi, culture advanced swiftly and reached at least one kind of climax between A.D. 1100 and A.D. 1300.

During this period the monumental towns of Mesa Verde, the unfortunately named "Aztec" in northern New Mexico, and the complex of towns in Chaco Canyon flourished. Domestic architecture reached a peak; the great kivas, or underground ceremonial chambers, far surpass anything of the present, and pottery reached a level seldom duplicated since. It should be noted that the still existing towns of Keres Acoma and Hopi Old Oraibi were founded in that age.

Very little is known about the religious life of those times. Surviving artifacts of ceremonial import do not seem to differ greatly from those in use today. By its nature, *Pueblo Gods and Myths* is based upon evidence from the historical period, and even there early reports are thin. Consequently, almost all of the book is based upon evidence gathered within the last one hundred years. Change, at least

---

[1] A. F. Bandelier, "An Outline of the Documentary History of the Zuñi Tribe," *Journal of American Ethnology and Archaeology*, Vol. III (1892), 46–47.

[2] L. W. Simmons, ed., "Southwest Issue," *American Anthropologist*, Vol. LVI, No. 4, Pt. 1 (1954). Beans were added to corn and squash, 1000 B.C.

until recently, was not rapid and much information about the gods can be projected backwards in time. Another loss is most lamentable; for several tribes there is not sufficient comparative material available to make a study of their gods. In consequence, this book is limited to a consideration of the views of Hopis, Zuñis, and Keres. The loss is acute, since, pantheon-wise, Pueblo religion seems to be a constellation of separate approaches to the supernatural world, rather than a single one.

At the time of Coronado's *entrada*, Castañeda estimated the Pueblo population at twenty thousand souls. Bandelier, who didn't like the man, thought this number was much too high, but after arranging all the population figures across the centuries, I think it not a bad guess. The U.S. Census of 1948 lists the Pueblo population as nineteen thousand. They are not, of course, all of the same tribes, nor do they all live in the same places. In the four intervening centuries extinction, starvation, pestilence, war, revolt, and exile have joined to make any correspondence between the figures nearly meaningless.

Nevertheless, the general drift of population statistics seems clear. In remote times there were large numbers of small groups, possibly clans, who were widely distributed and whose towns were often isolated. Sometimes these groups united to form larger units. Occasionally these were cities of a thousand or more people. These cities do not seem to be the result of a trend. Pueblo Bonito was such a place in the classic period; Pecos, now gone, and Sía, nearly gone, were cities in historic times. Today Acoma, Laguna, Santo Domingo, and Zuñi have populations over one thousand. Even there and under present circumstances, they tend to split up once more, either into summer farming villages, or into religiously based units.

Cliff Palace in Mesa Verde was a town of about four hundred, which was perhaps an optimum population for Pueblo society. Near by were other smaller villages, who doubtless joined in ceremony, friendship, and trade. A similar pattern exists today, for example on the Second Mesa at Hopi. Three pueblos exist there in proximity, but with elbow room. One had a population (1932) of 266, another of 123, and the third of 307. My guess is that such an arrangement was a basic pattern, close enough for defense and spread out enough to utilize farming possibilities and allay hostilities which grow in an isolated group.

In their *entrada* the Spanish carried a double-edged sword into New Mexico. On the one side it presented the Four Horsemen of the Apocalypse to the Pueblo Indians. On the other side it presented new crops, new methods of farming, and above all, domestic live-stock. The positive force of these innovations was not immediate. Notably Pueblos do not ride horses. Those who took to sheep over-grazed their land, and cattle are not a Pueblo road, but I do think that these Indians must admire a burro, when it carries his load.

At some time before the arrival of the Spaniard, other enemies entered the Pueblo world. It would be inexact to say that they lived in peace before, but beginning at some time before the historical period the Pueblo world was entered and surrounded by tribes most famously known as Navaho-Apaches, Utes, and Comanches. Accommodation is the Pueblo's great skill. Among the variety of enemies the Pueblos were forced to choose a number of strange alliances and techniques which were to turn some Pueblo groups against others.

By the mid-seventeenth century Comanches, or similar people, had forced the abandonment of Piro and Tompiro pueblos east and south of the Manzano Mountains. As a culture they are lost to us. In the Pueblo Revolt of 1680 the Pueblos, stung by suppression of their religious and cultural life—possibly also by the use of Indians as slaves in Spanish mines, and certainly in households—revolted and drove the Spaniards entirely out of New Mexico for a long decade.

The rebellion was a considerable feat of organization on the Pueblo side, but only by their own non-military standards. As a warlike operation it was just the reverse of that first encounter between the two races at Zuñi, except that this time it was the Spaniard who was disorganized and uncomprehending in the face of sudden and seem-ingly unwarranted attack. I quite agree with L. C. Powell in his suggestion that a monument be erected to Popé, the leader of the revolt. From what he could have known a much greater Pueblo vic-tory must have seemed within reach. Perhaps he did win one point which was worth winning. I note that many of the Pueblo land grants from the king of Spain, which are still valid under our law, are dated 1689.

On the other hand, the victory was ephemeral and costly, culminating in the extinction of the Piros, as a cultural group, the abandonment of many towns and mass migrations from others, as well as the usual cleavages and devastations of war. Prior to this war a document found by F. V. Scholes,[3] dated 1664, listed the Pueblo population at slightly above 20,000. If the list is limited to the three tribes considered in this book, his total comes to 6,766: 1,200 Zuñis, 2,966 Hopis, and 2,600 Keres (of whom 800 were at Sía).

During the eighteenth century the effects of the rebellion were reinforced by a series of famines and pestilences which kept the entire Pueblo population hovering around 10,000 persons, and these had no very certain future. Almost every Pueblo group has stood on the rim of extinction at one time or another, and not all of them have stepped back. While the totals for the Pueblo population in the seventeenth century and today are similar, the Hopis, Zuñis, and Keres have about doubled their share of Pueblo numbers, since they are now 13,000 strong.

The population figures indicate that at no time were there more than a few hundred adults in any pueblo. It is startling to think that such small groups could face the universe nearly alone, could cope with a most unpromising environment and call it to a draw on terms of physical existence, and still find the energy and ability to challenge and meet so many of the religious or philosophical questions which trouble mankind. In the final chapter I hope to outline some of the problems common to Pueblo and contemporary thought.

The successes and failures of the Pueblos have often been related to their agriculture. In prehistoric times food was, of course, an absolute; on this fact they built an agrarian religion. Today live-

---

[3] F. V. Scholes, "Documents for the History of New Mexican Missions of the Seventeenth Century," *New Mexico Historical Review*, Vol. IV, No. 1 (1929), 46–50. For contemporary population statistics of New Mexico pueblos, see S. D. Aberle, *The Pueblo Indians of New Mexico, Their Land, Economy and Civil Organization*. For population figures on the Hopis of Arizona, see Stanley A. Stubbs, *Bird's-Eye View of the Pueblos*.

stock has in some cases altered the picture, but agriculture rather than grazing is still the base. Let us look at a few more bald figures. Zuñi has 2,833 acres of agricultural land to support a population of 2,671. The Western Keres' pueblos of Acoma and Laguna have 2,979 agricultural acres for 4,341 inhabitants. These three pueblos also have extensive grazing land.

The Eastern Keres have very poor grazing, but good agricultural land. The pueblo of Santa Ana has 585 acres of good irrigated soil —enough to make three or four farms by midwestern standards— but there are 273 people who must live for the most part off that land. The Hopis are not as well off as the other two tribes. They depend upon rain, seepage, or flood water to irrigate their crops. Something of the limitations imposed on plant growth by short seasons and tenuous rainfall can be seen in the peach "orchards." At Zuñi these grow about four feet tall and in clusters that remind one of abandoned family orchards. On the Hopi mesas in winter they barely protrude above the swirling sand, and they look like something the Japanese might have grown in pots for ornament. The fruit they bear is more a sign of man's triumphant struggle with nature than something one would wish to eat—if there were a choice.

The Pueblos do have recourse to outside jobs and to arts and crafts for income. Except for a few individuals, such income merely provides coffee-money. For the majority, who survive by working a small plot of land, there will never be enough of anything to make the friendship of the gods unnecessary. But if the Pueblos' economy is spare, their ceremonial life is rich. In the following pages I hope to show something of this richness in so far as it applies to their gods.

Over the past half-century or more, the names of Pueblo gods have appeared in a variety of transliterations. Some of these versions are simple Anglicizations, while others are based on differing phonetic systems. The latter have a place in linguistic studies, but create an unnecessary problem for the general reader. For example, if you know ahead of time that capital "C" indicates an "sh" sound, all is well. If not, you fall into the error of some writers who have come to believe that the Zuñi Shalako ceremony is spelled and pronounced Calako.

I have rather arbitrarily selected the forms of the names that I have preferred for one reason or another, and the reader will not always find the same spellings in other works. Since the spelling of the name of the Hopi god Masau'u is subject to an impossible number of transliterations, I have taken the liberty of changing these, even when they occur in quotations. The general reader should be aided by this change, and the student is warned to check the texts before he uses them.

I use the word "tribe" often in the very loose sense of "social group," much as Kroeber in *Zuñi Kin and Clan* speaks of a Zuñi "tribal ceremony." The stricter meaning of the word tribe, that of a group based upon real or supposed kinship, certainly does not apply. The most meaningful grouping of Pueblo subdivisions is that based upon linguistic classification. There are no political groupings, since each town is a completely independent entity.

Fortunately, Pueblo linguistic units parallel cultural groupings. That is to say, for example, the seven Keresan towns share a common language and have a very similar, though not identical, religion.

The linguistic groups which concern us are three in number. (These as well as others are correlated with their respective towns at the end of this volume.) Zuñian is a language apparently unrelated to any family of languages and is spoken today only in the single town of Zuñi. Keresan may also be an unaffiliated language, as Boas thought, or it may belong to the Hokan-Siouan group. There are seven Keresan towns: Acoma and Laguna lie between the Río Grande and Zuñi; Santa Ana and Sía (also commonly spelled Zía) are on the Jémez River; San Felipe, Santo Domingo, and Cochití are on the Río Grande. The third linguistic group which concerns us, Hopi, is a Shoshonean language in the Uto-Aztecan stock. The Hopis are represented by seven historical towns distributed on three Mesas, and also by a number of modern offshoots. The names of the basic towns will be found on the map in this volume.

Hamilton A. Tyler

HEALDSBURG, CALIFORNIA
JANUARY 23, 1964

CONTENTS

The Pueblo World   ix

I. The God Masau'u, or Skeleton Man   3

II. The Dead   49

III. The Creators and Their Creations   81
    Sho'tokunungwa   98
    The Emergence   103
    The Flood   108
    The Migrations   115

IV. Earth Goddess   116

V. Germinator   125

VI. The Divine Sun   136
    Paiyatemu and the Corn Maidens   142
    Pautiwa and the Sun Kachinas   148
    The Hopi Sun Kachinas   150
    Winter Solstice Ceremonies   151
      Acoma Winter Solstice   152
      The Hopi Soyal Ceremony   154
      The Zuñi Winter Solstice Ceremony   156
    The Calendar   161
    Battle of the Seasons   165

VII. The Cosmos and the System of the Six Directions   169

VIII. The Godliness of Place   180

IX. Clowns and Gods   194

X. The Little War Gods   209

XI. Snakes and the Horned Water Serpent   221
    The Snake Myth   240
    The Horned Water Serpent   244

XII. The Face of Animism   250
    Freud   273
    Buber   282
    Table for Relating Town Names to
    Tribes and Linguistic Groups   291
    Bibliography   293
    Index   301

Map of the Pueblo Territory   xiii

PUEBLO GODS AND MYTHS

Chapter One

THE GOD MASAU'U,
OR SKELETON MAN

The Masau'u kachina, who does not really
represent the god, but is associated with him.

DEATH, to the Western mind, is so definitively an ending that the
reader may be surprised to find a god of death placed squarely at the
beginning of this book, where he will cast a certain shadow across an
otherwise cheerful prospect. The answer is that to the Pueblo Indians
the antithesis between life and death, and in particular the distinction
between this world and the other world, does not have the same force
that it has for us. The very nature of the god Masau'u will explain
some of the differences in attitude, for he is not only the god of
death, but is as well a god of life in many of its essentials. Western
man is a nomad, in thought at least, if not in fact. We think of our
past as a series of migrations and intellectual pilgrimages across other
continents, and as we think backward in time the places become less
certain and the issues more nebulous. For a moment we are arrested
here, or there, or wherever, but at death we move on again, and although the destination is not certain it is certainly far away, at least as
far as the sky and perhaps farther than that.

Not so the Pueblos; the Hopis, to whom this god belongs, emerged
from the ground very near to the villages in which they now live.
During his life the Pueblo is surrounded by a number of spirits who
may be confined within the visible seats of the gods of the four horizon
directions of a Zenith centered above; and the town itself rests above
a Nadir which contains below the roots of life. After death the
Pueblo returns to the underworld through an entrance within walking distance from his own village. That local underworld is not
only the place from which the race emerged and the place to which
its individuals return, but it is as well the storehouse of all life-
giving crops which are in season drawn up to nourish the living.

In a cosmos so compact, where life and death are intermingled
and cyclical, there is no need to separate beginnings from endings.

3

One may enter the Pueblo world at any point, and soon grasp the concepts and constructs which in varied elaboration delineate the Pueblo cosmos and the gods of mixed descent who govern there.

As we shall later see, there are gods who live on the distant ranges of the mind. Before meeting them, we face an immediate god whom some call Skeleton Man, the god of the Hopi underworld and of the surface of the earth, whose name has been variously transcribed by different writers as Masau'u, Masau, or Massua. In early accounts Skeleton Man was an anthropomorphic god, though in size he was said to be somewhat larger than mortal man. Despite his spectral nature as the god of death, Masau'u is, nevertheless, a very humane and reachable being, a quality which has made him an attractive gathering point for attributes perhaps not originally his own. Primitively he may have been a god of death and fire, a fearsome personification, something like our view of a Hades or Satan, who was kept at bay by the magic of fire rituals, but any such thought will have to be modified or abandoned as soon as we meet him.

To begin with we shall see him on his home fields as the original owner of all the good things of the earth, limited though they may be in Hopi land. In the dark he tends a fire by which he warms himself; and the same fire, which seems to be something of a Sun symbol, causes his crops to grow with magic speed. Very soon we shall hear of him as a general fertility god, a sort of male Demeter, then as a god of boundaries, of property, and of travelers. Masau'u is also a trickster figure. After the turn of our century he emerges as something of a tribal war god for the Traditionalists, and in our own day he is firmly set as an omniscient and omnipresent supreme god.

Since it is difficult to believe that Masau'u was always so complex, I will try to indicate both the historical and psychological links which account for the combination of such seemingly disparate qualities in one deity. The immediate purpose, however, is not to begin with speculation but to recount in Hopi words where they are available, their vision of this god, how he helped them, and in what manner he is worshiped.

In the view of the Pueblo Indians, mankind has existed from near the beginning of time, but formerly underground, blindly, trampling upon one another's toes. "At this time no sun existed and it was dark everywhere," not only in the underworld, apparently, but in the upper world as well. The darkness was so universal that the narrators are uncertain, some starting their story in the night above, and others in the blackness below. For those who use the latter sequence the Hopis were still underground, the seeds of their race, awaiting the proper season or divine gesture to bring them crowding through the crust of the earth into this upper world. At this time they heard someone walking around over their heads, up there. The Pueblo emergence was not only marked by great effort, but was as well a scene of wild confusion.

"It was still dark, and as there was no sunshine it was also cold, and the people began to look for fire and for wood, but as it was so dark, they could find very little wood. They thus lived there a while without fire, but all at once they saw a light in the distance and the chief said: 'Someone go there and see about it . . . .' So someone went in search of the light, but before he reached it he became tired and returned. Another was sent out and he got there. He found a field in which corn, watermelons, beans, and such crops were planted. All around this field a fire was burning, which was kept up by wood, and by which the ground was kept warm so that the plants could grow."[1]

The god they found there was Masau'u, but in this account from the Second Mesa town of Shipaulovi his appearance is unusual, in that he is not the specter of death most often seen. He is rather in the guise of the handsome man of many folk tales. As a god he can assume this appearance at will.

"The messenger found a very handsome man there. He had four strands of turquoise around his neck and very large turquoise ear pendants. In his face he had two black lines running from the upper part of his nose to his cheeks, and made with specular iron. By his side was standing his friend (a mask) which looked very ugly."[2] The ugly mask is Masau'u's normal visage which he has here set aside.

What the mask and the being look like we learn from another

[1] H. R. Voth, *The Traditions of the Hopi*, 12.   [2] *Ibid.*, 12.

5

narrator, who does not choose to soften his story by presenting the god as essentially a handsome and bejeweled figure. In addition to the fire, the Hopis had also seen the footprints of a being larger than living man, and were naturally frightened at the sight. The chief decided that the way to meet the unknown creature would be a ceremonious approach, just such as is used today. Accordingly they held a smoke and made prayer feathers for the unknown being. The chief then called for volunteers to undertake the dreadful duty of carrying the offerings; four brave men accepted.

"Going over with the tray of prayer offerings they saw at first in the distance only a faint light and they were very much afraid. Coming closer, they could see someone sitting by the fire and facing away from them and they could only see the back of his head. This head was of rather a great size, like the biggest squash, and there was no hair on it. As they came closer they were more and more frightened, but at last they got to him. He would not turn his face toward the fire, so they called to him and asked him who he was, but he would not answer." (Four is both a ceremonial and a magical number for the Pueblos; if one is asked a question four times he is compelled to answer.) "Then he answered and said he was surprised to see that they had come to his fire because no one had ever gotten so near to him before.

"When he said this he turned around toward the light and his face was all bloody and he had a mask on; his head was big and his mask was terrible looking. These four men were very much frightened and all felt something creeping back of their heads."[3]

Since we have heard these two differing accounts of his physical features we may now turn to a third which gives another aspect of Masau'u's relationship with the Hopis. As this story is told the people had not come up yet, but were living underground in considerable strife. Wishing to escape from their confinement they had sent emissaries into the black void above, but these explorers found no one there. As a last resort the Hopis asked a bird named Motsni, possibly a shrike, to help them.

"So we have been thinking of leaving here, but these have not

[3] E. Nequatewa, *Truth of a Hopi and Other Clan Stories of Shungopovi*, 25.

6

found anybody there, so you go up too, and you find out for us, and if you find someone there who is kind and gentle and has a good heart, why you tell us and we shall go up there."

Motsni flew out of Shipapu, the point of emergence from the underworld, and past the mesa where the town of Old Oraibi now stands.

"There somebody was sitting, leaning his head forward, and as the Motsni came nearer he moved it to the side a little. Finally he said: 'Sit down, you that are going around here, sit down. Certainly you are going around here for some reason. Nobody has seen me here yet.' 'Yes,' the Motsni said." He then proceeded to tell the unknown figure that he had been sent by the Hopis to see if there were someone in the upper world who would welcome them there.

" 'Now you say, you tell me if you are willing, and I shall tell them so, and we will come up here.' " The seated being whom the Motsni had found was of course Masau'u, but unlike the previous accounts in which he was found living among beans, melons, and squash that grew magically in a single day, which is the picture of a limited Arcadia, the deity in this version lives in and promises the Hopis only the actualities of their present-day life in Arizona.

"Masau'u said, 'Now this is the way I am living here. I am living here in poverty. I have not anything; this is the way I am living here. Now if you are willing to live here that way too, with me and share this life, why come, you are welcome.' " The bird returned to the underworld and repeated the message of the god whose meager offering was sustenance for a time, and then death.

" 'What have you found out?' the Hopis asked the bird. 'Yes,' he said, 'I was up there and I have found him away off. But it is with you now; he also lives there poorly, he has not much, he is destitute. But if you are satisfied with his manner of living, why you are welcome to come up there.' 'All right' they said, and were happy. 'So that is the way he is saying, so he is kind; we are welcome, and we are going.' "[4]

While the three accounts just given vary in many details, they are all a part of the same cycle of stories in which the focus is upon the

[4] Voth, *The Traditions of the Hopi*, 18.

Hopis' venture into the unknown and their discovery of the benevolent, if ugly visaged, god. There is another group of stories in which the god actively intervenes in bringing the people up. The time was early in the mythologic age, when only the gods roamed the earth, which had just stopped shaking from internal commotion. These gods tried to avoid each other, but when they met there was a trial of strength and the victor took the land, until he was in turn overthrown. After a time Muingwu, one of the gods of the earth of whom we shall hear more in the fifth chapter, heard a mysterious rumbling in the earth and was disturbed enough to call all the gods together.

"Masau'u was pleased when he heard this and he determined to rescue from the wrath of the other gods all of those confined people who would live in his land and furnish him with occasional nourishment. In those days the gods had the power of discerning the thoughts of others. Thus it became known to them that Masau'u was about to search for the noises. He had said in council that these cries came from people, not beasts, and he wished to befriend them, but the other gods wished to kill them. The gods knew Masau'u to be in earnest and thought if he discovered and befriended the strange people, he would grow more powerful than any of them and would rule the whole land and leave no place for them."[5]

Thus far Masau'u has proven himself to be a most loyal friend to mankind, or at least to the Hopis. It is said that at the time of the emergence the god stood astride the orifice and as each Hopi made his appearance linked his arm in that of the Indian, helping him to the surface and greeting him with words of welcome. Despite this benign gesture Masau'u is, as the name Skeleton Man indicates, the god of death; and there is plenty of evidence that the god, as apart from his ceremonial impersonators, is regarded with considerable terror. To meet him face to face is a warning of death, and the sight of his flaming torch in the distance at night is almost equally dangerous.

The twin antithetic aspects of the god, that of inspiring fear and

[5] A. M. Stephen, "Hopi Tales," *Journal of American Folk-Lore*, Vol. XLII, No. 163 (1929), 52.

yet of being friendly to mankind, are combined in a recollection by Don Talayesva of Old Oraibi. As the Sun Chief, which is to say priest, he had the duty of carrying offerings to the shrine of Masau'u on a moonless night. His uncle of the Fire clan should have gone, but he was too feeble to undertake the task. At 2:30 A.M. Talayesva took a plaque which held piki-bread, raw rabbit, mountain tobacco, and cornmeal. On reaching the shrine he sprinkled the meal and prayed, "Great Masau'u, I have been sent over here to ask your help in our lives. Give us moisture and protect us; let the people increase, live to old age, and die without suffering." As he said his prayer and placed the offering a great breath of air arose from the shrine.

On his way back up the mesa in darkness he heard footsteps and thinking it was another messenger he threw a rock. Silence followed the sound of the falling rock. Scarcely had he realized his mistake than he saw to the southeast what he took to be another moon arising, "but it was a big, red fire, blazing out of the ground about three feet high on the very edge of the mesa point."[6] Recognizing that the event was a test put upon him by Masau'u, he tremblingly walked toward the fire, since courage would put it out. As he approached, the fire diminished and then went out. On the way back to the village he became lost and felt something dragging him back, but once he had reached the warmth of the kiva he remembered that the first man to live in Oraibi had spoken to Masau'u without harm.

A feeling of nearness to the infernal world, and the fright that such close contact with it engenders when one takes offerings and prayers to the god who represents both fertility and the underworld, are not limited to the Pueblos. The Greek traveler Pausanias experienced a similar feeling at a famous shrine in Boeotia. The shrine was dedicated to a local god, Trophonios, who was said to be a son of Demeter-Europa. The shrine, which had been in existence at Lebadeia at least since the time of Herodotus, was said to have been constructed after a prolonged drought. The later purpose was oracular, and a visit to it was undertaken to ask for health and long life.

The important effect gained from a visit to this place was that of

[6] Don Talayesva, *Sun Chief: The Autobiography of a Hopi Indian*, 286–88.

having made contact with an underworld power. Two hermae, representing Hermes as the conductor of dead souls, led the suppliant to an underground chamber of stone, within which a movable stone covered a tiny chamber representing the very underworld, much as the foot-drum plank over the hole in a Pueblo kiva does. The shrine was calculated to frighten; the upper chamber was filled with snakes, and the lower cavern was barely large enough to hold a man. While the experience was said to be terrifying, Pausanias was more impressed with the power of the place. According to his account, "The descender lies with his back on the ground, holding barley-cakes kneaded with honey, thrusts his feet into the hole . . . . After his knees the rest of his body is at once swiftly drawn in, just as the largest and most rapid river will catch a man in its eddy and carry him under."[7]

In both of these accounts the supplication is for long life and for rain, and it is addressed to gods who represent the nether powers. Notably, in each case, there is the feeling of being dragged back, or sucked down. Not all contacts with the underworld involve the same degree of fright or terror. Sometimes the fear gives way to humor, as in any account of a young man passing a graveyard at night. The Hopis are much like everyone else in this respect. They can be truly moved by an encounter with the god of the dead, or a similar confrontation can be a matter for humor and satire, as the two following stories show.

The analogy between Masau'u and the Christian Devil has not escaped the Hopis, whether they were Traditionalists or Baptists, and the fancy was much to their taste besides. Perhaps these stories do not belong properly to religion, but they belong to the god we are studying, and Pueblo gods do not require continuous solemnity on the part of their worshipers. A growing god collects many stories about him and only history decides whether he will be modified thereby, or whether the stories will become winter's tales.

"In the long ago the Hopi Masau'u, like the Pa'han Masau'u, the White Masau'u, had a tail, a long tail that dragged in the sand, and Masau'u used to carry it, held the bight of it in his hand. This tail

[7] Pausanias, *Description of Greece*, ix, 39–40.

was offensive to children, they dreaded it and used to weep and fall into fits of terror at it, so Masau'u cut off the tail, chopped it into little bits and flung them in the sea, for this occurred in the far west, where the great water is . . . . The chopped bits of tail became the fishes that are now in the great water." The speaker then turns suddenly from this fancy to a serious concern about the appearance of the god. "His feet are shaped like a man's, but are about the length of the forearm. He is always black, shining black."[8] In all early accounts there is never any doubt as to Masau'u's visibility, and each narrator has a definite, though often particular, vision of what he looked like.

Another whimsical tale of recent origin concerns an anthropologist of the last century, the famous Dr. Fewkes, who reported to the Bureau of American Ethnology that he had been forced to leave Walpi with nothing to report, because of a smallpox epidemic. The Hopis, who lack many things, but never imagination, have another version. It was mid-winter in the glorious and desolate village of Walpi, which is a precarious and almost invisible aerie, aloft over deserts that to the south pass the horizon, and in this village the learned man was writing up notes on the ceremonies he had seen. Then someone told him he must go away and lock himself up, for Masau'u was about to appear and that part of the ceremony was too sacred for outsiders to see. The doctor did as he was told, locking himself in his house.

"Now suddenly he had a queer feeling, for he felt that there was someone in the room, and he looked up and saw a tall man standing before him, but he could not see his face for the light was not good . . . .

"He said, 'What do you want and how did you get in here?' The man replied, 'I have come to entertain you.' Dr. Fewkes said, 'Go away, I am busy and do not wish to be entertained.'

"And now as he was looking at the man, he suddenly was not there any more. Then a voice said, 'Turn your head a moment,' and when the Doctor looked again the figure stood before him once more, but this time its head was strange and dreadful to see.

"And the doctor said, 'How did you get in?' and the man answered

[8] A. M. Stephen, *Hopi Journal*, I, 150.

11

and said, 'I go where I please, locked doors cannot keep me out! See, I will show you where I entered,' and, as Dr. Fewkes watched, he shrank away and became like a single straw in a Hopi hair whisk and he vanished through the key hole.

"Now Dr. Fewkes was very much frightened and as he was thinking what to do, there was the man back again. So he said once more to him, 'What do you want?' and the figure answered as before and said, 'I have come to entertain you.' So the doctor offered him a cigarette and then a match, but the man laughed and said, 'Keep your match, I do not need it,' and he held the cigarette before his horrible face and blew a stream of fire from his mouth upon it and lit his cigarette. Then Dr. Fewkes was very much afraid indeed, for now he knew who it was.

"Then the being talked to him, and finally the Doctor 'gave up to him' and said he would become a Hopi and be like them and believe in Masau'u, and Masau'u cast his spell on him and they both became like little children and all night long they played around together and Masau'u gave the Doctor no rest.

"And it was not long after that Dr. Fewkes went away but it was not on account of the small pox as you now know."[9]

After having met Masau'u as the benevolent friend of the tribe, as a genial fellow who cuts off his tail to please children and as a being who is a considered satire on Christian pyrotechnics, it comes as a sudden, sharp break to think of him as centrally the god of death. Nevertheless, however humane he may appear at times, he does wear a horrible, bloody mask and is the just god of the dead.

"Masau'u has a two story house . . . Masau'u is death. The graveyard is Masau'u's kiva, Maski. [Maski means shrine, and may be associated with Muski, underground.] The surface we see is the roof of the second story, we will not see the interior until we die. . . . The grave is the entrance to Maski, the dead go to the lower stage or story where the houses are as those we live in. The plan of the house was brought from the underworld and what is called dying is a return

[9] E. Nequatewa, "Dr. Fewkes and Masauwu," *Hopi Customs, Folklore and Ceremonies*, 72–73.

to the early house; men and women follow their usual avocations there."[10]

The conception of the underworld as a partly protruding grave-yard is, of course, very different from the elaborated underworld which will be met in the next chapter, but Masau'u is the god of both these realms. Perhaps the image in the passage just quoted can be clarified by explaining a burial practice sometimes resorted to by many Pueblos. When the towns were large and multistoried, there were often abandoned rooms which were used for the disposing of refuse, particularly of ashes, which accumulated in great quantity. At times these ash-chambers were used for burial purposes and then closed off, so that some of the dead might very well be "living" in the lower rooms of the town. The conception of death as a return to "the early house" is a recognition of the many great ruins which modern Indians acknowledge as a part of the dead Pueblo past, a theme which we will meet again. The somewhat puzzling thought that Masau'u's kiva protrudes to the roof of the second story is again explained by certain ruins which have crumbled.

In 1700, which was just after the failure of the Pueblo Revolt against the Spaniards in New Mexico, the Traditionalist Hopis destroyed one of their own villages on the plain, because it had accepted alien ways. The destruction of Awatobi is of interest here because "legend declares that the men were all in the kivas and were killed by the hostiles; but the women and children were taken to Maski Skeleton House, now indicated by a mound in the plain, and were divided among the participants in the massacre. All those women who refused to go with the captors were killed, but the others, of diverse clans, were distributed among the villages."[11] This ruin, because of the tragic and spectacular events associated with it, became a shrine.

It has already been said that even to catch sight of Masau'u may be a portent of imminent death. Sometimes he works his power from a distance: "He is frightful; he frightens people, and no one dares

---

[10] Stephen, *Hopi Journal*, I, 151.

[11] Jesse W. Fewkes, "The Butterfly in Hopi Myth and Ritual," *American Anthropologist*, Vol. XII, No. 4 (1910), 579.

to disturb him. Merely to see him will frighten you. He will not shoot you, yet you will fall asleep. He emits a horrible stench. Consequently everyone is afraid of him . . . ."[12] (There are specified groups who are exempt from fear of the sight of the god.)

The event most to be feared is the touch of Masau'u. He is spoken of as "the one whose touch destroys." "When his child is sick, the moki [Hopi] prays Masau'u to come and look upon it and pass by without touching it. To come and look upon his cornfield and garden and pass by without touching them."[13] Because his touch causes change the god has, according to the same student, taken on a broader attribute which is the important link between the forces of death and the forces of life. Masau'u has the power of causing all the metamorphoses of nature, a factor which sets him apart from many other Pueblo gods. The creators provide the cosmic setting and thereafter remain aloof; other gods of varying importance play specific parts. Massau'u alone provides the vital elements which keep in motion the Hopi cosmic drama, several scenes of which we will see in other chapters.

Those who may look upon this god without fear are members of the Kwan Society. The members of this One Horn Society have a special set of relationships with the god of the dead and also with the other underworld god, Germinator, who may be called either Muingwu or Alosaka. The members of the society are charged with the awful duty of conducting the spirits of the dead to Maski, and for this duty they gain not a reward, but a penalty when they themselves die. The other dead may leave the underworld in vaporous forms and, becoming cloud-people, pass over their former villages to bring rain, but the Kwan men live forever in the underworld as the servants of the dead and of their special god.

At this point I may anticipate somewhat a future discussion on the similarities between Masau'u and the Greek god Hermes. The latter

[12] W. D. Wallis, "Folk Tales from Shumopovi, Second Mesa," *Journal of American Folk-Lore*, Vol. XLIX, No. 191–92 (1936), 6.

[13] A. M. Stephen, "Hopi Indians of Arizona," *The Masterkey*, Vol. XIV, No. 3 (1939–40), 103.

is often referred to as the Psychopompos, or the guide to dead souls on their journey to the nether world. The same function is served by these Kwan men, who not only serve the god of death, but may also stand in for him as impersonators. Something of their nature is seen in the following account from the town of Old Oraibi on Third Mesa.

"Of the four Tribal Initiation societies, the Kwan stands most apart; and the others are taught to regard it with awe and dread. This is due to its intimate association with Masau'u . . . . Indeed, a Kwan man is very commonly referred to not only as Kwanitaka (Kwan man), but also as one of the Maskwakwantu (Masau'u's Kwan men). Furthermore, on Third Mesa the control of the Kwan division is in the hands of the Masau'u clan, so that normally, the chief of the Kwan is the head of the Masau'u clan. Accordingly, he regards Masau'u as his *Wuya* [i.e., his clan ancient or progenitor] and does not fear to impersonate him or to assume his functions, as the leader of the Kwan society must do throughout the rites. Thus when fire is kindled on the first day of the [initiation] observances, the Kwan chief is present as the personation of Masau'u, the deity who first taught the Hopi the use of fire."[14]

On the fourth night of the Wuwuchim ceremony, which is celebrated not only for initiations, but also for the return of the gods in November, the souls of the dead—or perhaps more literally, the dead—are invited to return to their villages. All the roads to the villages are closed in the ceremonial fashion, by sprinkling cornmeal across them, except of course the road to the Maski. One half of the village is vacated so that the dead may enter there and find a house. Everyone must stay inside and darken the windows, which accounts for the fact that Dr. Fewkes was confined to his room on that night when the god visited him. Not even animals are permitted in the village. These arrangements were considerably disturbed by the construction of a modern highway across some of the mesas. David Monongye, after admitting the benefits, felt that the destructive elements far outweighed the advantages.

[14] M. Titiev, *Old Oraibi, a Study of the Hopi Indians of Third Mesa*, 134–35.

"During one of our sacred ceremonies, the One Horn and Two Horn Societies close all the roads that lead into our villages. They do that so as to clear the spiritual highway which leads from there to the rising sun. This is a road over which they walk to offer their prayers to the Great Spirit . . . . During that special day it must not be broken by someone traveling across it. If it is broken, something unfortunate happens."[15] The One Horns of this account are the Kwans and the Great Spirit is Masau'u, but how the concept of the ceremony became reversed must wait in the telling.

As Parsons describes the lengthy ceremony in 1919, the deserted streets on the fourth night are patrolled by the Kwan and the Horn men who keep up a fearful din, the Kwans with bells and the Horns with hoofs and tortoise-shell rattles. Those here called Horns are of the Two Horn Society, who are related to the other underworld god, Germinator, or Muingwu. The patrols challenge and club at anything they see, except the proper dead. These patrolmen go back and forth through the village in an anti-sunwise circuit; since the dead are the reverse of the living, the performance must be the opposite of normal behavior, which also accounts for the fact that Masau'u impersonators wear their garments and other articles of dress in the reverse of customary order. The ceremony grows towards a climax.

"As the night grows later, the pace waxes swifter until as the Pleiades reach the Zenith both Horns and Agaves [Kwans] are encircling Walpi at a furious run and this they maintain until the Pleiades and Orion are in the place they occupied when the Singers and Wuwuchimtu finished their songs on the previous night at the [kiva] hatch."[16] It is now after midnight, and all go into their kivas, except a few sentinels who continue their rounds of the village until sunrise.

What takes place in the kivas is not known, as no white person is allowed to see this part of the ceremony, but it is known that Masau'u is there. Titiev suggests that he touches the tyros with his club, symbolically killing them as children, so that they may emerge from the initiation as adult members of the tribe. In any case it is evident that

---

[15] G. Yamada, *The Great Resistance, A Hopi Anthology*, 52.

[16] E. C. Parsons, *Pueblo Indian Religion*, 613.

like our Halloween, much of the ceremony is directed at the children, but by no means lightly so. It is assumed that the dead enter the kiva to which they belonged while living, and this is made vivid to the novices in a startling way. Some time earlier four Kwans are delegated to visit the local graveyard, unknown to anyone, of course, "and to strip four recently interred corpses of their burial garments. There the four Kwan members dress in the foul smelling grave-clothes, and soon after, they appear before the startled neophytes in dimly lighted kivas where they are readily mistaken by the terror-stricken novices for the very dead men whose apparel they wear."[17]

Such drastic behavior is necessary because each village needs its dead and needs to know that they are able to find their way back to the homes of the living. This is true because the shades of the dead, which are like cloud-shadows or smoke, can also take on vaporous forms and float back over the village, either for the pleasure of seeing it again, or more importantly, to bring rain for the nourishment of crops which sustain the living. In this way a perfect cycle is maintained, working back and forth between the two worlds, between the living and the dead. So that no one may be lost, and so that the dead will remember, the road must be kept open for them each year in this ceremony. Then they will find room there and they will be fed as well in this early winter rite, so that in summer when summoned by prayer-feathers they will pass over again.

Masau'u's role in this initiation ceremony brings out another of his qualities: he is the god of fire and he is often spoken of as the giver of fire to the Hopis. In the account just given he kindles what is sometimes called the "new-fire" in the Wuwuchim ceremony. He always carries a blazing torch. Fire is not only a symbol of the sun, but it is also the logical and practical alternative to that light, and in this way Masau'u becomes the antithesis of the sun god. The god generally walks only at night, when he lights his way with a fiery cedar bark torch. In all accounts he is proscribed from day, as befits a god of underworld darkness, or the pre-sunlit upper world of blank night, though this is not true of his impersonators. His habits are bat-like, being blind by day, unable to face the sun, and perhaps he

[17] Titiev, *Old Oraibi,* 136.

does not even like to look into the fire, for in the first accounts we have given he warms his back by his blaze, facing the lifeless world beyond his flame-warmed fields.

Perhaps he was not always the god of fire, since in a recent statement by Hermequaftewa, chief of the Bluebird clan at Shongopovi, he is not. "We came to his land only after receiving permission from our Great Spirit, Massau'u. He was living on this land with the Keeper of the Fire, who is the Spider Woman . . . ."[18] I suspect, however, that the arrangement is a late construct designed to preserve a place for Spider Woman and the War Twins in the face of a rapidly developing monotheism.

However that may be, there is no doubt about Masau'u's blindness in daylight, which is preserved in a story concerning the genesis of the god's bloody head. It seems that Masau'u had spent a night of successful hunting, and toward dawn he hid himself and his game in a swale north of Walpi, where he was discovered by a group of hunters out early in search of rabbits. When surprised, he dashed madly in one direction and punctured his head upon a sharp rock. After repeating the same blind error in the other three directions his head became the bloody mask which is now his characteristic visage.[19] This same inability to face the sun is used in folk reference, where one who sleeps after daylight is jokingly referred to as a Masau'u.

The god is not highly elaborated in relation to fire, if we may judge by the ceremonies. His impersonator's specific function in this regard is to use a fire spindle to kindle a blaze in certain ceremonies, but that seemingly minor event is the nexus which links together the two most important sides of Masau'u. Although it may at first seem puzzling and incongruous, the god of death is also a fertility god.

It is difficult to decide whether the aspects of death or of life are uppermost in his nature, but it is notable that when he is impersonated, *memento mori* are less apparent than fertility symbols, and in recent years he has very nearly lost his touch with death altogether. The conjunction between the powers of death and the powers of life is not an uncommon one. Probably the most notable example is that

[18] Yamada, *The Great Resistance*, 52–53.
[19] Voth, *The Traditions of the Hopi*, 123.

18

of Demeter and her daughter Kore, or Persephone, where the one goddess represents the growing season, and the other the dormant part of the year; or to state it another way, Persephone, like a seed, spends a part of the year underground, during which time she is married to the god of the underworld. During the other part of the year she spends her time with her mother, who is the essence of the ripe grain ear. Hades himself, perhaps because of his marriage to Persephone, takes on the same kind of duality in a male role. Hades, according to Rose, "as Pluton has become (whatever he was originally) a god of terrestrial fertility as well as death."

In the instance of Masau'u, the fertility role is complicated by the existence of another fertility god, Germinator, who may be called either Muingwu or Alosaka. Germinator is highly specialized as a fertility god, and his underworld aspects are closely confined to the subject, although the Two Horn Society members represent him on the night of the dead. The connection between the two gods is rationalized by the Hopis, to some extent, by linking both with Sand Altar Woman, an earth-mother. She is said to be the wife of Masau'u and the sister of Germinator, but the content of available myths does not bear this out.

Of the two fertility gods, Masau'u seems by far the more important, which leaves the question of why there should be two gods with the same function. The best theory, since it is the only one, comes from Dr. Fewkes. In his book on designs on prehistoric pottery he has a cryptic footnote: "Eototo, also called Masau'u, was the tutelary of Sikyatki, as Alosaka or Muinwu was of Awatobi."[20] Sikyatki was a village some miles north of Walpi, and it was abandoned sometime before 1540, which is to say in highly traditional times when there was no outside influence, while Awatobi was the Christianized village destroyed in 1700. If there is any truth in the statement it would mean that Masau'u had not only an earlier, but also a more favorable, background.

Unfortunately, little faith can be put in these theories, even if told by Hopis. For example, in the Walpi Flute ceremony, part of the

[20] Jesse W. Fewkes, "Design on Prehistoric Hopi Pottery," B.A.E. *Thirty-third Annual Report* (1911–12), 275.

dramatization is a recognition of the important connection of the Bear clan with Masau'u, and yet, when the Bear and the Snake clan welcome the arrival of the Horns, he is not the god to welcome them. "And Alosaka of the Bear and Snake who always sat on the house tops watching, spied us before we got off the north mesa . . . ."[21] Various groups arrange the stories to include their own tutelaries in similar roles. What is likely is that converging groups clung to their own names for gods of similar function, and to some extent variant aspects of each were also allowed to stand. In other instances two gods were completely identified, as must have been the case with Alosaka and Muingwu, who are now one being with two names.

While Germinator is a god of vegetation, Masau'u is a general fertility spirit. When the Hopis first met him he was nursing his small paradise of vegetation inside his ring of fire. The blood upon his head is literally that of rabbits, or perhaps formerly of deer, which is to say that he is in part a god of game animals. Human fertility is also within his realm of activity, in the sense that human methods of fertilization are thought to be archetypes of vegetal reproduction. Fewkes early noted the phallic element in impersonations of the god: "Masau'u came down a ladder as if a stairway, making his way back of the line of dancers, came forward between two of them and squatted before the fireplace. The second personator followed, unmasked, but with two black streaks painted on his cheeks. He took his seat by the side of Masau'u, assuming the posture of a man planting, holding one end of the planting stick to the floor as if it were soil . . . ."

Fewkes goes on to say, "The foregoing rites and the nature of the prayers addressed to Masau'u lead the author to regard him as a god of germination or a personification of fire as a symbol of life."[22] Before continuing with the symbol of fire, let us again consider the god's bloody head. It is impossible to use the word blood without thinking of "life's blood." Beyond that generality there are specific relations between blood and fertility, notably menses in the human female. It may be noted that Masau'u wears a woman's dress, which

[21] Stephen, *Hopi Journal*, II, 768, 810.

[22] Jesse W. Fewkes, "Hopi Katcinas," B.A.E. *Twenty-first Annual Report* (1899–1900), 38.

may indicate an attempt to combine a female with a male element in the same fertility spirit. Nevertheless, he is a male god with markedly phallic qualities—the slightly enlarged size, the head shaped like a squash, and the fact that before the emergence the Hopis "heard him walking around up there."

If we return to fire as a symbol of the generation of human life, we find two widespread connections. Fire is associated with the masculine sun whose generative powers are obvious to all. Less obvious to us, perhaps, but very widespread, is the association of the fire drill, and hence fire, with the male element. Robert Graves mentions this in explanation of why the Greek god Hermes became a fire god. "The invention of fire-making was ascribed to Hermes, because the twirling of the male drill in the female stock suggested phallic magic."[23]

Masau'u brought fire to the Hopis in the same magical fashion as the Greek god Hermes did in his day. "Al [Two Horn] and Kwan men kindle two fires with rotating drills. During this part of the ceremony, the Kwan chief, impersonating Masau'u, is concealed behind blankets; and when the fire is brought to a blaze, the pine-needle strings are thrown into the flames as sacrifices to Masau'u. At this point, an Al man, wearing the two-horned headdress of his order, lights a cedar bark torch at the fire and hastens out to touch off fires at all the other participating kivas."[24] The lances and drills used by the Kwans in this rite are made from a wood called "pilakho" which is said to have grown around Shipapu, the opening of the underworld through which all Pueblos emerged, and the material is supposed to be gathered from there still.[25]

Masau'u's relation to fertility magic is manifest in occasional impersonations that fall outside of the strict cycle of ceremonies. An impersonator may be called for at important times during planting or harvesting when the event is ritualistic enough, but is a matter of individual or group concern rather than part of the tribal calendar. The impersonator is smeared with rabbit's blood, and in some accounts he carries a small cylinder filled with seeds with which he clubs people until the sack bursts and the seeds spill out. On the

[23] Robert Graves, *The Greek Myths*, I, 67.
[24] Titiev, *Old Oraibi*, 131.   [25] *Ibid.*, 135.

Second Mesa the sack is filled with cotton, while at Old Oraibi it is a short club covered with an inverted rabbit skin.

To be a Masau'u impersonator of this sort is such a difficult task that the ritual has lapsed at times for lack of anyone willing to undertake the part. Any Hopi who has fields to plant or harvest, which is done by a community work party, may call for Masau'u to be present. One of the village chiefs arranges for an impersonator, who then goes into seclusion, sleeping in a darkened room by day, fasting, "so as to become skinny and a good runner." There are also sexual taboos during the period which extend for several days thereafter. Each day, at some hour past midnight he goes out and runs a counterclockwise circuit about the mesa, which is not only an arduous, but may also be a frightening experience to the impersonator. Every day the circles become smaller until he is merely running around the villages on the mesa top. "All this running about is good for the crops." The circuit is narrowed suggestively to bring the rain clouds, and doubtless the god's bounty in general, nearer to the mesa.

On the third day a ceremonial rabbit hunt is held, and the first rabbit each man kills is given to Masau'u, or actually to the women who will prepare it for him. The following day a party of friends goes early to the field to be planted or harvested, and about noon the impersonator and another man from the same society go to a cave in the rocks above the field, where the impersonator is dressed. His body is painted red with rabbit's blood; he wears an old worn out woman's manta around which is hung a sash of multicolored ears of corn. His face is streaked with specular iron, but is covered with the mask which is bloody and has corn husks fashioned into rings around the eye and mouth holes.

"About the middle of the afternoon Masau'u goes out to the fields. As the working party returns he hides in the washes, jumps out suddenly, and chases people to frighten them . . . he may go straight to a field being planted, chase the workers and then plant a few holes with mixed colored seed corn."[26] He attempts to strike the workers with his cylindrical sack. Sometimes they fall down as if dead, or they may make a desperate attempt to avoid his touch of

[26] Ernest Beaglehole, *Notes on Hopi Economic Life*, 46.

death. The whole thing takes place at the end of the working day, and often a great deal of elaborate horse-play goes on. For example, a daring girl may entice Masau'u to ride behind her on her mount.

When the people return to the village, the workers eat at the arranger's house, while the impersonator again makes four counter-clockwise circuits of the village. The villagers, having eaten meanwhile, come into the dance court. Masau'u kachina dancers, who are not impersonators of the god, come there to entertain while the real Masau'u rests—as well he might. The kachina dancers leave and he returns to the court. Challengers, consisting of anyone who volunteers, appear in costumes which travesty Hopi, alien Indian, or white cultures. They may be dressed as cowboys or Utes, or kachinas, or in any other way they fancy.

"As each appears, Masau'u chases him with clownish antics and finally hits him with his cylindrical sack. The man falls down as if dead and Masau'u strips him of his clothes, putting them on himself, but in the wrong manner, ties the sash on the left side instead of the right, puts moccasins on the wrong feet . . . ." For a time all is nonsense and jollification, but when no more challengers appear, which is likely to be after darkness has fallen, the "ceremony" takes a new turn.

In the darkness men bring a bundle of juniper bark into the court. "One lights a piece of this and advances with it toward Masau'u, who being afraid of light and fire, falls as if dead. The men carry Masau'u to the mesa edge [in places like Walpi there is a dizzying drop which appears vertical, although it is not], and roll him over, but he jumps up and chases the men back to the court. This is done four times but on the last time Masau'u walks back slowly and stands in the court while men and women give him prayer-feathers and meal for long life, rain, good crops and many children."[27] On First Mesa his skins and garments are buried, which is called "killing and burying Masau'u." Thus in this unofficial rite we see the perfect blend of the qualities of the god which on the one hand represent the forces of life and fertility, and on the other the power of death which must be put down.

[27] *Ibid.*, 47. There is also a good account in Titiev, *Old Oraibi*, 184–87.

There are other ambiguities in connection with the god, not the least of which is shown by the Masau'u kachinas who took his place while he rested. These are "funny" kachinas, almost clowns, whose usual purpose is to entertain, although they may also have a war-like role. They wear a helmet with twigs on top to which prayer-feathers are attached; the face of the mask is covered with multicolored discs supposed to represent clouds. There are corn-husks around eyes and mouth, the latter having teeth of squash seeds to fill out a skull-like appearance. The legs and arms of the dancers are painted red and spotted black. A rabbit skin robe is worn, and around the neck hangs a necklace, which at Walpi is made of human bones. These kachinas, like the impersonators of the god, reverse the normal order of Hopi life, in that they are the only kachinas allowed to appear during the proscribed summer period. (Fewkes has a colored picture of the kachinas.)[28]

Titiev has an excellent account of one of these out of season dances by Masau'u kachinas, the theme of which was a burlesque of women's ceremonies in which gifts are often thrown to the crowd of onlookers. "A laugh arose whenever a Katcina appeared bearing a roasted sheep's head, and one dancer aroused huge merriment when he solemnly disclosed a prairie dog roasted whole."[29] This dance, involving twenty-one Masau'u kachinas, was apparently entirely for pleasure; but Stephen describes the same figure in a different role, also related to women. In a February ceremony a single Masau'u kachina came dancing into a kiva in a halting movement, alternately singing and growling: "he danced frantically round and through the blaze of greasewood the women were burning for its charcoal."[30]

The relationship between these kachinas and the god is not at all clear. In the planting and harvesting rite they seem to be only an entr'acte to hold the audience while the major performer gets a much needed rest. Their use in summer entertainment is due to the fact that no other kachinas can dance then, but the dance through the fire

[28] Fewkes, "Hopi Katcinas," *loc. cit.*, 76. See also Harold S. Colton, "Hopi Deities," *Plateau*, Vol. XX, No. 1, (1954), reprinted in *Hopi Customs, Folklore and Ceremonies*, 48.

[29] Titiev, *Old Oraibi*, 236–38.   [30] Stephen, *Hopi Journal*, I, 316.

certainly has a serious intent and is related to Masau'u as a fire god. It may be noted that the Zuñi fire god, Shulawitsi, or firebrand-youth, is likewise covered with multicolored discs and carries a cedar bark torch.

There remain two seemingly minor characteristics which have been associated with Masau'u since ancient times; he is the god of travelers and the god of boundaries. I say seemingly minor, since it will prove that these lead to his role as guardian of the land, which is of equal importance to his standing as a god of death and of fertility, and in our day has led to a complete transformation of the god by the Traditionalists. These points also provide the basis for a rather complete analogy between Masau'u and the Greek god Hermes. A number of students of Pueblo religion have remarked that it was something like Greek religion, without amplifying their remarks. We shall soon see how two distantly placed gods were alike, and, more importantly, why they combined similar elements.

Masau'u is the god of travelers, which probably derives from the fact that he is very importantly the god of boundaries. The Hopis were extensive travelers and traders, and each time they left the comparative safety of their mesas, they went into a wilderness dominated by the Navahos, Apaches, or the Utes. Until recent times these tribes were overtly hostile, and many stories are told of the perils and fights attendant to trips to other pueblos, or to a white town. Except in the case of an actual war party, the Hopis traveled in small groups, or alone. Sometimes the trip was only to their fields, but these might be many, many miles away.

Along the trails near the villages were shrines devoted to Skeleton Man where the returning traveler left votive offerings, quite simple ones, such as a stick of wood or a curious rock, left in thanks to the god of death. On First Mesa there is an etiological tale to explain the origin of these shrines. When the people of the Snake clan were migrating, they halted near Walpi, but Masau'u refused to let the people approach the springs; "he closed the trail." Then the Snake people built him a shrine there and he relented. "Nearly every trail, now, has a cairn upon it at some point, and when a tired Hopi passes it he takes a bunch of grass and rubs his head, arms, legs, etc., and places the tuft and a small portion of his burden on the heap, placing a stone on the tuft, or a bit of wood to hold it secure. At the same time he asks Masau'u to protect him; if returning from a journey he thanks Masau'u for his protection."[31]

Since the Greek god Hermes, whose name means "he of the stone heap," developed from a similar stone cairn which served both as a shrine and as a boundary marker, we are justified in looking for the alternative symbol, which is an upright stone post often called a "herma" in English. The point is a rather obscure one, and has hence attracted little attention from students of the Pueblos, but as it provides a key to various aspects of Masau'u's nature any information is valuable. It is known that boundary stones were used by the Zuñis to mark their fields, and at least one such object has been found at Pueblo Bonito, but its meaning is silent.

The point, however, is not to establish the existence of boundary stones, but their identification with the god. I have found three such references, the first in a footnote by Parsons, the editor of Stephen's *Hopi Journal.* "Stephen made no study of land holding. In 1888 he notes the use of certain field marks and of a boundary stone between Shumo'pavi and Oraibi lands, a figure of Ma'sauuh [Masau'u]. Two brothers lived, one at Shumo'pavi and one at Oraibi. The latter placed the monument here and it was agreed when Shumo'pavi increased sufficiently to need more farming land this monument would be moved toward Oraibi."[32]

The stone, which by good fortune is illustrated, is two feet high. The two brothers are likely a narrative device—there are always two brothers, or sisters, just as any period of time is indicated by "four years." Parsons adds a further note to the effect that a native knows no further meaning, and that the head and holes carved in the face for eyes and nose were put there to keep children and Navahos from destroying it. The latter part of the statement contains a good deal of truth, for the eternal watcher must stand in place in order to guard the boundary.

A second herma representing Masau'u seems to be a different one, although I cannot be as positive as I would wish. In any case, this

[31] *Ibid.,* I, 151.   [32] *Ibid.,* I, 390 and Fig. 220.

stone appears to be south and slightly west of Oraibi, whereas Shongopovi is east, so that the second herma would be a considerable distance
from the present Oraibi-Shongopovi border. At Old Oraibi the chief
of the Bear clan was the village chief, and he held a large tract of
floodwater farm land in the Oraibi wash. "The western limit of his
holdings was marked with a boundary stone on which a Bear claw
was carved. A similar stone, marked with the head of Masau'u, com-
memorated that deity's original claim to the entire domain, and
boundaries and shrines were erected at the south and northeast
corners."[33]

There is a third source which comes from *Folk Tales from
Shumopavi.*[34] "He gave them land as he had done at Oraibi and
marked off their respective tracts. He put up a stone to indicate the
boundary line. (A stone never moves; put up a stick and it will rot
and be gone.)" These three instances do not prove a widespread use
of Masau'u as a figure on boundary stones, but they illustrate the
fact that the concept was familiar on at least two mesas and over a
long period of time.

Perhaps the point seems small, but it rounds out a parallel with
Hermes. There is no actual connection between these two gods who
lived centuries apart and on different sides of the globe, but if they
share a complex of qualities, it can only mean that the complex has a
logic of its own. The traits which both Hermes and Masau'u share
look backward over the material so far covered, and forward to two
qualities yet to be discussed. The process which brings the bits together runs something like this: both are gods of the dead and the
underworld; both are gods of fertility, and fertility, whether vegetal
or human, is often represented by phallic images. These images may
take the form of stone cairns or pillars which have a double purpose;
they have a magical effect in fructifying the field by which they stand,
and they may also serve as its boundary marker. In relation to the
former idea is the concept of fire as a generating life principle, while
the boundary marker is also subject to two ideas. After you have passed
your boundary, or that of your village, you are a traveler and subject

[33] Titiev, *Old Oraibi*, 62.
[34] Wallis, "Folk Tales from Shumpovi," *loc. cit.*, 14.

to the dangers which that entails, among which is the great possibility of death, a thought which brings the complex full circle and ends in the underworld where it began. The phallic boundary stone may become a tombstone.

The boundary stone may also branch off in another direction which we have not yet considered. A boundary is a marker of property limits, particularly in land, and any matter relating to land ownership or use is subject to a good deal of trickery, if not downright thievery. We will find that both gods are tricksters and cozeners of men. To these items one must add the fact that both had an undeveloped tendency to become gods of war.

Undoubtedly the arrangement just presented is too neat, but it may prove useful. To begin with, it convinces me that Masau'u is indigenous in the Hopi world, rather than a death spirit borrowed from the Navahos, as Parsons suggested. A whole complex, whether it relates to a ceremony or to a god, is seldom borrowed intact. The borrower selects bits which impress him and fits these selections into already existing ideas where their logical place is uncertain. I think this thesis can easily be proved by examples of inter-Pueblo borrowing, but that would carry the chapter far afield. A whole complex takes a long time to grow up, and if the Greeks and the Hopis arrived at a similar set of relationships in one god, it would be because as primitive town dwellers they faced similar problems. The nomadic Navaho is not likely to have associated concepts of boundaries with concepts of death and fertility, since boundaries, to say nothing of markers, would be meaningless in their mode of life.

Since the particular analogy between Hermes and Masau'u has been chosen, I will list again the traits of the early Hermes. Like Masau'u, the Greek god underwent many changes; and some of these first come to mind when we think of him, as very soon many Hopis will think of Masau'u, only as the Great Spirit and savior of Hopi ways. The following is a composite picture drawn from Farnell's *Cults of the Greek States*, of the early Greek god Hermes, who was once conceived as of larger nature, as one of the "chthonians" or earth-divinities of vegetation and the underground world. "In old Arcadia it is probable that Hermes was once himself a high god

28

of life and death. The chthonian functions then that he still retains in the historic period may be regarded only as the shorn heritage of his original power and place as lord of the lower world."

As a god of travelers Hermes remained identical with Masau'u. The custom "had long been prevalent in Hellas of honouring Hermes, the god of ways, by piling up a heap of stones . . . Cornutus merely says that each passer-by added one to the heap." Of actual hermae we find: "Again, we may connect with the earliest period of his worship the fashion of setting up the agalma [these were at first just pillars with a phallic symbol on them, but later the head of the god was carved on top] of the god on the boundaries of land: the presence of the earth-god, or way god, which is thus secured, sanctifies the rights of public as of private ownership, establishing a *tapu* [taboo] that secures the place from violation."[35]

From that last statement we may begin an examination of two aspects of Masau'u which we have not as yet considered. The mere thought of a "boundary" is immediately transferrable from an individual field to the lands belonging to the town members as a group, and then to the lands of a number of towns which make up a "nation." The purpose of at least one of the hermae of Masau'u is to distinguish between the lands which belong to Old Oraibi and those of Shongopovi. In Greece the borders of the town of Megalopolis were guarded by Hermes at two places, while the people of Lampsakos set a herma on their border with Paros. Hermes never became a protector of all Hellas, but Masau'u has become the protecting deity of all Pueblo lands, at least in the eyes of the Hopis. More particularly he is the god of Hopi lands. In 1885 Ten Kate gave the Hopis a name, which I shall not transcribe, meaning: "the land of Másawé." *Mastutc'kwe* seems still to stand for Masau'u's land.[36]

The second aspect, which I believe is related to the former, is the difficult concept that the god is a trickster and a thief. The fact is indeed difficult to accept. In his study of Hermes, Farnell can almost be heard to sigh when he says: "Here is a fact that gives us

[35] Lewis Richard Farnell, *The Cults of the Greek States*, V, Chap. I.

[36] John R. Swanton, *The Indian Tribes of North America*, B.A.E. *Bulletin No. 145* (1953), 352.

pause and reflection. How did Hermes become the patron-god of thieves, liars, and defrauders?" In the face of literary evidence as old as Homer he admits the antiquity of the fact and hopes that *Hermes Dolios* was the result of license which prevails on carnival days, in "which the usual licence included some merry form of picking one's neighbour's pocket."[37]

Stephen must have had a similar difficulty with Masau'u, for he does not include this information in the *Hopi Journal*. He collected these items from what he called "kiva talk," which I gather implies an informal conversation about the god in which the speakers would not be thinking about the ritual role of the god, and these were published as "Hopi Tales." The material is blunt enough.

"Masau'u is a thief, a liar, and very jealous, also a persistent practical joker. He made trees grow gnarly and crooked and twisted men's faces into ridiculous shapes so that he could laugh at them. He not only played tricks upon men and inanimate things, but upon the other gods also." That, of course, is the very picture of Hermes.

The most famous instance of Hermes' thievery is recounted in the Homeric hymn, "To Hermes," a delightful and sophisticated work in which the unknown poet, who lived long after Homer, was careful to include all of the attributes of the god. The god, while still a babe, stole the sacred oxen of Apollo. When he is caught his plea is in essence: "Am I a cattle-lifter, a stalwart person? . . . I was born yesterday." His trick, as told by a master teller of folk tales, involves, in addition to the act itself, other elements. The fertility motif is light. As Hermes is herding the stolen cattle he is seen by an old farmer to whom he says: "Old man, digging about your vines with bowed shoulders, surely you shall have much wine when all these bear fruit, if you obey me and strictly remember that you have not seen what you have seen." (On the island of Lesbos statues of Hermes were placed in vineyards, doubtless for the dual purposes of fertility and guardianship.)

The theft involves a question of property. Since he was the god of the boundary stone, the divine power whose representation had a magic virtue in the defense of property, the inversion needs some

---

[37] Farnell, *The Cults of the Greek States*, V, 23–25.

explanation. Probably the alternative roles of thievery and the defense of property are based upon some such folk logic as "Set a thief to catch a thief." Certainly the beginning of all knowledge is the realization that it takes considerable cunning, and trickery, either to gain or hold property. There is no need to go into the question of Indian lands here.

Since the property stolen by Hermes belonged to another god, the question becomes a contest among gods and eventually a concern for the whole family of gods. Apollo promises to throw this "prince of robbers" into Hades and let him be a leader there—an allusion either to Hermes' role as psychopompos or to his aboriginal role as a great god of the underworld. After the cattle are discovered, physical contests of a magical type follow, in which Hermes outwits the god of the silver bow. In the end he is given the right, by Zeus, "to establish deeds of barter amongst men throughout the fruitful earth." Thereafter he is honest with the gods but, though he "consorts with all mortals and immortals; a little he profits, but continually throughout the dark night he cozens the tribes of mortal men."

According to the Hopi tale, Masau'u likewise began his career among the other gods. "He was made from nothing and came from nowhere. A very long while ago a number of gods came to this world, and from where no one knows. They assembled in council near the San Francisco Mountains. They tried to make a partition of the land, but they could not agree and separated full of jealousies, each determining to hold all the good land he saw." The land that Masau'u saw becomes of great importance, since his guardianship gives the Hopis a kind of riparian right to the land. I will return to that subject later, but first let us hear of the tricks of this god, which were certainly childish enough. Hermes was a babe, and it will be remembered that in the interview with Dr. Fewkes, Masau'u and the doctor "both became like little children and all night long they played around together."

The play of Masau'u is described in the following paragraph. "He would watch for their meeting in council, then getting upon a lofty crag in their view would mimic their songs and dances and throw the gods into confusion and bring their ceremonies to a standstill. The angry gods would then chase him, but he never could be overtaken. He would first disguise himself before playing those antics, when on seeing the other gods starting to pursue him he would run a little way, then, dropping his disguise, would turn and meet them, asking what they were chasing and vowing he had seen no one, but if he found the sacrilegious one he would bring him to their hands."

The trickster figure has many different aspects; in a later chapter on clowns we will see how some of these are related to fertility and mana. Here the fleeing, childish god is remarkably similar to the Hermes of the hymn. As the passage continues, we find that Masau'u sings or charms the gods to sleep. One will perhaps remember that the lyre and songs were gifts from Hermes to Apollo. "And next the goodly son of Zeus hymned the rest of the immortals . . . ." Only Apollo was not allayed—this was another situation—and he spoke to Hermes. "Slayer of oxen, trickster, busy one, comrade of the feast, this song of yours is worth fifty cows, and I believe that presently we shall settle our quarrel peacefully." Hermes offers the gift of song to Apollo; perhaps a division of labor between the arts and practical affairs is intended. Masau'u used the same device of song, but with a different result, perhaps because the story never became rationalized. Masau'u was more of a trickster than Hermes and his present victory over other Hopi gods may yet prove him right.

"One day the gods assembled in council and to sing and dance as was their custom at certain seasons. They were joined on this day by Masau'u who came carrying a bundle. The gods were surprised by his appearance but Masau'u soon disarmed all suspicious [sic] by his smooth talk; after much talking, one of the gods said that as the day was now well spent it was time they should begin to sing so that the ceremonies could be ended by sunset and permit the assembled gods to get some sleep as many of them had long journeys to make on the morrow. Masau'u at once began to sing and such was the soothing influence of his song that all the other gods immediately became drowsy and soon were all fast asleep. Observing this Masau'u still continuing his song, carefully undid his bundle upon which he had been sitting and produced from it an effigy of himself

32

which he arranged in a posture similar to the rest, with head on knees, fast asleep. Masau'u then went to the mountain top and putting on his former disguise began rolling stones down the mountain side. The noise soon awoke the gods but they were at a loss to account for it for there was the mischievous god sitting fast asleep."

While the device of singing the other gods to sleep was effective enough, his pranks which challenged them were not: "One of them presently endeavoring to awake the fictitious Masau'u disclosed the effigy. They were all enraged and their passion was increased when they discerned the disguised figure mocking them from the mountain top, but they were now assured that this mocking one was Masau'u. They determined to chase him and administer a severe punishment and for many days they followed him, but could not overtake him. One day, however, Masau'u, thinking himself far in advance and being very tired, lay down in the shade of a rock to sleep. The pursuing gods speedily coming up heard him snoring loudly and seized him. They stripped him and beat him and taking away everything he had on his person they left him to go where he would."

While we are in the midst of a tale, it should be noted that the story is parallel in some ways to the agricultural rite of planting or harvesting recounted earlier, in which Masau'u strikes down his challengers and strips them of their clothes, until in the end he also falls down as if dead. Then he rises to accept prayers and gifts. On one level this is a mime depicting the life cycle of the corn plant; the ear is stripped from the plant, the cob is stripped of its seeds, and some of these are buried—it was his clothes, "the killing and burying of Masau'u"—but he, as a corn symbol, rises again and accepts the thanks of the people. As the present tale continues, he needs the fertilizing companionship of lightning in order to recover.

"Masau'u's knowledge and cunning soon enabled him to get in good condition again and then he turned his thoughts on revenge. One morning he counseled with Sun, saying, 'I am but one against many. I would like to have an active friend, a brother, to assist me against my enemies.' Sun said he could not join him, but advised him to consult Shotukinunwa. Masau'u said he had little knowledge of the god of the skys and asked Sun to carry his request to him, to which Sun agreed. After some days of talk, Masau'u making many promises, the god of the skies sent him a companion, a brother, to assist him."

The quarrel with the gods is ended, as was the case with Hermes, and further trickery practiced by the god is directed toward humankind, but "cozen" is hardly the word which should be used here:

"They then each got a club and a round stone and went forth and everyone they encountered was knocked down and robbed, none escaped. Some of the Hopitu who were lazy and wicked and refused to plant corn for Masau'u and his brother were knocked down and robbed." In that last sentence there is a sudden shift of emphasis; Masau'u is no longer a liar, a cheat, and a thief; he has become an example and a threat.

"Today, however, Masau'u comes to us in the daytime and shows us by his pantomime how he used to treat his enemies and teaches us that he would treat us in the same way if we grew lazy and refused to plant corn."

The trickster has become, in the short space of one tale, a culture hero and the defender of the Hopi way, and a defender of those who grow corn with vigor. He has even become a daylight god. In the beginning of this tale the struggle among the gods was motivated by the division of lands, and the narrative ends upon the same subject. The claim, in the name of Masau'u, to a large tract of land is rather ambitious in the light of present day circumstances with the Hopis, but it is still stated in much the same way. This is the conclusion of the tale:

"Masau'u first travelled south, then circuitously to the eastward until he reached his starting point. He called this area his land. The exact limits are unknown, but it is surmised he started from a point about where Fort Mojave now is situated, thence south as far as the Isthmus of Panama, skirted eastward along the Gulf of Mexico and northward by the line of the Río Grande up into Colorado, thence westerly along the thirty sixth parallel or thereabouts to the Rio Colorado, meandering along its course and so on southward to his starting point at Fort Mojave. This was Masau'u's land originally."[38]

[38] Stephen, "Hopi Tales," *loc. cit.*, 55–57.

There remains one more characteristic of the older Masau'u: he may at times function as a war god. Hermes likewise had this capacity. One of his epithets at Athens was Hegemonios, meaning "Leader of the host to war." The quality was not developed in either god, and I think it would be safe to assume that the occasional use of a god of the dead as a god of war is based upon the obvious association of war with death. There is also the possibility that individual clans or societies may add their patrons as additional war spirits to the universally recognized War Twins.

To see Masau'u as a war god, one must go back to the year 1891, at which time the Hopis and the United States government were at odds. The latter proposed to take the Hopi children away from their parents and send them to distant boarding schools as a part of a program which we would now call brain-washing. The parents were, of course, bitterly opposed to the process. A unit of cavalry was sent to take the children, but Oraibi, which was then not irrevocably divided between Friendlies and Hostiles, made a show of resistance. When the troopers arrived, with some hostages they had captured at the foot of the mesa, they found the villagers on their housetops with bows and arrows and a few ancient guns.

"Before the lieutenant knew what to expect, the Hopi began to make a formal, ceremonial declaration of war. To this end they had 'dressed three of their number to represent the three War-gods. . . . The first two, arrayed in prescribed costumes, appeared in the plaza . . . . The last mentioned, or the the Little War-god, did not appear . . . .' The proceedings began when 'A man, clothed to represent [Spider Grandmother] approached the force drawn up on the plaza and advised them to leave, stating that trouble would result if they did not do so. The next personification to approach represented the God of Death, clothed to represent Masau'u. He wore a black mask painted with spots and carried various objects, among which was a bowl filled with a liquid medicine that had been prepared for the occasion, and as he passed along the line of soldiers he sprinkled them all with this medicine, using for the purpose a feather. He peremptorily ordered the soldiers to leave the pueblo before the appearance of the Little War God, when hostilities would immediately begin."[39]

On that particular occasion the soldiers departed as Masau'u had instructed them to do, but whites are not vanquished by ceremonial warfare, and it was inevitable that if Masau'u and the ways for which he stands were to survive under these new circumstances, the nature of the god would have to undergo changes. Some of these changes are rooted in the past which I have described; other aspects of the god are almost new. Most notably, perhaps, the physical presence of the god must subside. If an impersonator of the god sprinkles the enemies of the race and they disappear, well and good, but if that medicine fails of its power, as under the circumstances it must, the physical presence of the deity becomes more of a handicap than a benefit. On the other hand, the power of an abstract god can remain an incalculable force. In most of the accounts so far given Masau'u is thought of as a markedly solid being; he may magically materialize out of a keyhole, but in the end he is an anthropomorphic god.

Even in Stephen's day, however, there existed the makings of an abstract divinity; Masau'u was ubiquitous. Pauwati'wa told Stephen: "He goes everywhere, has always been present everywhere .... Wherever is a man or woman; there also is Masau'u."[40]

Something of the vastness of the changes in concepts which have taken place can be seen if we recall a statement quoted earlier. There a man of our generation mentions that the roads to the village are closed "to clear the spiritual highway which leads from there to the rising sun. This is a road over which they walk to offer their prayers to the Great Spirit." It will be recalled that the closing of the roads was in actuality part of an All Souls ceremony for the dead, and in it Masau'u, who has now become the Great Spirit, was most certainly connected with the dead and the underworld, rather than with the sun. The new arrangement is not made out of the whole cloth, however, as the idea is old, but it belonged to the initiation of a new village chieftain. Since the town chief was supposed to be on good terms with the cloud-people, or spirits of the dead, a Kwan man closes the ceremony with these words: "Now I make you a chief

[39] Titiev, *Old Oraibi*, 77.   [40] Stephen, *Hopi Journal*, I, 150.

36

and now I give you a good path to lead us to the Sun. Now you are our father."[41]

From now on we will hear very little of death, or even of fertility, and much of a sky god who is a supreme being. In the *Hopi Hearings,* a source of information which will be discussed later, old and new attitudes are combined. Simon Scott, whose name hides a Hopi, at one point says: "This supreme being who is over all of us is here with us and listening to all of us in this meeting and will be with us until this meeting is adjourned." Despite the Christian tone, the statement is not far removed conceptually from the remark Stephen quoted, but some days later the same Hopi leader added a few ideas: "It is the Executive Supreme Being who created the world and created the human for a holy purpose. It is this Executive Supreme who made two humans. One has a white flesh and the other is red."[42] Since he was referring to Masau'u, the latter statement contains something quite new; as every Hopi knows, the world was created by Huruing Wuhti, Hard Beings Woman, and in all the accounts we have heard there is no suggestion that Masau'u was a creator, either of the world or of mankind. Furthermore, the god has been changed by the competition of white politics as well as white religion. Our Chief Executive must have been an appealing idea, both in phrasing and thought content.

Before examining the new material on Masau'u, I should mention its main source. The Hopi Hearings were held in nine villages in July of 1955, by the Bureau of Indian Affairs. Any Hopi who wished to was allowed to speak for as long as he or she chose on any topic of concern. These proved to be largely matters of land, livestock adjustments, the past and present injustices of white administrators, and the like. Each speech was taken down verbatim. Whether the Hearings were of use to the Bureau or not, for the student of Pueblo religion they are invaluable, as they bypass the paid informant and reach the leaders who are shaping thought.

The first thing one realizes in reading through the transcripts of the Hearings is that the Hopis are badly divided over the issues which were just beginning when the Masau'u impersonator, who was

[41] Titiev, *Old Oraibi,* 64.   [42] *Hopi Hearings,* 31, 242.

dressed as a Masau'u kachina, bade the first group of white cavalry depart. The isolation which had protected the Hopis from both Hispanic and Anglo influences for centuries has now turned to their disadvantage, in that very complex adjustments must now be made within the short span of a generation or two. The Keres of the Río Grande have lived in close touch with alien cultures for more than three centuries and have evolved a workable compromise, consisting in part of outward compliance and inward secretiveness. When they want to close their pueblos for a secret ceremony they do so most emphatically. Also they, and Acoma and Zuñi as well, have been able to adopt a number of principles of scientific farming without greatly disturbing their agriculturally based religion.

On the Hopi Mesas there has not been time for such an adjustment, and the division seems almost absolute. The people are divided into "Friendlies" and "Hostiles." The former are willing to accept all, or almost all, white ways, while the latter want none of them, nothing but the true Hopi *wimi*. The *Hopi Hearings* present several brilliant expositions of the Friendly view, but the nature of this book confines our interest to the Traditionalist group. One exception is a very simple presentation of the Friendly position which is a direct echo of Masau'u's words to the first messenger from the people underground.

"So this is what has been planned and has been done. We are poor. We are still poor. We have nothing here. There is nothing here that we can have in the way of resources. There is no flowing stream here at all so naturally we will have to look to you and depend on you."[43] This Walpi man was speaking not to Masau'u but to the Bureau of Indian Affairs. Obviously a great many Hopis are no longer willing to live under the old contract made when they came up. "I have not anything; this is the way I am living here. Now if you are willing to live here that way too, with me and share this life, why come, you are welcome."

On the basis of the *Hopi Hearings*, there seem to be two villages where the old ways are intact and insisted upon, although many of the ceremonies continue in other towns as well and there are some

[43] *Ibid.*, 335.

Traditionalists in each village. The most important town is Hote-villa with a population of about 600, most of whom have descended from those ejected from Old Oraibi in 1906. The latter is now nearly a ghost town. The other Traditionalist center is the Second Mesa town of Shongopovi, which had a population (1932) of 307. A new village, Lower Moencopi, seems to have a number of strong Traditionalists. I gather that at least a third of the Hopi population support, to some extent, Traditionalist views, and I know that some off-reservation Hopis do so too.

Since it is rare to find information about individual Pueblo Indians who shape religious thought, it may be worthwhile to glance at two leaders from Hotevilla. They are outstanding in the *Hopi Hearings* and they supply much of the information on Masau'u. They are decidedly opposite types. Dan Katchongva, with whom the Hearings begin, is a mild and spiritual man; he has been to Washington and is sophisticated. I assume that he is the Qötchongva of Titiev's study of Old Oraibi. Titiev said[44] in the thirties that this man had the weakest claim to the village chieftainship. After the split at Oraibi the old man who led the Traditionalist party away soon gave up leadership and Yokioma became the new chief. He died in 1929. (In the *Hopi Hearings* his name is spelled Acuma.) Katchongva's only claim to leadership was that he is Yokioma's son, so that his succession is contrary to Hopi theory in that Yokioma's sister's son was a more logical successor, while the best claim belonged to a nephew of the original leader of the split. However, the matrilineal principle may never have been as strict as the ideal, and Katchongva is a leader. He not only became the spiritual and theological leader of the Tra-ditionalists on all the Mesas, but has proscribed all non-Hopi religions in Hotevilla and excluded their protagonists, with the possible ex-ception of the Ba'hai, a sect of Islam.

His speech begins: "I am a Hopi, Dan Katchongva, a descendant of some people who came to this land first. I belong to the Sun Clan, and I am the son of the Fire Clan. In the life pattern the Sun Clan leaders are placed perhaps at the very last in line of leadership."[45] He then goes on to explain the system whereby, if the traditional

[44] Titiev, *Old Oraibi*, 211.   [45] *Hopi Hearings*, 5.

leaders fail to defend the Hopi way, the duty falls to the next in line, and so on down to the Sun clan.

The other speaker, who has a great deal to say about the new Masau'u, about the plan of the god and the stone tablet in which it is embodied, and about an eventual apocalypse and purification day when the lost brother returns, is one Simon Scott. He is an irascible man. The following quotation does not do his long arguments justice, but it shows something of his personality. He is playing on the image of the "Two-Hearts," the false ones, or witches of Hopi ideology.

"So, I have come with this part of the Hopi heart, and I have here someone else's heart, and I want to show this here today. This one heart I am going to show you belongs to the white man. With that heart he has forced many of our own people to abandon their land and property in trying to take it away from them, and it has caused much hardship on our own leaders for trying to keep within the principles of own own way of life. [Throws a pistol and loaded cartridge belt on the table.] The white man also has another heart. It is a jail. These two make him strong. I have showed these two hearts under the Sun's witness who is looking upon us today, and we are not speaking just merely to be speaking, but this is our instruction."[46]

These two men, and a few others who are like-minded, have shaped a new Masau'u; and into the new form have come a number of ideas of foreign origin, due mainly to a strong negative reaction by the Hopis. These ideas are so blended with native thought that it is never possible to make a clear distinction. There are three central themes in the new view: first, a stone tablet given the Hopis by Masau'u as a solid reminder of their "life pattern"; second, the Two Brothers have become very important, which is of interest since the elder is often identified with the god himself; third, an apocalyptic theme, which includes a Savior who may also be a purifier or destroyer and may also be identified with the god in some way.

The stone tablet that is so frequently mentioned has existed for a long time at Oraibi, but as there is no mention of comparable tab-

46 *Ibid.*, 30.

lets from other Mesas, it seems probable that the tablet formerly had to do with Oraibi landholdings, rather than with any sort of Mosaic mandate. My surmise is based upon the fact that other divinely given mandates represented in physical form, such as the "tiponi" or chief's staff of office, are found in duplicate for each village. Since there is no evidence that Masau'u originated in, or had a particular relationship to that one town, one would expect other villages to have similar signs of a divine contract.

The Life Plan, or pattern, which is so often mentioned in connection with the tablet is never spelled out in detail. The god appointed group leaders to uphold each of the various parts of the pattern. These would be the chiefs in charge of the various rites in the Hopi calendar, and so at base it is the Hopi religious system, but it also includes an admonition to maintain the Hopi way, which is a larger concept. Today the Life Plan also includes a day of judgment.

Dan Katchongva says: "We are following certain life patterns which we obtained from Masau'u . . . . We actually came face to face with him and talked to him. This took place at a point just a couple of miles north of old Oraibi around the bend in the road . . . . So he gave us a stone tablet which contains the instructions and on which was written all the life plan of the Hopi people."[47]

There is evidence that similar views were held by people much older than Katchongva. In 1912 an informant from Shongopovi gave the following account: "Masau'u gave this story inscribed on a stone, to the Hopi. He said: 'The whole earth is mine. As long as you keep this, it all belongs to you.' One piece of this stone is broken off. Ki'oma, the present chief of Shumopovi, has the stone now. 'When this story is forgotten, something disastrous will happen.' Perhaps the stars will fall down into the ocean, and the ocean will become oil. Then the sun will set fire to it, and the conflagration will consume everyone. Perhaps there will be an earthquake that will kill everyone. That is what my father's father told me."[48]

If that information were correct it would place the tablet well back in the last century. Cushing was told of this stone tablet in

[47] *Ibid.*, 23–24.
[48] Wallis, "Folk Tales from Shumopovi," *loc. cit.*, 16.

1883, and he then heard that it had been handed down from the ancients, but he did not see it. At the time of the Oraibi split the stone was in the hands of Loloma, chief of Friendlies. The tablet is briefly described in the *Hopi Hearings:*[49] "There were picture writings on both sides of the stone tablet. One side represents crops as earthly things which grow on this earth and the material life of this land, and once they saw this they worked harder to get Loloma to turn it over. If he was going to lead this life it is good and he would continue to hold it. So when we reach there this land will be purified as it shows on the stone tablet. A beheading might have to take place, because it is the evil man who must choose.

"The symbol of a snake was also provided on the stone tablet which represents the guarding of this land and life. As long as we remain fast and adhere to the teachings of the tablet the Snake will hold back the punishment that will take place in case we let go of this stone map."[50]

The stone itself may deserve some comment, because of its growing importance. There is a picture of it and Katchongva in a paper I take to be the *Arizona Republic,* for May 23, 1941. Apparently two corners are now knocked off the stone, which does not appear very well in the photograph, although the chief does.

A scientific description of the stone is given by Titiev. "This stone is supposed to have been kept in the custody of the Bear Clan from the beginning and is zealously shielded from profane observation because its markings are believed to convey Matcito's [the legendary first chief, who got his instructions and power directly from Masau'u] intentions regarding the control of Oraibi lands . . . . It is a rectangular block of greyish-white, smooth-grained stone, about 16 inches long, 8 inches wide, and one and a half inches thick, splotched here and there with irregular red dots which the chief interprets as points of land. On both sides are lightly incised markings which are explained this way.

"One surface is covered with miscellaneous symbols, including a row of eight little scratches, said to stand for the eight-day period during which the Soyal [Winter Solstice Sun ceremony] is observed;

[49] *Hopi Hearings,* 55. Sentences transposed.   [50] *Ibid.*

cloud and lightning emblems in a random arrangement; an unidenti-
fied Katcina figure; two or three sets of bear claws; an old-age-crook;
a poorly executed serpent, said to represent the Little Colorado River; and eight circles, arranged in two parallel rows, which the chief
explains as thunder because the sound of a thunder clap is like that
of a number of objects being struck in succession. Along the edge of
one of the long sides of the relic there runs a series of little lines
which were not interpreted; and along the other edge there is a
succession of conventional cloud and rain symbols to indicate that in
Matcito's lifetime there was always plenty of rain. The pictures on
the other side of the stone tell a connected story. A double rectangle
in the center is supposed to represent the Oraibi domain. About this
are grouped six figures which depict the Soyal officers. Reading from
the bottom in a counterclockwise circuit, they refer to the Village,
Pikyas, Parrot, Tobacco, Crier, and War chiefs. Each figure stands
with the left hand across the chest and the right extended downward
to cover the genetalia. This posture is said to indicate that the chiefs
are claiming land enclosed within the central rectangles. Along the
edge representing the east, there is a line of small scratches, inter-
spersed with occasional circles or crosses, which depicts the proper
Hopi path that the chiefs are supposed to travel. The War chief
brings up the rear to make sure that no one turns aside from the
correct road."[51]

Although the stone tablet is simple and crude in its representations
of ideas which were once much more specific and limited, it seems to
have gathered a rich set of affects, as instanced by the snake which can
be either the Little Colorado, or a protector against the day of Purification; between the two statements there is room for gathering a
great deal of esoteric lore. It has oracular powers now. Titiev obviously had a good grasp of its supposed meaning, but now it is said
that no white man can understand it and that it predicted World
War II.

The Two Brothers theme is related to the tablet at this point, in
that the returning brother will be able to read it. Katchongva wrote
in the newspaper of the same date as the picture: "The legend says

[51] Titiev, *Old Oraibi*, 60–61.

43

that someday a white brother will come who will be able to read the things on the stone. When he comes we will know him and he will enable the Hopi and all the other people of the world to share equally in the wealth that is given to us who are living." Some years later Katchongva, as we shall see, assumes that the brother who will return is Indian. To Hermequaftewa the one who returns is a secondary spirit created by Masau'u, while Monongye thinks of the Purifier as the god himself.

The brothers are closely related to a pair of sisters in Keresan mythology. The basic story is simple. Early in the migrations of mankind the older and younger parted, promising to return. The elder is foreign, but not necessarily white; he, or she, is always richer —"more of everything in the basket," except of course, the love of the gods. There is a contest between the two which can amount to anything, from whom the sun first shines upon, to physical contests. The Hopis make the contest quite simple. Masau'u sets a pile of corn before the two, and the elder brother naturally picks the biggest ear: "One little corn, the smallest ear of corn, was left and the Hopi came forth and picked it up."

After the brothers had gone their separate ways, which was shortly after the time of the emergence, it was known that one day the elder, or white brother, would return again.

"We were told that another person will come to us, and he will do many things to us. There will be a man of white skin who will come to us, and life will be very hard because he will do many things to us—things that you do not have no knowledge of because you are following a certain life pattern given to us by Spirit Masau'u."[52]

To Hermequaftewa the coming of the white man is not associated with the return of the elder brother. "However, as time passed on someone else arrived and Masau'u who knows everything, who is a spirit, also knew this person was coming. He came out from below. This man appeared to be a white man. His tracks were found and they followed them until they came to a field. When they came to the field they found life; however, the people who were there did not greet them in the usual way of welcome but rather asked who

[52] Hopi Hearings, 25.

44

are you. Here's where Masau'u first met the white man and they talked to each other face to face. When Masau'u met the white man he met him under disguise, and when they came together ... Masau'u asked him, 'What are you doing here?' to which the white man replied, 'Looking for land,' and asked if there was any life here already, to which Masau'u replied, 'Yes, and more than that—there are buildings already on this land and the land has been divided among the people who live here.' When the white man heard this his countenance changed and Masau'u knew right away that there was a change in his heart.

"He came back to the Hopi, having put away his disguise and appearing to them as another Hopi and he let the Hopi people know that the white man was now on the continent but also that the white man had great plans, that he was making great plans to bring or try to subject the people to."[53]

We come next to the concepts of the Savior and of the Purifier. The ideas are by no means identical, but they tend to become identified. The return of the white god bemused the Aztecs, while the return of Montezuma has been current in a variety of forms in New Mexico and Arizona. There is no certainty in Hopi thought as to who the Savior will be. Sometimes it is Masau'u himself, as in these remarks of Hermequaftewa:

"And the Hopi people asked him that since he is the first person here and that they came to him, he should be their leader in the new land, but Masau'u said no. He said, 'You have many intentions or plans that you want to do in this life. I will not be your leader now, until you have completed all the things that you want to do in this life; Then I will be your leader."[54] If the god were speaking to an individual the statement would be simple and indicate that at death the god of the dead would become the leader of the shade, but today the meaning is tribal, not individual, and looks toward a doomsday. Sometimes this is thought of as merely a threat to hold the Hopis to their ways, and sometimes it is a Calvinistic day of predetermined end.

[53] *Ibid.*, 86. For a Second Mesa use of the brothers, see 81.
[54] *Ibid.*, 80.

To Katchongva the Purifier is the elder of the Two Brothers, but he is Indian rather than white. "Now we are awaiting our brother who has been commissioned at the time we came here to do this duty which was placed on him. It is he, who, when he comes upon our land, will purify this land. That is his duty. He is the one we are waiting for . . . . Because we all know that we are heading to the day which the White man says is the last day, and to the Hopi is Purification Day. We are all going to that same point."[55]

For David Monongye the Purifier is Masau'u himself, and I believe that this is the common attitude among both Traditionalists and Progressives. "We must never make this mistake of losing this land and life because there is someone watching us and is hearing us speak these words and if we ever make a mistake He will know and will punish us. That is His mission and we must never allow ourselves to come to this end."[56]

The old Bluebird Chief, Hermequaftewa, is too kindly and too much of a pacifist to admit an inevitable doomsday into his thinking. "We were instructed that we are all moving towards the day of purification when the purifier himself will come. He will have the tool, but if we continue to follow this pattern that he has set up for us, his tool will not be able to be used. He will not have any use for it. As I said, the purifier will come upon this land if we make a mistake in following this new pattern of the White man's way of life. That's his mission—to purify this land when we make a mistake, but if the Hopis still remain in their own way of life in carrying on the same duties that were placed upon him by the Spirit that gave him this life, then the purifier will only strike an old can or throw up an old shoe."[57]

Each speaker sees the event in the light of his own personality, so it will not be surprising to find Simon Scott saying, "Whoever is going to come to correct this life, perhaps will destroy all of us." Another Hopi, taking note of our present age, quoted Masau'u as predicting that "a gourd full of ashes might fall from the sky and destroy all of us." Indeed it might. However, the god himself is usually like a kindly parent who, when angry, would rather kick up an old shoe than strike his child.

[55] *Ibid.*, 261. Sentences transposed.   [56] *Ibid.*, 53.   [57] *Ibid.*, 88.

In that light it may be remembered that even when identified with the Christian Devil, Masau'u cut off his tail rather than frighten the children. It was inevitable that the analogy with the Pagan Masau'u would not be lost in modern times. A speaker who belongs to the First Mesa Baptist Mission at Polacca seizes upon the idea. Converts to Christianity must move down from the Mesa and away from their ceremonies to Polacca, a shambles at the Mesa's foot. Lawrence Lomavaya speaking:

"At these meetings they spoke about their traditions, life plan of Great Spirit Masau'u. When they spoke of Masau'u, they do not explain who he is, what he is. I'll try and explain it. I was wondering during the meetings if these leaders really understand or know who they choose to follow. Do they know where he will lead them to? We have learned from the Bible this Masau'u is Lucifer, Satan, or the Devil, who is a deceiver of the world. He has deceived the first two human beings .... Masau'u, Devil, had evil mind being in the presence of God in heaven so he was thrown out from heaven down to earth .... We are all misled by Masau'u, Devil .... The Judgement is coming for sure which we all know. Where will you spend your eternity? Down in the lake of fire, or have eternal life in the new world?"[58]

Despite this passage, it does not seem likely that Masau'u will find his ultimate place in history as a Baptist Devil, but as an otiose god, a Great Spirit, shorn of all light and shade. Another speaker from Lower Moencopi answers the charges leveled at the god by the speaker just quoted. Thomas Banyacya for the defense:

"I became interested in my Traditional people because perhaps I have gone through the school where the Christian religion ruled and had the privilege of listening to the comparisons of different religions in the world. It was then I realized the Hopi had a great religion and it is very good and most other religions are very similar to the Hopi beliefs and for that reason I decided to follow the Hopi religion. When the missionaries came, I went along with them. Using the Bible version they began to compare the Hopi beliefs and as we went around to the different villages [during this hearing] I heard

[58] *Ibid.*, 367–68.

47

several Hopi Christians try to misinterpret some of the Hopi beliefs by using the Bible version. In one instance one of the men said something about Masau'u, saying that Masau'u was a lucifer, a bad man, and a wicked person and he went on to explain that this person called Masau'u had died and was buried, but I believe, I firmly believe that Masau'u means a spirit, a spirit that cannot be seen. It is just like the other religion which teaches practically the same thing. Masau'u is a good spirit which governs us and looks after us in this life and that is what the Hopis believe, that someone is guiding us and has given us all this land and life."[59]

In the former roll the god is a devil, while in the latter he is in danger of becoming a patron saint, but one thing is perfectly clear. A spirit who cannot be seen will never again be met face to face, about two miles north of Oraibi, around the bend in the road.

[59] *Ibid.*, 404.

Chapter Two

THE DEAD

Natacka Wuqti, the death symbol

MANY LIVING MEN AND WOMEN have been able to describe the underworld, because they have made visits to the homes of the dead and the sources of life. Very few people ever want to make such a journey, but events are often ruled by powers other than ourselves. During the delirium of a sick man the psyche may leave the body and explore the other world, or at times a person may seem to die, while his spirit leaves on a short journey to the underworld, only to be hurried back to his body again by agents of the gods. He may then tell what he saw on his way. Dreams may more easily and simply tell one what the next life is like. Then finally and far back, in the mythologic age when the Real Kachinas came and danced in the villages, there was naturally a freer intercourse between the human and the spirit world. A prominent young man might be invited to undertake the perilous trip so that he could return and tell his people what the opposite world was like. All such things served to alleviate the mystery of death and to mitigate the fear, not only of one's own passage, but of the power the dead might have over the living.

The race had scarcely emerged from the underworld when the tribes were faced with death and the necessity for some to return. A chief's child, probably a newborn babe, is the first to die. The chief suspects evil magic: "A Powaka has come out with us . . . ." He is persuaded to look down into the entrance and sees his child running around with the others down there. "That is the way it will be . . . if anyone dies, he will go down there and he will remain there only four days, and after the four days he will come back again and live with his people."[1]

Something remains to be explained in the last sentence, since the dead in general do not come back to live with their people; but before

[1] Voth, *The Traditions of the Hopi*, 20.

49

we begin to examine the dead and their journeys, let us pause to hear a Zuñi view of a basic problem, that of the relation of the unborn to the dead. Not all of the people came out of the underworld at the time of emergence, and perhaps these are the ones who are born today, while people who have come to the ends of their roads return again. The relation of unborn to living and to the dead is very well explained by a Zuñi:

"It seems—so the words of the grandfathers say—that in the Underworld were many strange things and beings, even villages of men, long ago. But the people of those villages were unborn-made,—more like the ghost of the dead, for as the dead are more finished of being than we are, they were less so, so as smoke being hazy, is less fine than mist, which is filmy; or as green corn, though raw, is soft like cooked corn which is done (like the dead) and as both are softer than ripe corn which, though raw, is hardened by age (as we are of meat).

"And also, these people were, as you see, dead in a way, in that they had not yet begun to live, in the daylight fashion.

"And so, it would seem, partly like ourselves, they had bodies, and partly like the dead they had no bodies, for being unfinished they were unfixed. And whereas the dead are like the wind, and take form from within of their own wills (yan'te-tseman), these people were really like the smoke, taking form from without of the outward touching things, even as growing and unripe grains and fruits do."[2]

These images are not just poetic fancy, but a part of the language in which human beings are often referred to as either "raw," or "cooked," depending upon their ceremonial status, and so the dead are like ripe corn which is prepared for serving, as well as like the wind.

To return to the earlier statement, that the one who dies will come back again, it is only true in one circumstance, which is in the death of a babe under four years old. These unfortunates may be offered a second chance by being reborn into the same family, in expectation of which they were often buried under the floor of the family room. Such a special status was granted them because until the fourth day they have not yet begun their roads, they have not been held up to

[2] Frank H. Cushing, *Zuñi Folk Tales*, 399–400.

the Sun father for him to admire and accept, nor have they been given a name. After that time the individual has set out upon his irretrievable road whose length is unknown; his comfort is to pray, "May all our roads be fulfilled."

The logic for the race was simple and easily comprehensible. A Cochití child died of sickness, an all too common occurrence; the chief of the curing society went to the great mother in the underworld to ask why. "If your people did not die, the world would fill up and there would be no place for you to live. When you die, you will come back to Shipap to live with me."[3] Her judgment does not refer to space in general, of which the Pueblos had an ample supply, but to food space. At best their diet was just sufficient, while in times of drought much of the population might die of starvation if little rain fell for two years in succession, after which time the reserve supply of corn would have been exhausted. Until the present century, it was perfectly clear that for every mouth added one must be subtracted. The limits were so tight that it has been suggested that the sacred corn ear fetish, which each person kept by him through his life, held, in addition to its mystic power, a reserve of corn seed. To violate such a symbol of one's own life and of the Corn-Mother would be a desperate act, but the fetish did contain the seeds for a new cycle which could at any time spring from her and lengthen the roads.

Any culture is willing to accept the inevitability of death, but after the fact there follows a series of problems for those still living, which they may meet in a number of ways. Some degree of fear of the dead is a basic human emotion; the reality of the recent aliveness of a person does not stop at the moment we designate death. The life of the dead lingers for some time among the living, and under certain circumstances it can be for a very long time. What such an afterlife is no one knows for certain; it is as invisible as the wind, and as powerful. Among uncertainties are several negative possibilities: the dead are the opposite of the living and so very well may wish to harm them, or the very love they bear for their former families may cause them to draw the living members to them. Such possibilities must be put to rest as soon as can be managed.

[3] Ruth Benedict, *Tales of the Cochiti Indians*, B.A.E. *Bulletin* No. 98 (1931), 5.

In our own background we have gone from the very real fear of the early Greeks, through an intermediate time when the Romans, who were so much like ourselves, assumed that the dead were peaceable so long as all the proper rites had been performed. At first this was done by the family, but in time it came to be hired. Today our needs are simpler, satisfied by a mortuary firm, and with whatever degree of religious overtone is requested. In short we have conquered ghosts; their context is most often comic, something in which children half believe, mostly at night and only near a graveyard.

But this was not always so. We are at one extreme, while many peoples have lived at a point where the pendulum began on the opposite swing. Fear of the dead can become so all engrossing that it stultifies a culture. The Pueblos stand between. The physical fact of death is a matter of haste for them; a death interrupted not only a family, but the community. Any breach must be mended as soon as possible, so that the balance of community life may continue.

As a sign of this haste, the dead must be buried before sundown, if at all possible, partly I presume to keep their Sun Calendar accurate. The Sun in his journey must count each day how many have been born, and how many of his people have died that day. Since life is a ceremony, it will only be well if all the acts are carried out on time and in the proper order; otherwise there will be a disturbance in the configuration of the universe, jarring the places of men and of gods.

Among the Keres of the Río Grande there are native priests who are called in to attend the dying, and officials who take care of the physical tasks connected with burial. Among the Hopis, at least in Oraibi where the ceremonial organization has decayed, death and burial are a family, or even an individual, matter.

Don Talayesva had an uncle who was thought to be a hundred years old. He had been lingering between life and death for some time when on a November afternoon, during the Soyal ceremonies, Don's sister came to tell her brother, " 'There is a little breath left in him. I have covered his face with a blanket.' I removed the cover, placed my ear close to his mouth, and listened. Then I said to Naquima, 'His breath is about the length of my finger, and he is getting cold. He must be on the road to our dear ones. I hate to bury him

52

in the dark. I will prop him up against the wall so that the breath will escape quickly. Let's not worry, for he is too old and weak to feel any pain; and it is better for him to be on his way!' As I raised him, the last breath came out. Old Naquima was frightened and said, 'This is the first time I have ever seen a person die. I think I had better go.' He crawled out quickly and left me alone with the dead.

"My brother Ira soon joined me. 'You are just in time,' said I, 'and this is a good chance to help with the burial.' I wondered if he were brave enough to do it. He smiled uneasily and said that while I prepared the body he would go hobble the horses and hurry back. I put water in a tub and washed the hands and face of our uncle and painted both arms and legs to the ankles with white dotted lines. I also made a left curve over his left eye with points turned up like a half moon, to signify to the spirit people that uncle was a Special Officer. After washing his hair with yucca suds and combing it, I spun new string and fastened a soft prayer feather to the top of his head and to each hand, and placed on his feet one and one on his breast. Then I filled his hands with corn meal, closed his fingers and tied them fast. Rubbing meal over his face, I covered it with a white cotton mask with holes for his eyes and mouth. This represented the billowy clouds that would hide his face whenever he returned to drop rain upon our parched lands."

Don then delivered a speech to his dead uncle, while the people had taken their children indoors so that they would not see the body as it was carried away. "It was late afternoon, and I knew we must hurry or darkness would overtake us. By splitting some yucca stems, I bound the robes about the body in the old-fashioned way and bent uncle's knees so that he could sit in the grave." Don mentions that a non-relative might have done this work and the burying, but then he could claim a share of the estate.

"I had bound a rope," he continues, "around the shoulders and thighs of the corpse and made a carrying loop to fit over the head of the bearer. It is best to bear the dead back to back, since the legs of the bearer are less encumbered in walking." Brother Ira carried the body, while Don brought the digging tools.

"As I reached the edge of the mesa, Ira was descending in a stooping trot. Approaching the grave spot, I saw him standing there staggering under his load. 'Drop it,' I called; 'uncle will feel no more pain.' . . . . The clouds were heavy overhead and threatening a snow or hailstorm . . . ." Don then dug the hole. "On the west side I hollowed out a cave for the body, letting Ira throw out the last shovels of dirt. I handed him some corn meal to sprinkle on the bottom, dragged the body close, let it down into the hole, and pressed it back into the cave in a squatting position and facing east." They covered it with dirt and enough stones to keep coyotes and museum collectors out, then set a planting stick as a symbolic ladder and put food and water near by.

When they returned to the Sun clan house the women had boiled juniper boughs in water for a purifying bath; after the men bathed, the bowl containing the spiced water was broken.

"Returning to the house, we placed a piece of piñon gum in a broken dish, lighted it with red-hot coals, and stood under a blanket so that the smoke could pass over our bodies and drive off the evil spirits." They next washed their hands in yucca suds and the women burned their clothes. Sexual continence is maintained for four days, and had the death occurred during the growing season neither man would have tended his crops for the same period.

"On the third day . . . I made two prayer sticks and five prayer feathers. Mabel boiled some beans, and I took them on a plaque with piki wafer bread—and went to the grave. Placing these offerings on the pile of stone, I made a path of corn meal leading eastward and left as quickly as possible, for I did not need to make another speech. On the next morning our uncle arose, no doubt, ate the food, and departed for the House of the Dead."[4]

Thus the old uncle left this world in a manner that would not seem too strange to any people, although some elements are particular—the cotton cloud-mask over the face, the ground maize, juniper water, piñon pine smoke, and the prayer-feathers. The reversal of direction is notable; facing east toward sunrise is not the direction in which the dead journey and must indicate an emphatic feeling of rebirth. On the other hand the absence of any community participa-

[4] Talayesva, *Sun Chief*, 312–16.

tion does not sound characteristic, so we may add a few notes from the Keres where the arrangements are more formal.

When a person is dying, ground turquoise mixed with cornmeal is sent by the family to the head of a medicine society, by way of notification. The task of preparing the body and digging the grave falls upon the Bickaris. They bear the corpse on a ladder and after burial they walk around the grave in a sinistral circuit; again this should take place on the same day as the death.

The ceremonial part of the funeral takes place on the fourth day at the home of the deceased. Members of a medicine society arrive, an altar is set up, and songs are sung while a feast takes place. The central object on the altar is the Iarriko, or corn ear fetish—which is beautifully adorned with feathers. This object is both particular to the person, who has kept it with him all his life, and is as well an image of Iyatiku, the Corn-Mother of the Keres. On the present occasion the fetish symbolizes the heart of the deceased. At Cochití there are on the altar, in addition to the Iarriko, images of Bear, Eagle, Serpent, Turkey, and Chaparrel Cock, spirits of the directions who will help the dead on his journey to the underworld. At Santo Domingo there is a stone figure representing Paiyatemu as well. He is the demigod of music and butterflies whom we shall meet in a later chapter. Perhaps he is there as an associate of the Sun only, or again he may, as a phallic spirit connected with the Sun, represent regeneration.

A line or "road" of meal is made to the door of the house and food is placed upon it. The corn ear fetish of the deceased along with his rattle, dance kilt, and the like, as well as some food, are wrapped in a blanket and taken out by a "doctor" who walks along the meal line. These objects are then buried. Afterwards, "Two doctors with their eagle plumes go to the houses in the pueblo that have been recently visited by the deceased and exorcise the spirit: 'they sweep the floor and walls with their plumes and go like they were driving out flies.' "[5]

In Keresan Acoma a bowl of water is broken over the grave, with the overt indication that the body should sprout again. Today one

[5] Leslie A. White, *The Pueblo of Santo Domingo, New Mexico*, 87.

can see many of these broken pots in the graveyard in front of the famous and empty church there.

When we come to consider Pueblo mortuary behavior, exorcism presents nothing unique as it is nearly universal. Flexed burial is also common enough, but when combined with the typically Pueblo item, a ladder, and in some cases at least with the cloud-mask over the face of the dead, we get a combination presenting a particular view of the dead.

Historically there are two important methods of handling the dead, and these are to some extent directed toward the kind of expectation a culture or individuals have of an afterlife. As we shall soon see, these are by no means disparate alternatives. If a physical resurrection is anticipated, the body may be buried, along with useful objects, such as food, weapons, jewelry, and ceremonial objects—in short, such things as the living need and prize. If it is thought that only the spirit survives, and it should be noted that spirit may imply no more than the pale wraiths of Homer, cremation is practiced; there is a feeling that fire both purifies the body and sends the spirit outward, if not upward.

Despite the hazy nature of the unborn, and the windy essence of their dead, the Pueblos seem never to have practiced cremation. Casteñada's account of the Coronado expedition leaves some doubt. When discussing Cibola—Zuñi—he says, "They bury their dead, and throw the implements used in their work into the fire with the bodies." Possibly he had in memory mixed the Zuñis with tribes further west.

Pueblo attitudes toward burial do not lend themselves to any neat opposites; they represent a compromise of possibilities which is the peculiar genius of their race. When the dead are borne to their grave on a ladder, or a symbol of a ladder is buried with them, the intent is clear; one physically climbs out of his grave as he would climb out of a kiva, or in former times, out of his house. The position of burial, flexed, that is with knees drawn up to the chest, has been used for many centuries. Sometimes it is in a sitting position, or it may rest on its side, but in either case the body is in a foetal posture, an image which indicates a physical rebirth. To be sure, burial in this manner takes less space, but in such a serious matter the amount of labor is unlikely to be the prime consideration.

Against these signs of physical rebirth must be balanced the thinness of spirits—at Santo Domingo only the spirit goes back to the mother. The cloud-mask and the conception of the dead to which it relates, the cloud-people, are highly *aitherialised forms*. While there is some folly in explaining why people don't do what they don't do, I will accept the risk and make an assumption. To the Greeks *aither*, which means blazing, was an acceptable home for departed spirits. To the Pueblos, water rather than fire represents the purest essence of the heavens and the likely transfiguration of the dead. They insist that should they incinerate the bodies, there would be no rain, for their dead are the *u'wannami* (rain-makers). Incineration, they believe, would "annihilate the being." In Talayesva's (Hopi) account, which we will soon give, it is the smoke from the gum of piñon pine that purifies him from contact with the dead, and smoke is not fire, it is a replica of clouds and mist, and ultimately of life-giving water. All that is claimed here is that such a view would have an inhibiting effect on the use of cremation and not at all reduce the feeling that ultimately only the spirit survived.

We must now take both the body and the spirit on a journey into the unknown, and as one could expect, there is little certainty about either the paths or the destination; if all three tribes are considered together the contradictions abound. The Keres have the simplest and most Arcadian picture. The dead first go north, in a kind of reversal of the mythologic journey south from White House; and having paid this respect to their history, they then go west to Wenimats. "It is a place like the most beautiful mountains. In it are royal pines and trees of all kinds, game, lakes, and meadows. Here there are two estufas (kivas) where the *shiwanna* guard their flashes of lightning. There is also an immense bowl of the shape of a funerary bowl."[6] The shiwannas are the dead in their role as rain-makers, and the great bowl doubtless contains the water they distribute. Wenimats is also the home of the kachinas, or at least of many of them.

[6] Nöel Dumarest, *Notes on Cochití, New Mexico*, 173.

The Keres also believe that the dead go to a great lake to the north of New Mexico. Under the lake lies Shipapu which is ordinarily the point from which mankind emerged, but in this instance it represents the seat of the Great Mother Iyatiku who there judges her children.[7] Her home is in the underworld. While the good go directly to Wenimats, those who have been evil go through a purgation, either in a fiery oven, or by confinement to a narrow circle of shells.

Zuñi deceased likewise go to a Lake of the Dead under which resides the Council of the Gods. The residence there in the underworld is called Ko'thluwala'wa, a name which also identifies the lake. This mythic lake is often identified with a small actual lake, called Listening Spring, which lies at the junction of the Zuñi and the Little Colorado rivers.[8]

The Hopi dead, who had no river to contemplate during their life, have no lake through which to enter the underworld, but by way of compensation they enter somewhere in the vastness of the Grand Canyon and make their way west. Like the Keres, there are two ways; the Sun Trail is broad and strewn with pollen and meal; but for evil men there is waiting and purgatory or Hades.

At first sight one might be tempted to attribute these accounts of purgations and Hell, which are found in Hopi and Keres accounts, to Christian influence, particularly since the Keres have lived in intimate contact with Río Grande Catholicism for centuries. However, not all of the elements are Christian—the lakes and actual openings into the underworld are not Christian items, so we must be very cautious about claiming as a specific borrowing what may be rather a widespread set of beliefs. To illustrate, let us examine a few parallels between Greek views of the dead, and Pueblo, with the certain knowledge that there can be no connection between the two.

We have already heard one account of the living looking down a crevice leading to the underworld, related in the story of the chief whose child had died. The Greek writer Lucian tells of a chasm which opens in the earth. He "plucked up his courage, caught hold of a tree

---

[7] White, *The Pueblo of Santo Domingo,* 84n.

[8] M. C. Stevenson, "The Zuñi Indians," B.A.E. *Twenty-third Annual Report* (1901–1902), 305.

that stood near the edge, and looked over, where he saw all the lower world lying spread before him, including the mead of asphodel, where the shades of the blessed were reclining at ease with their friends and relations, arranged according to clans and tribes. Among these he recognized his own father, dressed in the clothes in which he was buried." There is irony here, but the passage is based upon a widespread belief.

In the Pueblo town of Hano on First Mesa they tell the tale of a man whose wife had died. The people "had put a round cactus over the hole they came out. He pulled away the cactus and looked down into the hole. His wife was way down underneath, she was combing her hair."[9] Again there is an account which is the very "mead of asphodel": "That deceased chief and three other chiefs were living in blossoms that were standing one after the other. 'Thanks' said the Kwanitaka [the one-horned bell ringers we shall soon meet again] 'these were never bad in Oraibi, they were always good, therefore they are here this way now. Now, then, let us go and look there, too.' So they again entered. There are all kinds of grasses and plants and blossoms of every description."[10]

It may be noted here that the uncertainty between placing the dead in the underworld, or on meadows and forests, with only slight effort to reconcile the difference, is common to both cultures. In Homer some men go directly to the Isles of the Blest, which, like Wenimats, is a pleasant grove, somewhere toward the setting sun. But when Odysseus visits his own dead mother, it is in Hades, or the symbol of it in the form of an underground trench filled with sheep's blood, although this too is in the far West.

The sacred lakes of the Zuñis and Keres are direct entrances to the underworld, and similarly the Greeks had "certain spots hallowed by tradition as particularly favorable to intercourse with the dead, or even as being actual entrances to the lower world." Sometimes this was a pool, as at Cyane, up the Anapus River from Syracuse, or on a larger scale: "Lakes and seas also were frequently believed to be entrances to Hades."[11]

[9] E. C. Parsons, *Tewa Tales*, 172.   [10] Voth, *The Traditions of the Hopi*, 112.
[11] Lacy Collison-Morley, *Greek and Roman Ghost Stories*, 33–34.

More to the point, perhaps, are detailed accounts of the journey to the underworld. Let us compare a Hopi account with the sixth book of Vergil's *Aeneid*. In each a visitor travels to the underworld, and the first dead to be met are those striving with slight success to complete their journey. In Vergil's story they stand pleading to be ferried across the river, but are arrested as in a dream, and their struggle to the fork of the road will take a hundred years.

In the Hopi account, the young man meets the dead who are on a treadmill. They beseech him to carry them on a bit: " 'Now you carry me,' said the one who was sitting there, 'at least four steps. There you set me down . . . .' " Since four steps, like anything counted in fours, imply simply a long period of time, one might as well say a hundred years. In another version the arrested individual said, " 'I did not follow the straight road; I did not listen, and I now have to wait here. After a certain number of days I can go on a little, then I can go on again, but it will be a long time before I shall get to Skeleton House.' "[12]

Although these stories come from opposite sides of the earth and are separated in time by two milleniums, both tell of the dead who must bear a burden of stone as a purgatorial punishment. In the Greco-Roman Hades the stone must be rolled, while the Hopi dead carry grinding stones in baskets, or by carrying bands around the forehead.

In either case the road the dead travel forks; in the classic underworld the road to the right leads to the meadow of Elysium, the road to the left to Tartarus, "encircled with a rushing flood of torrent flames. Vergil's account here follows that of Plato at the end of the *Republic*, where he has the just go to the right and the unjust to the left. The Hopi directions are reversed, the broad path of the good leading to the left, while to the right the Hopi youth sees a column of smoke rising in the distance; some are there purged and become smoke, while others fall in soot. The Hopi shades are shadows so light that they can climb ladders of sunflower stalks and yet they can burn.

The first point to be made in regard to the correspondence between the Classical and the Pueblo underworld is that we need not look

[12] Voth, *The Traditions of the Hopi*, 115.

to Christian influence to explain the Pueblo conceptions, and even less do we need suppose that they read the classics. The accounts given here all come from the turn of our century; and among the Hopis, if not among the Keres, Christians had made almost no headway at that time. If these were indigenous theories a second question arises. Why is the fork in the Hopi trail the reverse of that assumed by the Greeks and Romans?

In our language the right hand, with which one does things, is first linked with physical might and hence moral right, and ultimately with more abstract ideas of justice; in the background is always the strong right arm. This series of associations may not be inevitable, but the Indian too pulled back his bow-string with the strength of his right arm, and strength and virtue are likely to be united in the mind. The best surmise I can make is that as Masau'u wore his clothes backward, and as the dead are the opposite of the living in every way, so the "right" road becomes the left.

When we come to examine the Zuñi Lake of the Dead we find that the myths connected with it are very much the Zuñis' own. Kiaklo is the myth-bearing supernatural of the Zuñi race, and like the other gods he has a human counterpart, a Pekwin, or deputy. The Pekwin who impersonates him is supposed to have memorized and be able to recount all of the beginning talk. Beginnings in this sense also fold back into endings, for as we have seen, the unborn are "haze-people," while the living and the dead dispute smoke and mist. In a "creation myth" a duck searches for the Lake of the Dead, so that Kiaklo may see for himself how things are, and tell the story to the Zuñis.

A duck is the form a god takes when he travels, but this particular duck may only have been an emissary of the gods. In due time she discovers the lake, and from its depths the lights of the *Kiwitsin*, or kiva of the *kaka*, or gods. Light began to gleam in the waters, and rising from them snout foremost was one "like to her own kind." The one like her referred to is the Salimobia kachina, whose mask has a long snout in front, and on top of the helmet an abstract duck is also fixed. (Two most beautiful plates representing the masks of the Salimobia of the Zenith and the Nadir are to be found in Stevenson's *Zuñi,* page 242.) There are six of these kachinas, one for each of the six directions, and they act as heralds and messengers of the gods. During earthly processions they also act as protectors of the impersonators.

The Salimobia of the North who rose from the water had been sent by the gods to invite the duck to dive down and deliver her message to the Council. "The duck followed down, down, into the great assembly halls . . . ." The gods ask her to lead the myth-bearer to them. Kiaklo is blind and mourning on the plain. The reason for his mourning, and for the existence of the lake itself, is explained without regard to time sequence, in the following manner. Kiaklo had fallen in love with his younger sister, Siwiluhsitsa, and had attempted to seduce her. He was repulsed and then tore out his eyes to make himself hideous. The lake was formed by an earthquake and flood which resulted when the sister stamped her foot in rage.

Under the lagoon of the hollow mountain which the angry sister cleft in two "dwelt in their seasons, the soul-beings of ancient men of war and violent death. There were the towns for the 'finished' or dead . . . the Abode of Ghosts . . . the town of many towns wherein stood forever the great assembly house of ghosts . . . ." To this underworld the myth-bearer is taken that he may learn of the life of the dead there.

Kiaklo's litter is borne with mournful singing "to the shores of the deep black lake, where gleamed from the middle the lights of the dead." The Salimobias rise from the lake and take him on their shoulders to the ladder of reeds; then, "scattering prayer-meal before him (he) stepped down the way, slowly, like a blind man, descending a skyhole. No sooner had he taken four steps than the ladder lowered into the deep; and low the light was instant darkened."

When the Salimobias of the directions brought Kiaklo into the central chamber of the gods, Shulawitsi swung his firebrand and lit the fires again. The blind Kiaklo was able to see by the light the gods and shades gathered there, Pautiwa, chief of the Council of the Gods, then made a speech:

"Sit down with us that we may tell you of much. As a woman

with children is loved for keeping unbroken the line of her kin, so you, tireless hearer, will be cherished by us and worshiped by men for keeping unbroken the Stories of Creation and all that we tell of past days and future."[13]

Next the children who were the first to die in the upper world and return to the lake perform a dance for Kiaklo, and he is told to comfort mourning mothers. He then receives all the myths he must bear and tell, and thereupon, like Aeneas, he is returned to the upper world.

The actual lake is called Listening Spring because one can hear voices within its depths, which would account for its associations. In rituals either the lake or the town under it are referred to by the archaic name *We'nima*, which must certainly be related to the Keresan Wenimats, or Elysian fields in the West, just as Zuñi shi-wanna—rain-maker priests—is related to Keresan shiwanna, the dead as rainmakers. Since the two languages are not related in the terms, perhaps concepts must have been borrowed, in one direction or the other.

Kiaklo's visit to the chambers of Ko'thluwala'wa is an integral part of Zuñi ritual. Folk tales tell much the same thing about the lake, but one may be recounted to illustrate the complete separation of the living from the dead. In a story called "The Trial of Lovers," a young man mistakenly kills his wife while she is struggling with an identical twin who is a witch. Though she is an invisible shade after her death, the husband follows her route by watching a feather she has tied in her hair. The central theme is an Eurydice story; on the journey back to Zuñi he can't refrain from kissing his wife, and she must return to the underworld. The point of interest for us is the lake to which he has traced her. On the shores of the lake an ugly old couple are always walking back and forth across the trails—closing them, I presume. The young wife "fearlessly walked into the water, and a ladder of flags came up out of the middle of the lake to receive her, down which she stepped without stopping until she passed under the waters. For a little—and then all was over—a bright light shone out of the water, and the sound of many glad voices and soft

[13] Frank H. Cushing, "Outlines of Zuñi Creation Myths," B.A.E. *Thirteenth Annual Report* (1891–92), 411–12. Paraphrased. For earlier quotations, see 399ff.

63

merry music came also from beneath it; then the stars of the sky and the stars of the water looked the same at each other as they had done before.

" 'Alas!' cried the young man as he ran to the lake side. 'Ah, my beautiful wife, my beautiful wife, only wait, only wait, that I may go with thee!'

"Toward the middle of the night once more he heard strange, happy voices. The doorway to the Land of Spirits opened, and the light shot up through the dark green waters from many windows, like sparks from a chimney on a dark windless night. Then the ladder ascended, and he saw the forms of the dead pass out and in, and heard the sounds of the *Kaka* as it danced for the gods . . . . Once he ventured to gain the bright entrance, but the water grew deep and chilled him till he trembled with fear and cold. Yet he looked in at the entrances, and lo! as he gazed he caught sight of his beautiful bride all covered with garments and bright things. And there in the midst of the *Kaka* she sat at the head of the dancers. She seemed happy and smiled as she watched, and youths as bright and as happy came round her, and she seemed to forget her lone lover."[14]

Before the Zuñi spirits arrive at the Lake of the Dead, they and their abandoned bodies have undergone rites which more nearly resemble those of the Keres than those described for the Hopis by Don Talayesva. The heads of the fraternity to which the dying member belongs are at the house. After death women who are not of the immediate family come into the room and howl. "Parents or sisters of a deceased person sleep at the side of the surviving spouse during the four nights that the spirit is supposed to remain in Zuñi. A grain of black corn and a bit of charcoal are put under the head of the mourner to insure against dreaming of the lost one, whose ghost would appear should the sleeper awake." A "road" for the dead to follow is made with a trail of black cornmeal, "to make the road dark," so that the dead will not return in dreams.[15]

After the first sharp feeling of loss, there comes a presentiment

[14] Cushing, *Zuñi Folk Tales,* 28–30.
[15] Stevenson, "The Zuñi Indians," *loc. cit.,* 311–16.

64

of fear. A tender Zuñi prayer for a dead wife is interrupted by a stern admonition to the departed:

> Now you have attained the far off place of waters.
> I give you plume wands,
> Plume wands which I have prepared for your use.
> Drawing your plume wands to you,
> And sharing my plume wands,
> Indeed, under no conditions shall you take anyone away.[16]

In this one verse among dozens the sentiment is expressed in an official prayer, rather than from a sense of personal fear, but it is only because the community has accepted and ameliorated the individuals' feeling. By and by we shall examine the method by which the Pueblo communities have transposed their ghost, and by turning their power upside down have made it work for the benefit rather than to the detriment of the living. Since the dead have become helpful, they are asked to return, rather than being shunted away; they become patrons, protectors, and rainbringers, and as represented by kachinas their dances are both helpful and entertaining. In this return to the community the departed spirit released the last of his individual pull toward the underworld, and joins the benign collectivity of ancestral spirits.

Before we examine the kachinas, however, there are two other aspects of the dead which need consideration. To begin with, there are some dead who have been gone so long that they have lost any personal meaning, but they are recognized. The mesas, deserts, and canyons of New Mexico and Arizona are littered with dead towns. Many of these are well known to modern Pueblos, and they recognize that their inhabitants were in some way ancestors of themselves. A second quality of the dead, and one not essentially related to the first, is their attractiveness to the living.

Ritual has allayed the power of the dead who may wish to draw living relatives along with them, but what if the willing is done by the living? The desire for death which results in suicide is willed

[16] Ruth L. Bunzel, "Zuñi Ritual Poetry," B.A.E. *Forty-seventh Annual Report* (1929–30), 633–34.

from this world, not the other. To the Pueblos, whose morality is built upon the unbroken flow of community life, suicide is a terrible lesion, so much so that it is as rare as homicide; and devious methods, such as hiring the Navahos to kill one, are used—at least in story. There is, nonetheless, an undercurrent of fantasy suicides—those which take place in the mind only. The following myth is an admonition against death wishes, and a recognition and explanation, on a folk-tale level, of the dead cities that hang on cliffs, or crumble on the plains.

As befits a good ghost story, the scene and mood are first established. "But, fearing that never again would the waters refreshen their canyons, our ancients who dwelt in the cliffs fled away to the southward and eastward—all save those who had perished aforetime; they are dead in their homes in the cliff-towns, dried, like their corn-stalks that dried when the rain stopped long, long ago, when all things were new."[17]

There are two published versions of this myth which warn against seeking the dead past. Cushing's version is a myth in high style, while Benedict's is earthy, rather simple, and contrives, by magic, to end happily. We will follow the former story, and add a few elements from the latter. In both, a youth takes the form of an eagle, and flies too high and too far from the center. The first is an Icarus-like story of a youth who ventures into the proscribed realms of the gods. He is an introvert who has fallen in love with a female eagle he has raised in a cage. (Caged eagles whose feathers are used in ceremonials are a familiar sight in many pueblos.) Since he prefers her to his own community of people, they soon flee together.

". . . The Eagle and the youth went on until at last they came to the great opening in the Zenith of the sky. In passing upward by its endless cliffs they came out on the other side into the sky-world; and still upward soared the Eagle, until it alighted with its beloved burden on the summit of the Mountain of Turquoises, so blue that the light shining on it paints the sky blue."

He there married his love and was given an eagle suit, but warned not to fly beyond a particular range of mountains on the horizon. As

[17] Cushing, *Zuñi Folk Tales*, 428.

he flew through the sky for a long distance, his sense of power overwhelmed him and he turned southward exclaiming, " 'Why should I not see what this is? Who can harm me, floating on these strong wings of mine?' So he flew over the edge of the mountains, and behold! Rising up on the plains beyond there was a great city, fine and perfect, with walls of stone built as are the towns of our dead ancients. And the smoke was wreathing forth from its chimneys, and in the hazy distance it seemed teeming with life at the moment when the youth saw it, which was at evening time."

The dead being the opposite of the living, become active only as dark settles down. Eagle Youth, by violating the first proscription in discovering the forbidden city, has put both himself and the eagle people under obligation. This obligation is based upon the Pueblo principle of initiation by trespass; if you happen on to things or rites you should not see you are obliged to join the society which was holding them. He and the eagles are invited to attend a dance, and they must not refuse although they are angry with the youth. Eagle Youth's wife lays a second proscription on him as the price of her forgiveness: he must not smile or laugh at anything he sees.

"A beautiful place it was, large and fine, with high walls of stone and many a little window out of which the red firelight was shining. The smoke was going up from its chimneys, the sparks winding up through it, and with beacon fires burning on the roofs, it was a happy, bustling scene that met the gaze of the youth as he approached the town. There were sounds and cries of life everywhere. Lights shone and merriment echoed from every street and room, and they were ushered into a great dance hall, or *kiwitsin* where the audience was already assembled."

The entrance of the girls down the ladder into the ceremonial chamber differs in the two versions, the latter coming abruptly to the point: "A girl dropped in down through the hatchway and hit the floor like a dead body. Blood ran out of her mouth. Another girl fell in through the hatchway and hit the floor like a dead body. They stood up like two fine girls with smooth plump arms and big black eyes."

In the first version the maidens, mostly beautiful ones, arrive in a group, joking and laughing as they descend the ladder into the room, "and as they danced down the middle of the floor they cried out in shrill, yet not unpleasant voices, as they jostled each other, playing grotesque pranks and assuming the most laughter-stirring attitudes:

" '*Hapa! Hapa! is! is! is!*' (Dead! this! this! this!)—pointing at one another, and repeating this baleful expression, although so beautiful, and full of life and joy and merriment." The youth in time inevitably breaks the second proscription by laughing and joining in the dance. At this his wife and the eagles abandon him and fly away. Although now alone, he is not lonely, as the two girls ask him to spend the night with them in their room. He lies in the middle and they put their arms over him. In the second version the ghastly facts appear before morning: "They were fine looking girls but he said to himself, 'These girls smell like rotten meat.' "

The first account sticks by the traditional concept of the dead being unable to live in daylight, and consequently the revelation comes to Eagle Youth at dawn.

"In the morning, when broad daylight had come, the youth opened his eyes and started. It seemed as though there were more light than there should be in the house. He looked up, and the room which had been so fine and finished the night before was tottering over his head; the winds shrieked through great crevices in the walls; the windows were broken and wide open; sand sifted through on the wind and eddied down into the old, barren room. The rafters, dried and warped with age, were bending and breaking, and pieces of the roof fell now and then when the wind blew more strongly. He raised himself and clammy bones fell from around him; and when he cast his eyes about him, there on the floor were strewn bones and skulls. Here and there a face half buried in the sand, with eyes sunken and dried and patches of skin clinging to it, seemed to glare at him. Fingers and feet, as of mummies, were strewn about, and it was as if the youth had entered a great cemetery, where the remains of the dead of all ages were littered about. He lifted himself still further, and where the head of one maiden had lain or the arms of another had entwined with his, bones were clinging to him. One by one he picked them off stealthily and laid them down, until at last he freed himself, and rising, cautiously stepped between the bones which were lying around, making no noise until he came to the broken-down doorway of the place. There, as he passed out, his foot tripped against a splinter of bone which was embedded in the debris of the ruin, and as a sliver sings in the wind, so this sang out. The youth, startled and terrorized, sprang forth and ran for his life . . . . Shrieking, howling, and singing like a slivered stick in the wind, like creaking boughs in the forest, with groans and howls and whistlings that seemed to freeze the youth as he ran, these bones and fragments of the dead arose . . . .

"He ran and ran, and the great cloud of the dead were coming nearer and pressing around him . . . ."

At this climactic point the two versions of the myth part from each other, but as both are tales well worth telling, I will give both, continuing with the first. The youth is saved from the dead by the Badgers, who will appear in the next chapter as those who finally scratched an opening from the underworld, so that mankind could emerge into the upper world. When the youth returns to the homes of the eagles his wife cries out:

"Why did you go and become enamoured of Death, however beautiful? . . . . Who would dance and take joy in Death? . . . ." In this strait the youth is worse off than when fleeing the dead, for he has lost not only his wife but his eagle garments. Her people ask her to take him back, so she gives him a ragged coat and they fly away from Turquoise Mountain, "downward and downward in very narrow circles." When his worn wings faltered his wife bore him up until, "in a moment of remembrance of his faithlessness, she caught in her talons the Eagle dress which sustained him and drew it off, bade him farewell forever, and sailed away out of sight in the sky. And the youth, with one gasp and shriek, tumbled over and over and over, and fell into the very center of the town in which he had lived when he loved his Eagle, and utterly perished."[18] And such is the fate of one who would leave the Pueblo community.

The second version illustrates the virtue of repentance and the power of magical rites. The youth first escapes the dead girls by purifying himself with ceremonial emesis, but he knows that the girls

[18] *Ibid.*, 39–53.

are still coming after him. He admits his folly to an old man who tells him to get white corn, turquoise, and coral to grind into prayer meal. "Take your bow and arrow and take your wife. Put her half a mile outside the southeast corner of that pueblo. Make a circle of prayer meal all around the town. Begin it at the east and close it to the southeast. Shoot your arrow into the circle and you will overcome these bad people."

Late in the afternoon "he flew down to the dead people's pueblo and waited for the sun to set. Just at sunset all the dead people woke." The parents of the girls noted that their arms and legs had been broken where the youth had kicked them off him. The people "came out into the streets and they saw that where the young man had made the circle of prayer meal the whole pueblo had been lifted up into a great mesa. They tried to get down the cliff but they couldn't. The young man set his lightning arrow to his bow and shot through the circle of sacred meal and the whole pueblo shot up into the sky on the other side of the ocean."[19]

Don't go too far West in your thoughts, is again the message; but this time with the hopeful addition that even if you have joined the dances of the dead, you can return and be rescued by the powerful rites of your living community.

When we turn to examine a Hopi visit to the underworld, we find the escape motif and reliance on traditional culture again present. This account comes from the dream of a man during delirium. Don Talayesva, the Oraibi Sun Chief, was taken from his parents and sent to the Riverside boarding school of the U.S. government. While at Riverside, Don became extremely ill and was put in the critical ward of the hospital. His feet were growing numb and he knew that his end was near.

"I began to think of the two-Hearts and to review all that I had heard about them. I knew that they were very unfortunate but powerful people, members of every race and nation, organized into a world-wide society in which they spoke a common language, and that they were able to postpone their own death by taking the lives of their relatives. I understood that Hopi Two-Hearts were leaders of

[19] Ruth Benedict, *Zuñi Mythology*, I, 130–36.

70

this terrible society, that they held their underworld conventions at Red Cliff Mesa northeast of Oraibi, and that Two-Hearts in Oraibi were probably the worst of the lot."

A tall human figure dressed as a kachina appears by his bedside bearing a blue prayer-feather in his left hand, the color blue signifying the West and the land of the dead. "I saw the door swing slowly back and forth on its hinges and stop just a little open. A cold numbness crept up my body; my eyes closed; and I knew I was dying . . . .

"The strange human being said, 'Now, my boy, you are going to learn a lesson. I have been guarding you all your life, but you have been careless. You shall travel to the House of the Dead and learn that life is important.' " First the ghost of Don walks, then he is swept along as by a gust of wind, and at last flies until he comes to the Hopi Mesas; after passing through a region of fog and little lights he goes to his own house, but his relatives don't see him. He then walks out to some rocks that rim a dam, and notices a large lizard run into them.

"As I drew near I saw peeping out from the rocks an ugly, naked woman with drawn face and dry lips. She looked tired, half-starved, and very thirsty. It was my old (clan) grandmother, Bakabi, my mother's sister." She denies that she has killed Don, but he nonetheless believes that she is the Two-Heart responsible. "From here to the House of the Dead," Bakabi tells him, "you will see people like me who can take only one step a year over a path of sorrow . . . ." He arrives at a place of monstrous steps, reminding one of the Great Stairway at Hungopavi, in Chaco Canyon. "I started to climb but seemed to float up on air, just touching my feet lightly on the top step. There a bell from the west side rang so clearly that I heard echoes out among the mesa walls.

"As the ringing grew louder, I looked and saw a man climbing up the mountain from the west, dressed in white buckskin, wearing a horn, and holding a spear and a bell. It was a Kwanitaka, a member of the Kwan or Warrior society." Don is then shown the two roads; the one on the left side is wide and sprinkled with cornmeal, while on the right "I saw naked suffering people struggling along the path with heavy burdens and other handicaps such as thorny cactus plants fastened to their bodies in tender places. Snakes raised their heads along the edge of the path." He is then shot up onto the mesa where he sees flowers blooming and hears birds singing—it will be remembered that he is dying in midwinter.

"In the distance were twelve queer-looking striped animals chasing one another. As I drew nearer I saw that they were clowns who had painted their bodies with black and white stripes and were joking and teasing one another." Don takes another left turning and arrives at a great canyon which he believes to be the Little Colorado. "On the walls across the canyon were the houses of our ancestors with smoke rising from the chimneys and people sitting out on the roofs." Here again is a vision of the cliff-dwellers living as an intact group, quite apart from the contemporary dead who are struggling between heaven and hell. The picture is of the distant past, and wholly serene even to the feverish mind of a sick man. These ancients are so settled in the past that their former lives on earth are no issue; they merely sit on their ghostly rooftops amid the wreathing of their smoke.

Such a static vision is a brief interlude, soon interrupted by the bells of the Kwan men ringing again. They now act as guides, one traveling before and one after him, to keep off evil spirits. By and by they arrive at a fire pit, "like that in which sweet corn is baked," where Two-Hearts are being pushed in by the people they had killed. "I stepped up close to the rim and saw an empty hole with a network of two-inch cracks broken into the walls through which flames of fire were leaping. In the center at the bottom were four black beetles crawling about, two carrying the other two on their backs . . . . 'That's the end of these Two-Hearts,' said he, 'and the fate of all their kind.' They will stay there as beetles forever, except to make occasional visits to Oraibi and move about the village doing mischief on hazy days."

The family of beetles which Don refers to has worn the badge of Hell in men's minds on other continents as well, which may serve as an excuse for an excursus on the Tenebrionidae, that may not be altogether irrelevant, since they do bother people on hazy days and do have a place in Hopi ritual. The Latin name of the family suggests not only shadows and the dark, but all things obscure, secret, or underhand and, of course, gloomy. According to Lacordaire, their historian, *La livree des Tenebrionides est en harmonie avec leurs moeurs. Un noir profond* . . . . or, "the servant's garb of the Tenebrionides is in harmony with their habits, a profound black."

In her Introduction to Stephen's *Hopi Journal*, Parsons states, "Something of a supernatural war character was attributed to Beetle and at least one of the old men opined that the dead, if bad enough, but not too bad, turned into beetles."[20] The war association, which is also found at Keresan Cochití,[21] where in a tale the tip beetle (same family) does the warlike work for a snake, is based in part on the fact that the beetle is an ingredient in the famous snake-medicine of the Hopis, although the association with the dead may have explained its use as a remedy for snakebite, rather than the other way around.

Voth says that *Asida rimata* is used in the snake emetic. Parsons says both this and the stinking tumble beetle are used, and one need not doubt their effectiveness for the purpose. The *Asida* has another association—it is conspicuous after rain and is thought to be blind, wherefore it feels about for a host plant, which is also used in the emetic. One genus, whose members are again flightless and awkward, and thereby prone to fall into abandoned kivas and pits, is *Eleodes*, the tip beetles. The largest of these, *gigantea*, is about the size of one's thumb. I have watched a half dozen of these trapped at the bottom of an old kiva, where they make the perfect picture of lost souls as they lumber about futilely looking for a way out.

Having noted the relationship between these beetles and the dead, we shall now return to the narrative of the dream. The canyon was by now full of smoke, and the Kwan men were hurrying Don back along his course to the world of the living. And now "when I peered down I saw a gruesome creature in the shape of a man climbing the cliff. He was taking long strides with his shining black legs and big feet; an old tattered rag of a blanket was flying from his shoulder as he approached swiftly with club in hand. It was big, black, bloody-headed Masau'u, the god of Death, coming to catch me." Undoubtedly this

---

[20] Stephen, *Hopi Journal*, I, xli.
[21] Ruth Benedict, *Tales of the Cochiti Indians*, B.A.E. *Bulletin No. 98* (1931), 127–28.

is a recollection of the flight Don recounted in the first chapter; at any rate, the Kwans push him so fast that he rises off the ground.

"When I reached Cole Canyon the clowns were waiting for me, standing in a straight line facing west with their arms about each other . . . As I approached them at full speed, they cried, "Jump, Masau'u is gaining!' I jumped and landed on the chest of the leader, knocking him down. They all laughed and yelled, seeming not to mind, for clowns are always happy."

The clowns are near the dead, in that they too do things backward, but they are of the living and Masau'u cannot overcome them. Don is advised to cling to the neck of his body when he returns to the hospital, in order to warm his flesh. His body comes back to life and the blue kachina spirit appears again.

"Eat," it says, "and regain your strength. Some day you will be an important man in the ceremonies . . . . I have shown myself to teach you this lesson. Now I shall leave you. Be good, be wise, think before you act, and you will live a long time. But I shall hold you lightly, as between two fingers, and if you disobey me I will drop you."[22]

In the accounts and myths presented so far in this chapter, fear of the dead has been uppermost, or perhaps it would be better phrased if we said avoidance of the dead, rather than fear. Contact is limited in both story and fact. Bury them as soon as possible, don't even dream about them, destroy their clothes and physical remains, don't go near their towns either in fact or in fantasy. And yet, despite all attempts to separate the two worlds, the dead remain with us and if they are to remain they must in some way be domesticated. One common method is to turn the departed into protectors of the living. The hero cults select a man of renown, now gone, and assume that his power over the living is used to protect his town, tribe, clan, or other group. Ancestor worship is a more modest and particular version of the same pattern.

What the Pueblos most desire on earth is fertility for their meager crops. If the dead have powers, they can be used to assure a good harvest. The idea is not unique; in central India the dead are buried

[22] Talayesva, *Sun Chief*, 121–26.

near fields to watch and protect them, that is, they are rustic rather than warrior protectors; in other parts of India they are not only responsible for the crop, but may be immanent in the grain itself. In the Central Celebes a prayer beseeches, "O grandfathers, have pity on us; if it is your will that this year we should eat, then give rain."[23] In this way what has been feared, or avoided, has become desirable and must be sought.

Considering the communal nature of Pueblo life, it is natural that a collectivity of the dead, rather than particular ancestors or heroes, would be sought. All of the dead are useful to everyone, just as the living are joined together. Since the dead return to the underground, both actually and mythically, they join with the sources of all agricultural crops. But for the success of these crops, two things are necessary: germination from underground and, on these deserts and mesas, rain from above to "fertilize" the sprouts. For the first act of sustaining their living descendants the dead are well prepared. They bodily climb out of their graves and live an underworld life comparable to our own, but below. But for the second office a transformation must be made, a resurrection, since they must come out of the underworld and as nebulous, ephemeral spirits pass above the living to bring rain.

The necessity of turning the dead into vapors accounts for a good deal in Pueblo ritual. Smoking, by analogy, produces clouds, as even we say; any connection with the fire which produces it is quenched. The pipes in which tobacco is smoked are shaped like a blossom and are called "cloud blowers." The blossom raises the cloud, which then returns the fertility. The burial party described earlier purified itself, not by fire, but only with the smoke of piñon pine. When the living smoke during their ceremonies, "this smoke goes down into the other world to the *tiponis* or mothers and from there rises up in the form of clouds." In order to float around as clouds the dead must be very light; they "never eat food, but only the odour and soul of food. That is the reason why the clouds into which the dead are transformed are not heavy and can float in the air."[24]

[23] J. G. Frazer, *The Fear of the Dead in Primitive Religion*, I, 103.

[24] Voth, *The Traditions of the Hopi*, 116f. For a good illustration of the "cloud blowers," see N. M. Judd, *Pueblo Bonito*, 300.

And what in addition to smoke is as light as a cloud? Feathers, of course, and these are used to invoke both the gods and the dead; "these we tie around our forehead and they represent dripping rain." The dead come over the villages in all kinds of clouds, in wind-blown cirrus clouds, or in the cumulus clouds replete with living waters. When the Zuñis ask for their rain-making dead they are not only saying a prayer, but are also constructing an altar with sand paintings:

> Four times we shall spread out the mist blanket.
> We shall fashion the house of the massed clouds.
> We shall fashion the life-giving road,
> Four times we shall fashion your spring.[25]

These words are chanted as the Zuñis paint the altarpiece.

Feathers of subtle meaning and infinite variety are the essence of every rite, private or public. As feathers are placed in this rain-seeking prayer to the dead, a priest chants:

> This day
> Desiring the waters of our fathers
> . . .
>
> We have given our plume wands human form,
> With the massed cloud wing
> Of the one who is our grandfather,
> The male turkey,
> With eagle's thin cloud wings
> And massed cloud tails
> Of all the birds of summer.
> . . .
>
> At the place called since the first beginning
> Rock wedge,
> Where our fathers,
> Rain maker priests,
> In their rain-filled inner rooms
> Were all gathered together in beauty
> To receive their plume wands.
> . . .

[25] Bunzel, "Zuni Ritual Poetry," *loc. cit.*, 657.

You will make your roads come forth.
Your little wind blown clouds,
Your thin wisps of clouds,
Your great masses of clouds
Replete with living waters,
You will send forth to stay with us.
Your fine rain caressing the earth. . .
With your great pile of waters
You will come together.

. . .

Then our children,
Our ladder-descending children,
Will gather you in.
Into all their houses.

. . .

Do not let anyone fall from your grasp
When he has gone but a little ways![26]

These last two stanzas express the mutuality involved; the living will let you, the dead, into all their houses and you in turn should not let the living disappear too soon. But the priest will soon again be chanting, "Stretch out your watery hands, let us embrace!"

The six-point cloud-people are the supernatural dead who come back to help their villages with rain. In that role they are usually equated with the dancing kachinas, who are spirits devoted to rain-making, and incidentally to entertainment. Once these kachinas were the "real kachinas" who came from their home in the West, but they no longer return to the pueblos in person, but are thought of as the cult of masked dancers who impersonate these spirits. Most of the kachinas are identified with the dead in a general way, but one who dies does not become a specific kachina.[27]

The problem of identifying the kachinas with the benevolent dead is confused, or perhaps one should say left unresolved, by the fact that not all kachinas are good. In a major ceremony at Acoma they even attack the town; at Cochití there is a "Bloody Hand Print

[26] *Ibid.*, 643–45.
[27] For a negative view, see White *The Pueblo of Santo Domingo*, 198–99.

77

Kachina," and at Laguna they even murder people. These facts may indicate either that it is hard to put the ghosts to rest, or that the kachina cult, at least among the Keres, has never been completely integrated into its benign and central role.

The kachinas, in a general way, represent the dead and some of them represent greater supernaturals as well. But how supernatural are they? Some of them are certainly gods commingling with the dead, but the masks worn by the living represent not only these, but other figures who may be merely entertaining grotesques of animals or insects; or they may satirize other cultures, or represent fragments from mythology. Some have modest functions, such as disciplining or amusing children, but all of them together, whether they represent gods or merely good fellowship, are very powerful spirits who share in the function of rain-making.

This leads to the interesting question of how far the dead, through the medium of the kachinas, are identified with the gods. Apparently not at all. However, one can debate the associations of kachinas with gods altogether. White, in his various studies of Keresan towns, seems to think of all kachina figures as gods. For example, when writing on Santo Domingo he says, "I endeavored to find out what a man feels and thinks during a masked dance. Impersonating a god is a serious business."[28] It is true that gods are imitated by Keresan kachinas: *Oshatsh* is the Sun; there are two sets of masks for Paiyatemu, while another group represents a set of female equivalents to the Chiefs of the Directions, and Yellow Woman of the North has the stature of a goddess which may be shared, by analogy, with the other directional spirits.

Against the godly conception of kachinas there is other evidence to be considered. A Zuñi woman told Erna Fergusson, " 'They are not gods,' said she; 'That word is wrong. The Zuñis have no gods; they are *Koko*.' "[29] Since Ko'ko is the Zuñi word both for masked dancers and for gods (kachina is a Hopi word, but is used generically in this text) her distinction is not clear, except for degree of power. Actually there is a closer correspondence between the pantheon and

[28] *Ibid.*, 101.   [29] Erna Fergusson, *Dancing Gods*, 98.

78

the kachinas at Zuñi than elsewhere, since the whole Council of the Gods is represented.

Since the Pueblos have not integrated or rationalized these concepts, we may leave them in their cloud-like state and only note that the Hopi word kachina derives from *kachi,* which means "spirit father, or life, or spirit."[30] A spirit father is naturally associated with the dead: "The awe which Zuñis feel for all sacred and powerful objects is intensified in this case by the fact that masks are representations of the dead and, indeed, the very substance of death. [Recall the non-representational cloud-mask of cotton Don put on his uncle.] Therefore the use of masks is surrounded by special taboos. One must never try on a mask when not participating in a ceremony, else one will die."[31] Among the Hopis, when the body is buried, it is addressed: "You are no longer Hopi, you are changed (*nih'ti,* grown into) a kachina, you are cloud (O'mauuh). You will eat once of this food [i.e., accept this food offering], and, when you get yonder, you will tell the chiefs to hasten the rain clouds here."[32]

Thus, although the pattern of thought cannot be made rigidly logical, there is a transformation made from the ugly aspects of the dead to the useful and beautiful, just as Masau'u took unto himself benevolent as well as fearful qualities.

Having now completed our journey through the lands of the dead and having met its denizens, both human and divine, we may leave this gloomy half of the Pueblo cosmos. The world of death was presented before the realms of life, since it could not serve as a fitting conclusion to Pueblo thinking in its entirety. The Pueblos are essentially a cheerful and festive people. Most of their rituals and myths have a religious character, but they are also social, and for three quarters of the year there is scarcely a break in the performing and enjoying of rituals.

When we leave the bell-ringing Kwan men, the smoke of vanished

---

[30] Frederick J. Dockstader, *The Kachina and the White Man,* 9.

[31] Ruth L. Bunzel, "Zuñí Katcinas," B.A.E. *Forty-seventh Annual Report* (1929–30), 845.

[32] Stephen, *Hopi Journal,* II, 826.

pueblos and their peoples, and the recent dead, we turn next toward the sunlight and those gods who inhabit the daylight world, first to examine creation itself and then to turn to earth-mothers and a male lord of crops. Then we will follow up to the sun himself, from which point we will be able to view all of the cosmos as it surrounds the Pueblo mind and life.

Chapter Three

THE CREATORS
AND THEIR CREATIONS

Sho'tokunungwa, the sky or star god

ULTIMATE GODS are by their very nature inscrutable; they are shrouded in secrecy. These powers are hidden not because they wish to keep their natures and intents withdrawn from mankind, but because they exist very far away in time and space. They tend to retire, or to be dethroned, as soon as the motion of life has begun. One Indian tribe in South America solved the question with pristine simplicity: the world was created by a dung beetle who rolled up this little ball of mud with his hind feet, and then went off and left it. On a more complex level, consider the familiar gods of Greece. Zeus is a well defined figure, but he is not a creator. His father Kronos is, as the name indicates, in part a personification of Time, and belongs with those other beginning powers called Night and Chaos. When we arrive at Phanes, who started the process of creation, according to many Greek mythographers, we find a very abstract being who is not "female and male," but "female and father," at least so say some orphic fragments.

Thus it is not to be expected that the divinities of this chapter will be as precise as one could wish. The three tribes in question differ more fundamentally on the nature of the creators than they do on other aspects of Pueblo religion. The ultimate Zuñi god, A'wona-wil'ona, is, like the Greek Phanes, a "he-she." Such a statement can mean either that the god is beyond sex, or that the being contains the attributes of both males and females. The Zuñi divinity in question is so abstract that one good scholar has doubted the existence of such a being, attributing the name to a collectivity of spirits. Unless one insists that all gods be personal and singular, the question is probably irrelevant. There are undoubtedly many individual interpretations, just as Night could be thought of as a personified female being, or as a void of powers in which Chaos coalesced into matter.

81

The beginning goddess of the Keres Indians is "Thinking Woman," or to use the spelling of Sía pueblo, Sus'sistinako. She seems to belong to the underworld, but her creative capacity for "thinking outward into space," a kind of silent Logos which brings everything into existence, indicates a close relationship with the upper, if not the heavenly, world. There is some ambivalence about the sex of Thinking Woman, as at Sía she is male.

The generatrix of the Hopis is "Hard Beings Woman," or Huruing Wuhti. She is of the earth, but lives, like the Sun, in the heavenly world where she owns the moon and the stars. She is definitely female, and curiously enough it is her son who becomes the earth-god of crops. Possibly the matrilineal system of inheriting power, which was strong among the Hopis until lately, has something to do with the arrangement. Hard Beings Woman is most often mentioned in connection with shells, beads, and the like, but these are doubtless signs of our great hard being, the earth. The emphasis in her character is not so much upon fecundity as upon solidity—she is responsible for the substance of the earth, that old shell-mound on which we all live. She does not give birth to, but creates, a youth and a maid.

The male youth she created was Muingwu, a god of crops who will be considered at length in the next chapter. The female counterpart of this god—sister is hardly the right word under these circumstances—is Tuwa'boñtumsi. She is Sand Altar Woman, and is also called Childbirth Water Woman. The latter is spoken of as the mother of kachinas. Apparently the division was made on the basis of a male god to guard the fertility of crops, and a female goddess to handle human fecundity, which seems characteristic of Hopi everyday reasonableness.

Hard Beings Woman lived in the very beginning on the only piece of solid land there was, a kind of world nucleus which gathered matter around its reefs.

"Aliksai! A very long time ago there was nothing in the world but water. Only away off in the west where Huruing Wuhti lived there was a small piece of land where she lived. She lived in a hill or bluff called Talaschomo. Huruing Wuhti owned the moon, the stars, and all the hard substances, such as beads, corals, shells, etc.

Away in the east lived the Sun, painted up very beautifully. The Sun was very skillful."[1]

Her house is a kiva in the western ocean where the Sun enters each night to be let down through a hatch that he may travel under and rise in the east again. We get so few glimpses of this goddess-paramour of the Sun that one which is not august may be worth including. The account comes as a part of the Snake Legend, a matter which belongs to another chapter. A young man is watching the waters slide along the Grand Canyon as he wonders where all of them go. To solve the riddle, the youth makes a journey down the river in a boat that eventually runs ashore. There he "got out, and saw that there was land, and also much water—the ocean. He also found many people living there. At one place he saw a hill out in the water. That was the house of Huruing Wuhti, the deity of such hard substances as beads . . . turquoise, etc. Presently a maiden approached him that was very pretty." At her invitation he "rowed to a hill in the ocean, that was clear and transparent, where there was a kiva from which a ladder was protruding."

The maiden takes him to the kiva of the goddess, although I think that in the mind of the teller she and the goddess are identical. The Snake youth has brought one prayer-feather for the Sun. "She asked him whether the sun was low, to which he replied in the affirmative. She then put him into another room, as something 'very living' was coming, as she put it. Presently the turtle rattle on the ladder rattled and the Sun came rushing down in the form of a handsome young man, beautifully painted and dressed up as the Flute players at the Flute ceremony are painted and dressed at the present day.

"The young man stayed over night with Huruing Wuhti, sleeping with her at her request. She had many beads—white, red and turquoise—wound around her arms. In the morning the young man found that she had turned into an hag."[2]

The last time we met that sudden nocturnal metamorphosis from maid to hag, it was as a symbol of death in the Zuñi myth of Eagle Youth. Perhaps it is only a stock item in a tale, but since the same

[1] Voth, *The Traditions of the Hopi*, 5.
[2] H. R. Voth, *The Oraibi Summer Snake Ceremony*, 349–51.

image appears elsewhere in relation to an earth goddess, we should not overlook its value as a symbol of fertility. In Greece, Demeter, the corn goddess (corn there being wheat, spelt, and barley—not maize), appears in a cycle which includes maid, matron, and crone; or, as it doubtless signified, green corn, the ripe corn, and the harvested corn, or hag. The snake, that universal communicant with the mysteries of the earth, was also involved, since Demeter sent Triptolemus out to sow the seeds of staple foods in a chariot that was drawn by serpents.

While the Pueblos did not elaborate a triple-goddess on the analogy of corn cycle, they were aware of its elements—though of course in fours—as in the Zuñi prayer:

> Dawn old women
> Dawn matrons
> Dawn maidens,
> Dawn girls . . . .
> Perhaps if we are lucky
> Our earth mother
> Will wrap herself in a fourfold robe
> Of white meal.

Cushing was aware of some similar analogy when he stated, "Further, the succession of beings in the becoming of a complete being may be regarded as an orderly personification of growth phenomena as observed in plants and seeds; for example in corn . . . ."[3]

But lest this aside, which might explain the transformation of Huruing Wuhti into a hag, confuse the reader, it must be noted again that she is no mother-of-crops. She is the mother of the Universe, standing coequal with the Sun, and perhaps even more powerful, but only perhaps.

There is a sublimely confused passage in which the mixture of relationships and generations is as boldly set forth as in the dreams of James Joyce's hero in *Finnegans Wake*: "One time Huruing Wuhti sent the moon to the Sun, throwing him through space so that he fell down in front of the Sun. He told the Sun that Huruing Wuhti

[3] Cushing, *Zuñi Folk Tales*, 401.

wanted him; then he arose and passed through the sky back to the west. The Sun also soon rose and followed the Moon to the west, at the house of Huruing Wuhti. 'Have you come?' the latter said. 'Yes, I have come. Why do you want me?' 'I have come because you wanted me.' 'Thanks,' the Huruing Wuhti said, 'thanks that you have come, my father, because you shall be my father.' 'Yes,' the Sun said, 'and you shall be my mother, and we shall own all things together.' "[4]

The surviving versions of the creation of the world as it is told at Oraibi and on Second Mesa are as bare as that in Genesis. "By and by these two deities caused some dry land to appear in the midst of the water, the waters receding eastward and westward." The Second Mesa version only adds to the context of the longer passage quoted above.

"After having passed through the opening, the Sun returned under the earth to the east again, and when he came out he turned over the land which belonged to Huruing Wuhti, and which had been under water, and by so doing made the world (tuwakachi) land."[5]

Before considering any further developments in the Hopi scheme of creation we must return to the Zuñi deity, A'wonawil'ona. "In the beginning A'wonawil'ona with the Sun Father and the Moon Mother existed above, and Shi'wanni and Shi'wano'kia, his wife below." The latter pair were "superhuman beings who labored not with hands but with hearts and minds."[6] There is nothing puzzling in this pair of spirits; they are simply the eponymous originals of the Rain Priests and the Priestess of Fecundity.

As has been noted, the existence of this divinity has been questioned. Bunzel insists that the name covers a collectivity of spirits in the manner of the Keresan word *Kopishtaiya*, and bases her contention on the fact that no one she asked during five years in Zuñi had ever heard of such a being. While her argument cannot be disregarded, think of turning to the man next to you on a bus and asking, "Could you set me straight on the relationship of 'the one who shall be nameless,' Jehovah, Lord of Sabaoth and Eli, or Elohim?" Un-

---

[4] Voth, *The Traditions of the Hopi*, 5.   [5] *Ibid.*, 1, 7.
[6] Stevenson, "The Zuñi Indians," *loc. cit.*, 23.

less the bus were going to a theological seminary, it is unlikely that one would get a very clear idea of how singular or collective the concepts of a deity were.

More to the point, the two great students of the Zuñis in the nineteenth century agree on the nature of A'wonawil'ona. Both Stevenson, quoted above, and Cushing were close to the priesthood and hence esoteric lore, and furthermore, they were in Zuñi when secrecy was not an issue.

Anyone who reads Mrs. Stevenson's great book will be convinced that she did not interpolate. In her account of creation, "All was shi'pololo (fog) rising like steam. With the breath from his heart A'wonawil'ona created clouds and the great waters of the world. He-She is the blue vault of the firmament. The breath clouds of the gods are tinted with the yellow of the north, the blue-green of the west, the red of the south, and the silver of the east of A'wonawil'ona; they are himself, as he is the air itself; and when the air takes on the form of a bird it is but a part of himself. Through the light, clouds, and air he becomes the essence and creator of vegetation."[7]

The passage has both simple beauty and a lofty philosophical content. If it is exceptional, it may be due to Mrs. Stevenson's brilliant companion, Wewha. However, there is nothing in the passage which is outside Pueblo thinking—the concept relating breath to feathers, to clouds, to divine force, seems likely enough. There is, furthermore, the independent testimony of Cushing. His language may be his own and he may have improved upon his sources, but that is conjecture.

"Before the beginning of the new-making, A'wonawil'ona (the Maker and container of All, the All-father Father), solely had being. There was nothing else whatsoever throughout the great space of the ages save everywhere black darkness in it and everywhere void desolation.

"In the beginning of the new-made, A'wonawil'ona conceived within himself and thought outward in space, whereby mists of increase, steams potent of growth, were evolved and uplifted. Thus by means of his innate knowledge, the All-container made himself in person and form of the Sun whom we hold to be our father and who thus

[7] *Ibid.*, 23–24.

came to exist and appear. With his appearance came the brightening of the spaces with light, and with the brightening of the spaces the great mist-clouds were thickened together and fell, whereby was evolved water in water; yea, and the world-holding sea.

"With his substance of flesh (*yepnane*) outdrawn from the surface of his person, the Sun-father formed the seedstuff of twain worlds, impregnating therewith the great waters, and lo! in the heat of his light these waters of the sea grew green and scums(*k'yanashot-siyallawe*) rose upon them, waxing wide and weighty until, behold! they became Awitelin Tsita, the 'Four-fold Containing Mother-earth' and Apoyan Ta'chu, the 'All-covering Father sky.' "[8]

These passages do not have the authentic ring of the simple one quoted by Stevenson, but that may be due in part to the style Cushing used. It is epic, and the last sentence of the first paragraph is a rather close echo from *Paradise Lost*, which would indicate that either Cushing or some Zuñi had read Milton.

Most of this book is concerned with chthonian gods, or those of the underworld, or at times the surface of the earth. Heavenly gods, beyond the Moon and Sun, are rare and necessarily vague. The Sky has been worshiped as a divinity by many peoples, but its nature and relationship in either space or time to the realm of mankind is never definite. The Greeks used two words, *Aer*, which signified the atmosphere and reached as far as the moon—the region of cloud-crofts and storms—and *Aither*, whose root means "blazing." It is the brilliant light beyond the clouds and is not necessarily identified with the Sun. While Zeus was normally identified with the cloud and storm god of the lower atmosphere, he is sometimes identified, as in some fragments of Euripides, with the divine brilliance of outer space, the *aither* which is the essence of gods and the souls of mortal mankind.[9]

Perhaps some such striving for order in the universe was at work in the mind of Cushing's Zuñi informant. The use of the Sun as a median between ultimate power and man would not be out of place

---

[8] Cushing, "Zuñi Creation Myths," *loc. cit.*, 379.

[9] William K. C. Guthrie, *Orpheus and Greek Religion*, 185. See also J. G. Frazer, *The Worship of Nature*, I.

at Zuñi, where the Sun cult is highly developed. Against the possibility stands the fact that in other accounts the Zuñi Sun is granted as always existing. In a final statement of related ideas Cushing includes an idea that most students agree is Yuman rather than Pueblo.

"Thereupon the Earth-mother repulsed the Sky-father, growing big and sinking deep into the embrace of the waters below, thus separating from the Sky-father in the embrace of the waters above."[10] These thoughts do not follow naturally from the image of the mist which coalesces and the algae which grow solid on it as upon a pond, or with a comparable image given by Cushing in which haze turns into a corporeal being, an analogy with the experience of the fire drill, where smoke appears first and then vanishes when the flame appears. None of this should imply that Cushing made up the embrace of the Sky-father with the Earth-mother. There were many traveling merchants among the Pueblos and they would certainly listen to the myths of their hosts wherever they went; and one place the Zuñis certainly went was to the south and west of their own region.

We find the beginning of the universe, as seen by the Zuñis, treated once more by Cushing, and this time in a simpler book where he does not feel the need of epic props. He adds it as a footnote to one of the stories in his *Zuñi Folk Tales:* "The universe is supposed to have been generated from haze (shí-wai-a) produced by light (of the All container, Sun-father) out of darkness. The observed analogy of this nature is the appearance of haze (both heat and steam) preceding growth in springtime; the appearance of the world, of growing and living things, through the mist seemingly rising out of darkness each morning. In harmony with this conception of the universe is the correlative one that every being (as to soul, at least) passes through many successive states of becoming, always beginning as a *shi-u-na hâ i* (haze being), and passing through the raw or soft (*k'ya-pi-na*), *the formative* (*k'yai-yu-na*), variable (*thlim-ni-na*), fixed or done (*ak-na*), and finished or dead (ä-shï-k'ya) states; whilst the condition of the surpassing beings (gods) may be any one of these at will . . . . There are many analogies of this observed by the Zuñi, likening, as he does, the generation of being to that of the fire

[10] Cushing, "Zuñi Creation Myths," *loc. cit.*, 379.

with the fire drill and stick. The most obvious of these is the appearance, in volumes, of 'smoke-steam' or haze just previously to ignition, and its immediate disappearance with ignition."[11]

However as one evaluates the various parts of these several descriptions there is no doubt about the central idea: that the air and the things in it, whether mists or clouds or light, are a divine force; and that other light things of the air, such as smoke and feathers, are at least symbols, if not actual aspects, of the divinity.

The earth, which appeared like a scum upon a pool of water, is naturally flat. It "is circular in shape and is surrounded on all sides by ocean. Under the earth is a system of covered waterways all connecting ultimately with the surrounding oceans. Springs and lakes, which are always regarded as sacred, are the openings to this system."[12] Hence the earth literally floats and as though to complete the image of forming scum we will find that it was soft when the people first emerged upon it. The similarity of this circular earth, with Zuñi at the center and the ocean on its border, to the Greek world, surrounded by River Okeanos and centered on Delphi, is apparent. The difference is that the Greeks, at least in historical times, used it only as a poetic myth and Delphi was certainly a late choice for the center.

When we turn from the ultimate deity of the Zuñis to the beginning one of the Keres, we pass from an abstract divinity to an anthropomorphic one. The original goddess of the Keres is Thinking Woman, Sûs-sĭstinnako, or Sus'sistinako, to use the Sía version of the name. She thought outward into space and what she thought became reality.

While we do not have to struggle with abstraction here, the difficulty as to the sex of the deity is as great as before. She was clearly an underworld goddess, but to some Indians today she is male. To make matters worse the Keres, whose villages are widely scattered, rather than unified as with the Zuñis, have probably scrambled the names of their spirits—a difficulty I hope to clarify in the next chapter

[11] Cushing, *Zuñi Folk Tales*, 400–401.

[12] Ruth L. Bunzel, "Introduction to Zuni Ceremonialism," B.A.E. *Forty-seventh Annual Report* (1929–30), 487.

when the lesser Keres spirits are brought forth. Until then the reader will have to stumble over both variants in orthography, and entirely different names, such as the Uchiti of the second account.

These stories, recorded by Boas, are drawn from relatively recent sources, chiefly from the village of Laguna, a pueblo which was rent in two by Christian missionaries at the end of the last century. The traditionalists moved to Isleta, leaving ceremonies and concepts in some confusion. With that warning, we begin with a Laguna Indian's view.

"Long ago Ts'its'tsc'i·' na·k'o [Sus'sistanako] finished everything, thoughts and the names of everything here on the earth, and she also finished all the different languages. And so our father, Y'tc'ts'it'i [Uchiti] and our mother Nau'ts'it'i [Nautseti] said they would make names and they would make thoughts. Thus they said. Thus they did and therefore everything was finished and the names of everything and the different languages. That made them all different."

In the same informant's account the creation of the world was in the hands of a male god, whose hands were shaking. "A long time ago there in the north at the place of emergence below there our mother, corn-mother worked miracles. Everything that has names developed, the sun and the moon, and the stars and rain storms and spirits and [kachina] and the shamans and game and the people were completed, then our mother Nau'ts'it'i [Nautseti] and our father Y'tc'ts'it'i said 'How is it . . . is it not yet done? Shall we not put out our children? . . . . 'No' said he, 'First I shall divide water and land.' . . . Then to a mountain top went our father Y'tc'ts'it'i [Uchiti]. Then there below he looked around. Then he divided water and land. He shook it. There it was shaking [like water in a medicine bowl]. Then he looked at it. Then he said, 'Earth and water have become good,' thus he said. Then he also said, 'only the earth will be ripe.' "[13]

Another view from the Western Keres comes from a curious man of the last century, John M. Gunn, who wrote a book on the many things he knew about Acoma and Laguna. Unfortunately he made no literal transcriptions, but he has this to say of Thinking Woman: "Their theory is that reason (personified) is the supreme power, a

[13] Franz Boas, *Keresan Texts*, 7, 1.

master mind that has always existed, which they call Sitch-tche-na-ko. This is the feminine form for thought or reason. She had one sister, Shro-tu-na-ko, memory or instinct. Their belief is that Sitch-tche-na-ko is the creator of all, and to her they offer their most devout prayers."[14]

However lofty a conception this goddess may be, it seems that when she has a form it is that of a spider, and in the popular mind she is often equated with Spider Grandmother.

From the Keresan village of Cochití a nineteenth century French priest of fine objectivity, Father Dumarest, who lived there, makes no mention of Thinking Woman; all is Spider. When the Indian sister wanted to make stars, they would not shine, so "She consulted Spider, the Creator." Again he reports of the sisters: "They lived with Spider Woman, their mother, at *shipapu,* under the waters of the lake, in the second world."[15]

Recently, at Santa Ana, L. A. White found out little about Thinking Woman except that "her function was to scheme or plan," and he adds in a note that an Acoma informant told him: "She must have been quite small, for she sat on Iatiku's right shoulder during her contests with her sister and told her what to do."[16] That note indicates that in the mind of the speaker she was definitely identified with Spider Woman. Perhaps that is an ordinary confusion, since an Oraibi citizen told Titiev that the goddess whom Snake Youth meets in the myth, which is to say, Hard Beings Woman, is also sometimes identified as Spider Woman.[17]

In the best account of Thinking Woman, which comes from the pueblo of Sía, she is a spider: "In the beginning there was but one being in the lower world, Sûs-sĭstinnako, a spider. At that time there were no other animals, birds, reptiles, or any living creature but the spider. He drew a line of meal from north to south and crossed it midway from east to west; and he placed two little parcels north of the cross line, one on either side of the line running north and

[14] John M. Gunn, *Schat-Chen: History, Traditions and Narratives of the Queres Indians of Laguna and Acoma,* 89.

[15] Dumarest, *Notes of Cochití,* 227.

[16] Leslie A. White, *The Pueblo of Santa Ana, New Mexico,* 82.

[17] Titiev, *Old Oraibi,* 153.

south. These parcels were very valuable and precious [they were indeed, since they contained the seed of the twin mothers of mankind and all their creatures], but the people do not know to this day of what they consisted; no one ever knew but the creator, Sûs-sĭstinnako. After placing the parcels in position, Sûs-sĭstinnako sat down on the west side of the line running north and south, and south of the cross line, and began to sing, and in a little while the two parcels accompanied him in the song by shaking, like rattles. The music was low and sweet, and after a while two women appeared one evolved from each parcel; and in a short time people began walking about; then animals, birds, and all other animate objects appeared, and Sûs-sĭstinnako continued to sing until his creation was complete."[18]

From comparing these Keresan accounts the first thing of note is that the act of creation is comparable to a ceremony as performed by a priest, who sings either over a medicine bowl which he shakes in order to foretell something by the shimmering of the water, or one who sings over medicine bundles. In singing one expels the breath, which is of the divine essence. The singing of a priest is a prayer, and with him, an especially potent kind of wish. It is possible to consider the expelling of such a wish through the breath as a literal "thinking outward into space." Possibly that is the image the Keres had in mind when they explained creation, but that is merely a surmise on my part. The more metaphysical interpretations are doubtless valid for those individuals—and there seem to be many among the Pueblos—who are speculative thinkers.

Before ending this rather lean account of the ultimate deities, we must return to Hard Beings Woman and consider one more point. Huruing Wuhti is sometimes a double goddess, one living in the East as well as the more familiar one in the West. The duality may be a late addition, but it is nonetheless believed in fervently by some in Oraibi. When Don Talayesva made his pilgrimage to Yale University we are told, "While in New Haven, he made a special request for an opportunity to worship the 'Lady of the Eastern Ocean.' When he was taken to the beach, he walked reverently to the water and prayed: 'Our mother of the Ocean, I have arrived from afar to pray

[18] M. C. Stevenson, "The Sia," B.A.E. *Eleventh Annual Report* (1889–90), 27.

to you . . . . Notify your spirits to hasten with clouds . . . . Let them arise and go ahead of me over the mountains, drop rain on Oraibi, and my people so they will be in good health when I return. I ask this in the name of my God, the Sun. May our lives be good.' "[19] He then splashed water on himself and smoked to send messages to the six-point cloud-people.

In this view Hard Beings Woman is quite evidently a sea-goddess, or at least a goddess of the littoral where all kinds of shells and beautiful bead-like things are found, and of the visible moisture of the sea.

The duality was, I believe, formerly between the Sun in the East and Hard Beings Woman in the West, as we find in an account from the Second Mesa town of Shipaulovi, in which the divinity of the East is the Sun who travels to the West, where he and Huruing Wuhti create the forms of life alternately, and give them to each other.

"From this time on the Sun always went towards the west, entering the house of Huruing Wuhti, passing out below, and returning to the east again. When he came there this time Huruing Wuhti said: 'Have you come,?' 'Yes,' the Sun said, 'land has come out everywhere, and everything is beautiful, and the water is beautiful, too. Now, tomorrow when I shall rise there will be blossoms and flowers and grass all over the land.' 'Very well,' Huruing Wuhti said, 'but let us make something now again. What shall we make?' Hereupon she fed the Sun honey, and other good food."[20]

In the process of the following creation, the goddess rubs off a part of her cuticle which is rolled in a ball and hidden under the blanket; first a maiden is produced and then a male youth. The youth is Muingwu, who will be discussed in the next chapter. Yahoya (the final element *hoya* means child or youth) is not mentioned elsewhere, so far as I know.

From the creation myths of these three tribes one can establish a vague pattern, even though the dissimilarities are more apparent and interesting. The ultimate gods are responsible for the creation of the world out of a watery element, and they also create one pair of human beings—with the Keres they are not a sexual pair. The beginning gods are seldom worshiped, unless we include the Sun, and seem-

[19] Talayesva, *Sun Chief*, 416.   [20] Voth, *The Traditions of the Hopi*, 7.

ingly never impersonated. They are of little importance in ceremonies or daily life. After their role in creation myths, they fade
rapidly into the mists from which the world was made.

Among the Keres there is a powerful intermediary between the
creator and mankind. She is Iyatiku, the Corn-Mother. Her Hopi
counterpart, Muingwu, is a male corn god, but he is of less importance, probably because Masau'u has usurped so many of his
functions. Another difference is that he seems to be one half of
the pair, a brother-sister combination, while Iyatiku creates the pair,
which in that culture is a sister-sister combination. The Zuñi pair
are vaguely thought of as husband and wife, but it is not a procreative
sexual relationship. The Zuñi divinities cling closely to the ceremonial
pattern of the culture and have little historical shape beyond that,
so that this pair are no more husband and wife than are the Sun and
Hard Beings Woman with the Hopis.

To the Zuñi pair was delegated the secondary creation of the universe. That is very unlike the Keresan pair, who are the actual mothers
of mankind, one white and the other Indian, or the Hopi Muingwu
who is sometimes thought of as the father of mankind, as his sister
(wife) Sand Altar Woman is the mother of mankind. The Zuñi
pair intervene early and directly in the process of creation: "After
A'wonawil'ona created the clouds and the great waters of the world,
Shi'wanni said to Shi'wano'kia: 'I, too, will make something beautiful, which will give light at night when the Moon Mother sleeps.'
Spitting in the palm of his left hand, he patted the spittle with the
fingers of his right hand, and the spittle foamed like yucca suds and
then formed into bubbles of many colors, which he blew upwards;
and thus he created the fixed stars and constellations. And Shi'wanni
was well pleased with his creation. Then Shi'wano'kia said, 'See what
I can do,' and she expectorated into the palm of her left hand and
slapped the saliva with the fingers of her right, and the spittle foamed
like yucca suds, running over her hand and flowing everywhere;
and thus she created A'witelin 'Si'ta (Earth Mother)."[21]

Six of the fourteen A'shiwannis are associated with the six directions, the priest of the North being the senior rain priest. The Shi'-

[21] Stevenson, "The Zuñi Indians," *loc. cit.*, 23–24.

94

wano'kia is associated with him, while others have female assistants of less definite character. The priest of the Zenith is deputy to the Sun-father.

The statement of the original Shi'wanni, "I, too, will make something beautiful," is a phrase which can serve to introduce another creator, Spider Grandmother, or Kohkang Wuhti as she is called by the Hopis. She is a helpful goddess—or at the very least she is well intentioned—and she very often comes in direct contact with mankind. Spider Grandmother is very powerful and a superior creative force, even if a comic one at times. It is notable that she is a figure common to Hopis and the Keres, and one is tempted to think of her as an older and simpler goddess who was supplanted. The only evidence is the fact that Sus'sistinako was obviously once a spider-goddess who wove the web of creation.

A similar image is brought to mind by a Zuñi figure. He is a water-strider who discovered the exact center of the universe. While he is no god, he was of such cosmic proportions that his legs stretched out beyond the horizons; and the paths they made when drawn in toward the center, his heart, are described as web-like: "like stays of a spider's net." While the tale is a poetic image to account for Zuñi wanderings and the final discovery of Halona at the center of the world, it is an image which could easily be elaborated into a concept of a deity.

When we turn to the Spider Grandmother of Old Oraibi we find a similar thought, but it is related to an undoubted goddess. Hard Beings Woman of the West invited her counterpart of the East to come and consult with her. They had asked the Sun to look for life on the world, but he could see nothing, so they thought that perhaps this was because he only traveled over the middle and might have missed life that lived to the North and South. After the Eastern Woman traveled over the rainbow to the West, the two created a wren by singing over a covered bit of clay and sent him out to search the earth, but he reported back that there were no living beings on it. Yet the wren had somehow missed Spider Woman, who was living somewhere on the southwest edge of the water.

Spider Woman had heard that the two women had created, first birds, then animals, and men; and she decided that she too would create something. "So she made a man and woman of clay, covered them up, sang over them, and brought to life her handiwork. But these two proved to be Spaniards."

Thus the bumbling Spider has created a thorn for the Indian's side, and that was not the end of the trouble she caused with her creations. She continued to make pairs of human beings, giving each a different language, which is bother enough, but to make matters worse she failed to create a man for a certain woman. " 'Oh my!' she said, 'How is this?' and then addressing the single woman she said: 'There is a single man somewhere, who went away from here. You try to find him and if he accepts you, you live with him. If not, both of you do the best you can about that.' " Naturally the lost couple meet, marry, fight, and separate, but they decide that living apart is even more difficult: "Who will work the fields for you?" The stock of this unhappy couple was mixed with the rest of mankind, much as the blood of the Titans was in some Greek thinking, and that accounts for present strife.

"Had these people not lived in that way, all the other Hopi would now live in peace, but the others learned it from them [and] these were the kind of people that Spider Woman had created."[22]

Spider Grandmother is various. In contrast to the highest gods she is often at fault and her faults are the source of human bane. She had been creating perfect pairs, but her drowsy error led to the strife we experience today. What her mistake brought about was not the fall of man, but merely his unfortunate tendency to stumble over ordinary obstacles.

In folklore she makes amends for the difficulties she has created by becoming a tutelary goddess devoted to the protection of mankind, or of lesser spirits, when they find themselves in trouble. She becomes a representative of the old ones, of ancestors, but of progenitors at least once removed, who are able to watch over you when the odds are bad—if you ask for help. She spins the old ways. She has lost her creative power, for the most part, as becomes old age. As a divinity her creations were faulty, but that is tolerable, since

[22] Voth, *The Traditions of the Hopi*, 3–4.

what can one expect from well-meaning old ones. But above all the old ones are there to advise and help; they know how, they hold all the tricks of survival, and prove it by their presence.

Spider Grandmother is by her nature small and disappearing, like the old ones. Sometimes she is a voice only, but full of the wisdom of ages, as well as of age. She appears on the shoulders of young men when they are in trouble, and the young, even young gods like the War Twins, are always in trouble, and in need of the advice, or of the magic of elders. Unlike uncles or parents she is at least once removed. Her advice is prophetic rather than admonitory—no room for the yucca whip—she is too tiny to offer a threat. She might say, "I am a small thing, perhaps a scornful thing, my only power is wisdom. I am your culture, which can stand on your shoulder and whisper in your ear when you need advice."

Andrew Hermequaftewa said: "We came to his land only after receiving permission from our great spirit, Massau'u. He was living on this land with the Keeper of the Fire, who is the Spider Woman, and the two grandsons or nephews who are guardians of the Life Plan of this Great Spirit." Here she is keeper of the fire in the sense of carrying the torch: "Then the Spider Woman, being very intelligent person, again cautioned us to be on guard, to never let go of the Life Pattern given to us by the Great Spirit."

Spider Woman, whom I take to be a very old earth goddess and culture heroine, seems likely to survive as the only other divinity in the Traditionalist pantheon, along with the newly remodeled Masau'u. She is the only other divinity, except for the Sun, mentioned in the *Hopi Hearings*.

Despite the fact that she appears in a kindly role in most tales, there is one account which shows that she has, at least potentially, a sinister possibility. The unusual again comes from Don Talayesva: "When I was four or five I was captured by the Spider Woman and nearly lost my life. One morning in May as I played in the plaza in my shirt my father said that he was going to his field. I wanted to go. But as he filled his water jar he said, 'You had better stay here, my jar does not hold enough for us both.' I began to cry. As he started down the south side of the mesa I followed along the narrow path between two great stones and came to the bottom of the foothill near the Spider Woman's shrine. My father had disappeared among the rocks. I happened to look to my left at a rock by the shrine where some clay dishes had been placed as offerings to the Spider Woman. There sat the old woman herself, leaning forward and resting her chin in her hands. Beside her was a square hole in the ground. She said, 'You are here at the right time. I have been waiting for you. Come into my house with me.'" She claims that she has a right to him; he has been walking on her trail, and Don is slowly drawn to her door. A man coming up the trail shouts to him:

" 'Boy, get out of the shrine! The Spider Woman may take you into her house!' I laughed in a silly manner but could not move."[23] That night the boy had a terrible dream in which he is hers, which is a sign that he will not live long. His parents took him to a "doctor" on Second Mesa who discovered that Don's father had not made a feather for Spider during Soyal, the ceremony in which the family was most prominent.

The story seems to belong to the realm of religious psychopathology. At the time Don was scarcely beyond his infancy; in his recollection the experience was highly hallucinatory and based, in memory at least, upon the failure of a religious duty—placing the feather—and upon the violation of a taboo against trespass upon Spider's shrine. While the experience may have been highly personal, it is nonetheless true that some such possibility existed in the nature of Spider Grandmother, which combined enough fright at the face of divine power to sicken one; a fear that was doubtless strengthened by the visual image of the trap-door spider's nest, which would seem to lead down to the secrets of the underworld.

Sho'tokunungwa

The god whose light is spread under this name is a star-god, a lightning-god, and above all a war-god; and as such does not properly deserve a place among the creators, except for the fact that a strong minority vote of both natives and Anglos gives him high place in the Hopi pantheon. Rather than rending him and his attributes

[23] Talayesva, *Sun Chief*, 47-49.

and scattering the bits, Orpheus-like, through several chapters, I will consider most of his aspects here.

The spellings of Sho'tokunungwa are various, the name often beginning with a "C" even before that letter became a common symbol, and a wretched one, for the phonetic "sh." There is an appealingly simple "Shotokwin," but I am not sure that it refers directly to the god rather than to his priest or representative. The name either means, or stands for, "heart of the stars" or "heart of the above," an epithet which gave him a special place in the minds of Christian missionaries and their converts.

The role of this god as a creator rests upon a very pretty winter's tale: "At the beginning, Co-tuk-inung-wa (the heart of the above), the all-powerful one, created a beautiful virgin, and all the supernatural ones strove with each other to obtain possession of her for a wife. From this rivalry, desperate feuds arose, which prevailed for a very long period, until Co-tuk-inung-wa to end the contention transformed the Virgin and she became the World. Her hair became the vegetation; her eyes, the springs; her teeth, gems (white shell beads); her bones, the rocks; her breath, the wind; her secretions, salt." Stephen breaks his outline at this point and concludes, "and so throughout her entire anatomy, each portion is disposed of in the geogony of the Hopitu. Co-tuk-inung-wa is chief of all, and at this transformation he assigned separate regions and powers to the other deities."[24]

"Chief of all' is not the same as creator of all, and his position as a ruling Zeus is probably not earlier than the first contacts of the Hopis with Anglo missionaries, but the influence of the idea has spread to non-Christian Hopis as well as to converts. As the god of the above, he was a rather natural choice when missionaries chose one deity from the Hopi pantheon to represent their god. I might also hazard a guess here that the early Christian pre-emption of this divinity had a considerable influence on the Traditionalist's choice of Masau'u for their "Executive Supreme." The two gods have several things in common, but the latter was untainted by outside influence and association with Christianized Hopis.

[24] Stephen, "Hopi Indians of Arizona," *loc. cit.*, 102.

Before considering his shape and probable aboriginal nature let us look for a moment at the new being. As early as 1893 Stephen added a note in his *Hopi Journal:* "It has been handed down from uncle to nephew from earliest times, that in addressing prayers to any of the spirits the great ruling spirit, the god of the Above . . . from whom we derive our existence, must never be forgotten."[25] Parsons points out that this has a missionary flavor, which it certainly has. For one thing, the note is appended to an account of war practices where it is indicated that before going on the war trail the warriors of the Reed and Patki clans offer him prayer-sticks.

In any case, the flavor has lasted. Mrs. Colton states in her notes to Nequatewa that this star-god is "the Supreme Being, or Heavenly God, who is served by all other gods."[26] That statement is much too extreme, although it may represent the view of some Hopi individuals. A more likely view, though it is by no means so precise, comes from an informant in the Second Mesa village of Shongopovi who spoke in 1912. I gather that he was "Christianized," but I doubt if any sect would claim his views.

"So'teknani gives the rain and makes the grass and seed grow. The white people call him God. He prays and sings all the time." After pointing out that Muingwu lives in the earth and has a sister with him, the informant continues: "The Earth is a female. Now Moing'iima lives with So'teknani (Heaven) who sends the rain. So'teknani married the earth. When they have intercourse, we get rain, for that is the fertilizing fluid. All the vegetation is the off-spring of the earth [Tiwa'kpomatamsi (Tuwa'boñtumsi), Sand Altar Woman]. So'teknani puts grass seeds inside of hailstones. When these melt, the seeds go into the earth, the sun shines with heat, and soon they spring up . . . .

"I am sure everything is as I have said. I believe in the white people's God because he belongs to the white people. That is why he is somewhat different from So'teknani."[27]

That Sho'tokunungwa is somewhat more than a little different

[25] Stephen, *Hopi Journal*, I, 96n.

[26] Nequatewa, *Truth of a Hopi*, 125. See also Colton, "Hopi Deities," *loc. cit.,* 21.

[27] Wallis, "Folk Tales from Shomopovi," *loc. cit.,* 13, 15.

from the Christian Dios is at once apparent, but before examining his nature further let us look at his person. His chief aspect is a single, curved horn rising from the middle of his head, an item which always distinguishes him from the earth-god, Muingwu. The single horn has two associations: one is with the Horned Water Serpent, who wears a similar horn and is also related to lightning; the second is with the One Horn Society. We have seen something of this group in the first chapter. They are played off against the Two Horn Society—if I may coin a name for the sake of clarity. The patron of the One Horns may be either Masau'u or Sho'tokunungwa, or even a third god, Tokonaka,[28] who is possibly to be equated with Masau'u, but as neither the natives nor the scholars are certain about the matter, we may leave it. Patron of the Two Horns is Muingwu or Alosaka.

The One Horns and the Two Horns are related in that they are relevant to dangerous things: to war and the hunt, and to the underworld. Contrariwise, they have important value as fertility symbols, the power of death being related to the powers of life. So in addition to the curved horn which indicates male lightning, or power for war, we find that Sho'tokunungwa is often represented with cloud and rain symbols for eyes, or in murals he may stand among such signs.

Lightning is the pivotal idea. In his right hand he holds a zigzag symbol of lightning, or a "bull-roarer" which represents thunder. In his left hand he may carry jointed sticks which are called a "lightning frame," or the netted gourd, related to fertility.[29]

While he does not rule over all of the gods, Sho'tokunungwa certainly has charge of two: the Little War Twins. Many of their prodigies were performed with lightning. With this aid, or its counterparts, arrows, they cleave mountains, form rivers, and destroy enemies. In a myth, which concerns the Horned Water Serpent and floods, the Twins are found wandering helplessly.

"Cotukvnangi, the God of Thunder, lived in the sky and saw the children and took pity on them." He appears in the terrible mask of a weather-god, all icicles, but in reality he is a handsome man.

[28] Titiev, *Old Oraibi*, 134n.
[29] Fewkes, "Hopi Katcinas," *loc. cit.*, 120 and Pl. LVIII.

After rescuing them, "Cotukvnangi remained with them that afternoon and after the sun had gone down he began to talk to them, talking to them all that night. Cotukvnangi is the great warrior chief, and he now gave these youths the lightning and the thunder, and he told them how to kill enemies . . . .

"They would do it, he said, but it would be he that would do it through them."[30] By a logical succession, the warriors in turn gain the power from the War Twins through the office of the war chiefs.

In another story a war chief is in need of help. He "took a bone whistle, went outside and whistled upwards, whereupon immediately a great noise was heard and a small man entered the room. This was Cotukvnangwuu, the Star and Cloud deity, living in the sky." The god does his work as expected, which in this instance consists of destroying sorcerers. "Hereupon he drew forth a ray of lightning, threw it among them and they were all torn to pieces, the kiva being filled with a bright light. When the lightning had done its work and it had become dark in the kiva the warriors waited until they felt the warm blood of their victims touching their feet."[31]

While Sho'tokunungwa is often referred to as a star-god, I have found no elaboration of that concept. The Hopi word for star is *sho'hü*, which may indicate some real or imaginary linguistic relationship. The relation of stars to warriors is common in other cultures; the various Morning Stars are particularly used to connect the two, and they sometimes add the serpent as another element. Two examples that come to mind are Racumon of the Carib Indians of Guiana, who is a war-god, a star, and a spirit who appears in the form of a snake with a man's head. In the other world Lucifer is called "son of the morning" and he likewise takes the form of a serpent. I do not know that he was a war-god, but the circumstances certainly suggest that he was.

Sho'tokunungwa appears in puppet ceremonies related to the Water Serpent,[32] where he shoots out a lightning frame. Although the serpents will be given a chapter to themselves later, a remark of Fewkes's may be noted here. "The distinctive fraternity of the Rain-

---

[30] Voth, *The Traditions of the Hopi*, 56–57, 59.
[31] *Ibid.*, 127, 129.   [32] Titiev, *Old Oraibi*, 124.

cloud clans now existing in Walpi is called *Kwakwantu*. The members of this society wear head-dresses with single horns called *cotokinunwu*, and carry in their hands wooden imitations of the Plumed Serpent. In a way we may say that they personate ancestors with symbolic likenesses to a Sky-God as a Great Serpent. In other words, the Serpent-Sky-god is the cultus hero of the *Kwakwantu*."[33]

Details of the lighting, serpent, war, and fertility association will have to wait for a later chapter. At this point it is safe to say that he is not a creator, nor the Christian God, but a deity who fructifies the earth by lightning and the rain it brings, and because of his lightning bolts he is also the patron of warriors.

The Emergence

The emergence of mankind is not a creation, but a bringing forth of people who already existed, though sometimes in an imperfect state. There are two contradictory feelings about the state of mankind underground. On the one hand it was a scene of social chaos, a motivating factor in the emergence. On the other hand, it was the beginning of our later life under the Sun, and it sent those stems up from underworld deities who directly gave warrant for present ceremonies. The first priests and officers were appointed underground, and the original paraphernalia was "brought up." Also the people were given their "instructions" shortly before they came up. Thus the images both of comforting authority and of escape are combined in one event.

It is notable that there is considerable certainty and even unanimity of accounts between the three tribes on the events relating to the emergence of mankind through Shipapu. To keep the proper order this section should begin with an account of the Little War Twins, the divine twins, demigods, sons of the Sun, whose first mission was to lead the people up; but the importance of these war gods and the richness of the mythology surrounding them will require a separate chapter.

Meanwhile, since we have heard much from the Hopis and Zuñis,

[33] Jesse W. Fewkes, "Minor Hopi Festivals," *American Anthropologist*, Vol. IV, No. 3 (1902), 499.

let us begin this account with a story from the Keresan Sky City of Acoma. The version is somewhat simplified (as it is at Keresan Sía as well) by the reduction of the usual fourfold underworld to a single one.

"In the beginning," starts the Acoma version, "two female human beings were born . . . . There was no light and they could only feel each other." These two grew up slowly and waited a long time. The goddess nursed them, taught them their language, and eventually gave them each a basket of seeds and little images of all the kinds of animals there were to be in the world.

"All of the four seeds sprouted, but in the darkness the trees grew very slowly and the two sisters became very anxious to reach the light as they waited this long time. They slept for many years as they had no use for eyes." At last one tree "pushed a hole through the earth for them and let in a very litttle light." The two sisters created a badger from the images in the basket and told him to make a hole big enough to let them out. Then a locust was created and instructed to cement the opening. The goddess Sus'sistinako gave them instructions on what to do when they emerged: "With the pollen and the sacred corn meal you will pray to the Sun. You will thank the Sun for bringing you to light, ask for a long life and happiness, and for success in the purpose for which you were created." The two were then taught the prayers and the creation song.

"On reaching the earth, they set down their blankets and saw for the first time what they had. The earth was soft and spongy under their feet as they walked, and they said, 'This is not ripe.' They stood waiting for the Sun, not knowing where it would appear. Gradually it grew lighter and finally the Sun came up." They prayed to the Sun as they had been taught by Sus'sistinako, and sang the creation song. They were then told, "You will rule and bring to life the rest of the things he has given you in the baskets."[34]

In this particular version the sisters create not only living things, but arrange the landscape as well, placing the mountains of the four directions, covering them with grass and trees. After that they "created," which is to say, took out of the basket beings already created,

[34] M. W. Stirling, *Origin Myth of Acoma*, B.A.E. *Bulletin* No. 135 (1942), 1–3.

the animals both large and small. The birth of the Pueblo race is delayed and roundabout in this story. In time the elder sister becomes impregnated by a steaming mist and gives birth to twin boys. The younger sister adopts one of the boys who, when grown, becomes her husband. These two in good time become the parents of the Pueblo race. The exceptional thing in this Acoma story is that only the sisters come out; men were created below, but do not really come into being until born on the surface of the earth.

Another Acoma account makes all the people come out: "They came out of the earth, from Iyatiku, the mother. They came out through a hole in the north called Shipap. They crawled out like grasshoppers; their bodies were naked and soft. It was all dark; the sun had not yet risen."[35] When the people, who are thought of as babies, came out, the mother Iyatiku lined them up facing east and caused the Sun to rise. When it came up it caused their eyes to open.

From Acoma's neighboring town of Laguna there are several fragmentary versions which include the common fourfold underworld, whose lowest level is white, and the succeeding ones red, blue, and yellow. In Gunn's account from Laguna, Shipapu is, as at Zuñi, filled with water. "Into this pit flowed four mighty rivers from the four cardinal points, and although these rivers flowed ceaselessly, never was the pit filled completely to the brim, but would rise and lower rhythmatically."[36] It may be noted that Laguna, as the name implies, was originally located on a fair sized lake or pond, but it was not as permanent as the Zuñi lake.

In a literally transcribed Laguna account mankind is "put out," an image which corresponds to our phrase, "the stars come out at night."

" 'It is good,' said she, 'let me put them out,' said she. 'I shall put them out with this,' said she, 'with rain-storms and with the kachina and with songs and with prayers and with shamanistic power and carrying prayer sticks and carrying in their arms corn and carrying in their arms altars and grinding stones and carrying in their arms

[35] Leslie A. White, "The Acoma Indians," B.A.E. *Forty-seventh Annual Report* (1929–30), 142.

[36] Gunn, *Schat-Chen*, 110–11.

mullers and having tied in their hair eagle feathers. 'My children will be thus . . . .' " The teller obviously had no central focus on the process of emergence. As a part of the shift of emphasis in the Laguna emergence story from the beginning to the end of the process, there is one version in which a flint shaman bores his way from the upper world down to the fourth level of the underworld.[37]

To continue the survey of Keresan towns, we find that at Sía they believe that the creation took place in the dark and the sisters are the first two created. It is not clear, however, whether or not the first pair are underground.

"These two women, being inspired by Sus'sistinnako, created the sun from white shell, turkis, red stone and abalone shell. After making the sun they carried him to the east and there made a camp, as there were no houses. The next morning they ascended a high mountain and dropped the sun down behind it, and after a time he began to ascend, and when the people saw the light their hearts rejoiced."[38]

Another small Keresan town, Cochití, produces only fragmentary emergence stories, but they indicate a certain concept of emergence and also of the leadership of the War Twins in that experience.

"The people were coming up from Shipap. Masewa led them, and after him his brother Oyoyewa. After them came our mother Iareku, the corn fetish. They came up through the doorway of the rainbow and after Iareku all of the Indians of the pueblos came together."[39] From Santa Ana comes a version which is archetypal: "The Cacique and the War Chief [here the town chief and the war chief stand for the Little War Twins who are their originals] were talking in the underworld. It was all dark down there. They were wondering if there was any light up above. First cottonwood went up but could not see any sunlight. Then the cedar tried, but came back down. Then the spruce tree was going to try. But spruce saw that he would need an opening . . . . So Woodpecker Boy flew up to the top of the spruce tree and began to peck at the ceiling." They needed to enlarge the opening, "So Eagle flew up to the top of Spruce tree and built a nest for Badger . . . . as Badger worked upward, Spruce was to grow so

[37] Boas, *Keresan Texts*, 34, 39.   [38] Stevenson, "The Sia," *loc. cit.*, 29.

[39] Benedict, *Tales of the Cochití Indians*, 13, 249.

Badger could reach his work." When the Twins reached the third level of the underworld they got the help of Whirlwind Old Man, by offering him prayer-feathers and honey. "Whirlwind Old Man caught up all the dust and held it in his whirl all day long." The spruce kept growing, and Badger reached the fourth world just before sunset. Spruce then said that he could not go any higher, was thanked for his work and told that his sprigs would be used for prayers. It remained for Douglas Fir finally to reach into the upper world and become the ladder on which the people emerged into the beautiful and sunlit realm.[40]

To this account of the basic mechanics of the emergence the Hopis and Zuñis add another element which has not appeared in these Keres narrations. The underworld was a very unpleasant place in which to live: "Thus the lowermost womb or cave-world, which was Anosin tehuli (the womb of sooty depth or of growth generation, because it was the place of first formation and black as a chimney at night time, foul too, as the internals of the belly), thus did it become overfilled with being. Everywhere were unfinished creatures, crawling like reptiles one over another in filth and black darkness, crowding thickly together and treading each other, one spitting on another or doing some other indecency."[41]

In Hopi accounts of the emergence the emphasis is not so much on physical confusion as on social disorder: "At times the wives of the lower class were visited by these men and by the priests and high priests, while the poor husbands of the women were away. Now all this kept on from bad to worse . . . . Then, gossip, quarreling and fighting started between the men and the women."[42]

The meaning of the emergence myths thus seems to be twofold: it explains how men came upon the surface of the earth and how they rose out of chaos. The first Zuñis had tails and no vents and the Hopis originally had no order. Thus, in addition to the obvious analogy to human parturition, the emergence myths point to an evolution of order, the achievement of biological order, social order,

[40] White, *The Pueblo of Santa Ana*, 89–91.
[41] Cushing, "Zuñi Creation Myths," *loc. cit.*, 381.
[42] Nequatewa, *Truth of a Hopi*, 7.

and the order that attends the religious and ceremonial functioning of Pueblo society. At the end of all these stories the newly emerged people face the Sun, who is the god that observes daily the functioning of human order. Each night he is asked, "And how many have died today and how many have been born today?" The Sun is called upon as a witness, because he has seen who has done well and who has not. Since the Sun counts heads and judges hearts it is fitting that the final step in the emergence of mankind is a facing of the Sun. The Zuñis say that when they reached the underworld just below us:

"There was rumbling like thunder and the people came up into the first world. It was light like red dawn. They were dazzled." Thinking that they had at last arrived upon the earth they asked the Twins if this was where they were to live, but the reply was, " 'Not yet.' The people were sad. They could see each other quite plain. Their bodies were covered with dirt and with ashes. They were stained with spit and urine and they had green slime on their heads. Their hands and feet were webbed and they had tails and no mouths or exits." After four ages mankind at last came to the surface.

"When they came into the sunlight the tears ran down their cheeks. Younger brother said to them, 'Turn to the Sun and look full at our father Sun no matter how bright it is.' They cried out for it hurt them and their tears ran to the ground. Everywhere they were standing the sun's flowers (sunflowers and buttercups) sprang up from the tears caused by the sun. The people said, 'Is this the world where we shall live?' 'Yes, this is the last world. Here you see our father Sun.' "[43]

It would be hard to put the struggle of mankind from the depths of his past to the flower decked earth on which we live more succinctly, or beautifully, and it is to be hoped that the politicians who hold our roads will remember that "this is the last world."

The Flood

Since stories of the great flood are universal, and as it is the world's

[43] Benedict, *Zuñi Mythology*, I, 3.

best known myth, there is no need to make a general introduction. A learned and detailed account of flood myths can be found in Frazer's *Folk Lore in the Old Testament*. What we are concerned with here is the individuality of the Pueblo stories. They place the event in very close order with emergence itself, and often the two are joined. With one exception, the waters do not come from rain, but spring miraculously from the earth. Most frequently the great flood is loosed by some form of the Horned Water Serpent.

The analogy between the emergence and human gestation and parturition was apparent enough to reach a conscious level in the Pueblo mind, and in many stories it is continued through childbirth water. In such stories the flood occurred, naturally, in the underworld. At Sía the rising of the waters came in the form of a flash flood, an image which certainly has outward reality for those familiar with Jémez Creek and its washes. It is said there that the creeks and rivers filled and surrounded the mesa, but in the myth this mesa is in the underworld. So Sus'sistinako placed a huge reed upon it for the people to climb into the upper world. The goddess went out first and was followed by the priests carrying their sacred objects in blankets. After them followed the people and then the animal kingdom, and last of all, just to make the story good for all ages, "the turkey was far behind, and the foam of the water rose and reached the tip ends of his feathers, and to this day they bear the mark of the waters."[44]

There are other accounts which are similarly oriented. In the story from Laguna, it will be remembered, Shipapu was filled with water which rose and fell without overflowing. A brief Hopi version states that the men and women had quarreled and were living on the opposite banks of a river. This was in the underworld, and the women were attempting to raise their crops without the help of men, which proved to be an infertile idea. "About that time a flood was coming closer, and the women began to build a tower."[45] The tower, as one might guess, fell down, but then even the men began to worry about

[44] Stevenson, "The Sia," *loc. cit.*, 35–36.
[45] Parsons, *Pueblo Indian Religion*, 237.

the flood. They planted first a pine tree and then a reed, which brought them above the flood.

If childbirth water plays a part in flood stories, so does the actual experience of overflowing rivers. The town of Zuñi is blessed with a river which divides the old part from the new and two stories seem to refer to actual floods.[46] There is a theme of punishment for not finding the exact middle, but the essence is, "Lo! the river to the southward ran full, and breaking from its pathway cut in twain the great town, burying houses and men in the mud of its impetuosity." The people were then forced to flee to the mesa top.

While these two simple elements are likely to be a part of most flood stories, the valuable content is the elaboration, the unique interpretation a people can wrest from an universal idea. The central theme of the Pueblo flood myths is ostensibly one of human sacrifice. There are four important accounts of the flood, two of which come from Hopi Second Mesa, but they are nearly a half century apart in the telling. The second two stories come from Zuñi. All of these are inset pieces connected with longer narratives of varying import, but the flood story is intact and very similar in each case. The myth is semihistorical in that it is placed in the legendary times of migration, rather than at the beginning of time. In each version a ghost is involved. He is the son of a priest, or a chief; this ghost turns into the Horned Water Serpent who floods a particular town—not the world —and thereby forces the survivors to migrate. Importantly, there is a sacrifice of a boy and a girl to the Serpent to allay the flood.

The story is known from Third Mesa Oraibi, but only as a kind of hearsay. Yokioma, the Traditionalist leader, alludes to it in two sentences. There was trouble with female sorcerers: "And so these wicked ones had increased very much until finally Palatkwapi was destroyed by a great water produced by the Balolookongs. Nearly all the people were destroyed, but a few succeeded in reaching dry land in the flood and they were saved."[47] The reason this story is scanted there is quite simple: it is a migration myth of the Patki, or

---

[46] Cushing, "Zuni Creation Myths," *loc. cit.*, 429. See also Stevenson, "The Zuni Indians," *loc. cit.*, 61.

[47] Voth, *The Traditions of the Hopi*, 25.

Water-Corn clan, who claim to have come from Pala'tkwabi, and at that time there were no members of that clan on Third Mesa.[48]

The town of Pala'tkwabi is said to be somewhere south of Flagstaff. If we take a short excerpt from a long story, it will be found that the people of this town were behaving very badly, so the chief decided to move. The handsome son of this chief disguised himself as a ghost, by the use of four masks, but after a time he was captured and exposed. He instructed the people to plant prayer-sticks at certain points in the village. These, as it turned out, became little Water Serpents. The populace soon realized that something evil was about to befall them.

One particular cause of the trouble that beset this town was the ill-treatment of an old man. The chief dressed this old man to resemble the Horned Water Serpent, dug a hole in the plaza, and buried the man there with a bowl of water and a whistle such as that used in some ceremonies connected with the Snake. The old man blew the whistle into the bowl and the people noticed that the prayer-sticks they had planted at the direction of the "ghost" were really Balolookongs. Where they entered the ground water was coming out, and every water vessel began to fill up and pour out as well. The old man emerged from his grave as the Horned Water Serpent; the town was flooded and many drowned. The handsome son of the chief and his beautiful sister were dressed in elegance and sent to quell the great Horned Water Serpent and his lesser counterparts. The young man went to the great Serpent, embraced him, and at the same time pushed him down into the water where these two and the sister disappeared forever. Very soon thereafter the flood subsided.[49]

There is a very clear, and probably ceremonially organized, invocation to the flood in this story, as well as the sacrifice to placate the same waters. The Pueblos, it should be remembered, are floodwater farmers. If the right amount of water comes down the washes and fans out over the cornfields to soak the sands, all is well. If there is too much water the fields are washed away, or if there is too little the life-giving corn dies.

[48] Titiev, *Old Oraibi*, 52, gives clan population figures.
[49] Voth, *The Traditions of the Hopi*, 48–63.

Water as a source of life must be supplicated, and if it is too abundant it must be placated, but that is hardly the whole story. The later account from another Second Mesa Village begins in agricultural terms. The people of Pala'tkwabi were "prosperous, on account of having water, and having an irrigating system from the river which flows through that country." But to that is added another theme: the wrongdoing of the people is sexual. The ghost theme—ghosts are stock symbols of disaster impending—is greatly elaborated. The ghost this time is the nephew of the chief and it is he who is buried in the hole in the plaza. The grave soon becomes boggy and on the forth day the Horned Water Serpent comes forth and sways to and fro in the plaza. Water pours out of the ground and the town is flooded. In desperation a six-year-old boy and girl, described as of "clean hearts and innocent," are sent to the Serpent. "When they had reached this monster he sprang up and coiled himself around the two children and sank with them into the water."[50]

The same story can be pursued to Zuñi, and there it is attached to a clan which may be a correlative of the Patki. The Patki clan is sometime called the Divided Water clan, probably because of elements in the flood myth already mentioned. More broadly, it is grouped as the Water-Corn clan, which indicates that two individual groups are involved. Sometimes such a link between clans is denominated a phratry. However we name the group, the Pueblo clans which signify water, whether they be Cloud, Snow, Frog, or Sky clans, are linked with Corn clans, for reasons which are natural enough.

Thus we find that at Zuñi very similar stories are connected with the Corn clan, probably not as a historical association, but as a logical one between the sources of water and of corn. Again there is a sexual implication. The Corn clan was the largest at Zuñi and the young people were very handsome, but they slept together. The evil which is always the reason for a flood is thus attributed to clan incest. One man, the son of a priest, was disturbed, so he called his dead uncle. There was moaning and rattling in the distance and the body came rolling toward him. They went toward Itiwana, but the uncle brushed against the boy and he became a dead man, which is to say a "ghost"

[50] Nequatewa, *Truth of a Hopi*, 85–102.

if we relate back to the Hopi stories. When this young man came to the wicked kivas the people cried out in fear of earthquakes (landslides). Everyone fled to Corn Mountain, except the son of the priest and his little sister and the grandmother.

"The boy carried his little sister on his back. When they came to Matsaka, they felt the earth rumble, and the boy who was now the apparition turned into Kolowisi [the Water Snake]. They said to their grandmother, 'Stay here, grandmother, and we will go on to Corn Mountain; it is too dangerous to wait for you.' The grandmother said, 'It is well. I have only a little while to live. Let the young ones go on quickly; I must die one of these days.' The young pair went on to Corn Mountain without her, and Kolowisi kept back the floods until they had reached the mountain. Then he let loose the waters and they filled all the valley."[51] The sacrifice of these children is not mentioned in this story, but it occurs in older versions, and the figures of these two are well known to the Zuñis in a natural, sculptural formation on the mountain.

Since the element of human sacrifice is central to each of the myths so far presented, we must face the question: do they indicate a recollection of an ancient time when a youth and a maid were actually sacrificed to the god of underground waters? Some people, including Indians, have thought so, and since such sacrifices are known from central America, the idea cannot be dismissed offhand. In my opinion there never were human sacrifices by the Pueblos. To begin with, their history is so short that any memory of such a practice would still linger among the whole tribe. Instead we find the story centered in only one clan among the Hopis. At Zuñi the sacrifice element is a common type of aetiological tale invented to explain a prominent rock formation resembling human figures. While these arguments are not decisive, an analysis of the psychological import of the myth yields an explanation of sacrifice which does not point to a sacrifice of human life.

The images in the story are patently sexual and when added together give a life history. The first element is a warning against sexual disorder, either of a type of promiscuity that would make the orderly

[51] Benedict, *Zuñi Mythology*, I, 11.

sequence of generations impossible, or against clan incest, which was felt to hold the same danger. In the Zuñi story just given, the young ones struggle up the mountain, and the grandmother dies. In so far as the flood theme is related to childbirth water, it is a two directional image which may refer backward to the time of one's origin, or forward to the birth of the generation which will in time succeed the present one.

Another Zuñi story makes the moral purpose of generation stories quite clear. There was a frozen pond near the town, and the people wanted to skate (slide) on this dangerous ice.

"The girls who had sweethearts slid with them and not with their mothers. After the meal they skated again. Those who had babies tended them first and then joined the rest. The bow priest and Pekwin [the officers responsible for the tribe] sat at one side smoking and the people skated for them. The people played harder and harder; the women pinched the men and the men ran after the women and some of them got separated from the others and lay together. Women who had children left them with their people and went off with the men they were playing with. Only a few people were left at the pond. Pekwin and the bow priest saw what was happening. The bow priest was angry. He called out, 'My people, come back to this place. We don't want you to scatter yourselves. Enjoy yourselves sliding on the pond.' "[52]

While a frozen pond is not comparable to a flood, these stories seem to have a common moralistic purpose. The youth must take family life with some seriousness, and the old ones must be left behind. The great Snake, who is a friendly water-god, holds back the waters so that the generations may pass safely. Between the young, who tend to be chaotic, and the departing aged there is a middle generation. The sacrifice consists in accepting the stages of life. The first step is the loss of youth and innocence. Some embrace the Serpent and willingly sink into the water with him. To other minds a monster rises from the water and coils himself around the young ones. In either case they have sacrificed their careless childhood days and enter a time of flood and earthquake, from which they may luckily escape

[52] *Ibid.*, 13.

114

to Corn Mountain, leaving their grandparents to drown in the seas of time. The middle generation watches, anxiously: "Come back to this pond—don't scatter yourselves."

The Migrations

After mankind had been created, after he had emerged from the underworld, he was still forced to wander about the earth until he found his center. The image refers to the omphalo certainly, but more importantly it indicates a search for stability and balance which can only be achieved in the true home where one's heart lies.

The migrations were certainly historical events leading up to present success, or at least to present equilibrium, but all of the migration stories have proved to be a confusion, rather than an illumination of actual history. They represent a kind of progress of the soul, or more simply a search for the basic securities of water, food, and safety from enemies. When the people first came up they did not do well. Eventually they came to White House, which the Keres believe to be somewhere in the North. The experience there was something of an initiation; the people took stock of themselves and their rites were amplified. With this gathered strength they again set out to locate the center. At Zuñi, as has been told, the water-strider is called in to help. "He touched the corners of the east and north, but could not touch the corners of the west and south. He said, 'You are very near. I will go and find the place where my arms will touch the horizon in all four directions.' The bow priests went with him. Water Spider said, 'I have to go back. Let us try Halona (ant place). My heart will be on an anthill.' He stretched out his arms and legs and touched the horizon at the north, west, south and east. He was in the middle of the world. He said, 'My people shall live here always. They will never be overthrown for their hearts will not be to one side of the world.' "[53]

[53] *Ibid.*, 5–6.

Chapter Four

EARTH GODDESS

Buli mana, or Butterfly Maiden

ONE WOULD EXPECT this chapter to be a simple account of the Pueblo equivalents of the Grecian goddess Demeter. Unfortunately the simple concept is surrounded with problems. The Hopi corn deity, Muingwu, is a male, and while one expects confusion as to sex among the great gods it is more troubling in relation to a "cornmother." The Keresan corn spirit, Iyatiku, presents an even greater puzzle, and, unfortunately, one of no general interest. It is simply that the names of Keresan deities are badly scrambled. The concepts are clear enough; there is a high goddess or god whom we have chosen to call Sus'sistinako, as the most common name for Thinking Woman. Below her, but of even greater importance in daily life, is the Corn-Mother, whom we choose to call Iyatiku. Between her and humanity stand the two sisters whom the Keres of Cochití call Uretsete and Naotsete.

For the reader of general interest the scheme of Keresan spirits could be left that simply, but for the student who intends to read or question further there is more to be said. The phonetic transcription of Pueblo names varies a great deal, according to the individual and the system used in writing down the words. With the Keres there seems to be, in addition, a dialect diversity from town to town. While difficult, neither of these barriers is insurmountable to the serious reader; you soon learn to correlate "Sussistinako" and "Sitch-tche-na-ko." The serious problem when considering these Keresan divinities does not lie here. It is rather in that they have taken these four basic names, and in the different towns have applied them in seemingly random fashion; so that, for example, at Acoma the name of the highest goddess-god is the same generally used for the eldest of the two sisters.

116

I must apologize both to Iyatiku and to the reader for beginning her account with a list of names, but it will make the quotations more intelligible.

In this list Santo Domingo and San Felipe are left out because they do not differ from their close neighbor, Santa Ana. As one reads down the list it will be seen that only in two recent reports from Acoma does the name for the Thinking Woman vary, which seems sufficient reason to accept some version of Sus'sistinako as the original and correct name.

> Cochití (Recorder: Dumarest)
>> High Deity: Sussistinako
>> Corn-Mother: Uretsete
>> Two Sisters (Indian): Uretsete
>>   (Alien): Naotsete
>
> Sía (Recorder: Stevenson)
>> High Deity: Sus'sistinako
>> Corn-Mother: Utset
>> Two Sisters (Indian): Utset
>>   (Alien): Now'utset
>
> Santa Ana (Recorder: White)
>> High Deity: Tsityostinako (Thinking Woman)
>> Corn-Mother: Iatik
>> Two Sisters (Indian): Utctsityi
>>   (Alien): Nausity
>
> Acoma (Recorder: White's Informant)
>> High Deity: Utc'tsiti
>> Corn-Mother: ———
>> Two Sisters (Indian): Iatiku
>>   (Alien): Nau'tsitic
>
> Acoma (Recorder: Stirling's Informant)
>> High Deity: Uch'tsiti
>> Corn-Mother: Tsichtinako
>> Two Sisters (Indian): Iatiku
>>   (Alien): Nautsiti

Laguna and Acoma (Recorder: Gunn)
   High Deity: Sitch-tche-na-ko
   Corn-Mother: E-yet-e-co (Meaning "Earth")
   Two Sisters (Indian): Nau'tsity (Recorded in Laguna by
                              Benedict and Boas)
               (Alien): I'tc'ts'ity

When we come to the middle goddess, the Corn-Mother, we find that something like Iyatiku is used as the name in Santa Ana, Santo Domingo, San Felipe, and Laguna and perhaps earlier at Acoma; in Gunn's account he does not distinguish between the two western towns. We also find that the pueblos of Cochití and Sía use a word which generally designates the Indian sister to indicate the Corn-Mother. A ready explanation, though not necessarily the right one, for the change is that the sisters were a simple division of the mother, and that the Indian sister was thought of as identical with her.

Another explanation must be found for the variance in names in recent Acoma accounts. When White gives his version of the Acoma pantheon, he places Iyatiku where he thinks she should be, i.e., as the corn goddess.[1] While I agree with him, there is no doubt that current Acoma usage places that name on the Indian sister, which becomes a reverse complement to the Cochití and Sía system of identifying the younger sister with the mother.

Why did the people of Acoma transpose these names? For one thing, Acoma is far to the west of the Keresan pueblos on the Río Grande; and for another, the modern informants have suffered through the boarding-school era. Stirling's informant was taken far from home as a child and indoctrinated with Christian, which is to say foreign, ideas. Under these circumstances a child might remember the concepts of his parents, but confuse the names. The error is also logical, in that if Uch'tsiti is removed from the top of the column Tsichtinako will rise to the top as the high goddess and Iyatiku will take her place as the Corn-Mother.

The sisters are less of a problem. All of the alien sisters have some variant of the same name, as befits a late coming and unwanted sibling, with the exception of Laguna where the names of the two sisters

[1] White, "The Acoma Indians," *loc. cit.*, 64–66.

have been transposed. The Indian sister, as we have seen, is often identified directly with the Corn-Mother in name.

Since the sisters are intimately connected with the Corn-Mother, we may examine their story first. In the following account from Acoma the reader must keep in mind that the speaker is Iyatiku: "For the first time they [the sisters] asked Tsichtinako why they were on earth and why they were created. Tsichtinako replied, 'I did not make you. Your father Uchisiti made you, and it is he who has made the world, the sun which you have seen, the sky, and many other things which you will see. But Uchtsiti says the world is not yet completed, not yet satisfactory as he wants it. This is the reason he has made you. You will rule and bring to life the rest of the things he has given you in the baskets."[2]

The Corn-Mother, who named the Indian sister first, thought a long time for a name for the other. The two were waiting to pray to the Sun when it came up. Finally Tsichtinako noticed that the other had more in her basket, and told the Indian sister to call her by this name, so she "called her Nautsiti which meant 'more of everything in the basket.' "[3]

These sisters, the reader will probably have realized, are the counterparts of the Hopi brother pair which figured prominently in the first chapter. The elder in each case is foreign, powerful, and rich. The change in sex can be traced from east to west. At Laguna, which is Keresan, but nearly midway between the Keres villages of the Río Grande and the Hopis on their Arizona mesas, there is a compromise in that the older sister is transformed into a brother. Boas states that all of his Laguna informants agreed upon this; the white man has a father, not a mother, a development which he attributes to Catholic influence.[4]

In other Keresan stories there is no doubt that a pair of sisters were involved, and that these siblings were not long on the best of terms. "Naotsete and Uretsete quarreled from childhood because Naotsete, the elder sister, mother of Whites, was jealous of the younger, Uretsete, mother of Indians. Both sisters wanted to go to the south to people that region. They were to have a contest to determine who

[2] Stirling, *Origin Myth of Acoma*, 3. [3] *Ibid.* [4] Boas, *Keresan Texts*, 221.

had the right to go."[5] At Sía there was a contest between the two sisters, the elder being a Navaho in this case, and the contest was of a most elemental kind.

"After a time the younger sister ran to the park and cried, 'This is enough; fight no more.' [Referring to the people of the two tribes.] 'Let us descend to the park and fight.' And they fought like women—not with bows and arrows—but wrestled. The men formed a circle around them and the women fought hard and long. Some of the men said, 'Let us go and part the women;' others said, 'No; let them alone.' The younger woman grew very tired in her arms, and cried to her people, 'I am very tired,' and they threw the elder sister upon the ground and tied her hands; the younger woman then commanded her people to leave her, and she struck her sister with her fists about the head and face as she lay upon the ground, and in a little while killed her. She then cut the breast with a stone knife and took out the heart, her people being still in a circle, but the circle was so large that they were some distance off. She held the heart in her hand and cried: 'Listen, men and youths! This woman was my sister, but she compelled us to fight; it was she who taught you to fight. The few of her people who escaped are in the mountains and they are the people of the rats;' and she cut the heart into pieces and threw it upon the ground, saying, 'Her heart will become rats, for it was very bad,' and immediately rats could be seen running in all directions. She found the center of the heart full of cactus."[6]

I have quoted this unparalleled display of violence to illustrate the effect of actual history on myth and legend. The contest usually amounts to a test of whose face the Sun will shine on first, or a test of identifying game tracks, and while the alien sister loses she goes free. The violence of the feeling against the elder sister at Sía can probably be explained by the fact that they have experienced the worst of both white and Navaho worlds. After the Pueblo Revolt the Spanish in 1689 fought a great battle at Sía, "killing six hundred and capturing seventy. Also, many were burned to death rather than surrender. This battle reduced the Zía to a more or less peaceable

[5] Dumarest, *Notes on Cochití*, 212.
[6] Stevenson, "The Sia," *loc. cit.*, 34.

state . . . ."[7] To make matters worse, this state put them in opposition to the still resisting Pueblos from Jémez and Zuñi and their Navaho allies who continued to raid the town. It was a battle to the death, and despite the story, it was not the heart of the alien sister that was plucked out, but the heart of Sía itself.

While these two sisters, the earthly counterparts of the underworld Corn-Mother, do the actual planting of trees, releasing of animals from their baskets, and most importantly appearing as the actual mothers for human kinds, Iyatiku remains beneath in the four-chambered underworld, from which she first passes on information at the time of the Emergence. Later she receives the dead back again when they return to her realm. Thus once more, as with Masau'u, the deity of fertility is identical with the deity of death: "When the deceased arrives at Shipapu, at the end of four days he is received into the ante-room of *uretsete* [which is to say Iyatiku]. Two guards examine his *hachamuni* and let him in to his mother."[8]

In Sía mythology Iyatiku adventures into our daylight world long enough to endow mankind with a start in agriculture, but she does not remain long in the upper world. In this respect her rule is the opposite of the Greek mother and daughter pair, Demeter and Persephone, where it is the daughter who spends part of the year underground while the mother reigns from above. However, in both the Greek and Keresan versions the mother and daughter are often simply aspects of the same goddess. At Sía she leads the people in the emergence: "Sûssïstinnako placed a huge reed upon the mesa top and said: 'My people will pass up through this to the world above.' Ûtsĕt [i.e., Iyatiku] led the way, carrying a sack containing many of the star people; she was followed by all the theurgists, who carried their precious articles in sacred blankets, on their backs; then followed the laity and all animals . . . ." Then, after the customary items of the emergence are given, it is stated that "Ûtsĕt is appealed to, to the present time, as father and mother, for she acts directly for Sûssïstinnako, the creator."

After she has led mankind up from the underworld Iyatiku's role

[7] Paul Reiter, *The Jémez Pueblo of Unshagi, New Mexico*, 37.

[8] Dumarest, *Notes on Cochiti*, 172.

as mother of crops comes to the fore: "Their only food was seeds of certain grasses, and Ûtsĕt desiring that her children should have other food made fields north, west, south and east of the village and planted bits of her heart, and corn was evolved (though Ûtsĕt had always known the name of corn, corn itself was not known until it originated in these fields), and Ûtsĕt declared: 'This corn is my heart and it shall be to my people as milk from my breasts.' "[9]

In this instance we find a continuation of the image which Sus'sisti-nako represents, but instead of thinking outward into space and the thought becoming a reality, this time it is a name that was known, a Logos, and the name became a reality through the division of the goddess' heart. The reality is both corn and the cultural advance which raised the Pueblos from the level of seed-gatherers to that of a town-dwelling agricultural people. That change naturally involves a great deal more than the simple acquisition of a basic food plant.

In his study of Acoma White states that there Iyatiku is not specialized for food; she is life itself, or a most important deity representing life, or the forces of life. While prayers and bits of food are offered to her before each meal, she is remote and is never dramatized in ceremonies. "In certain rituals one speaks of getting the breath of Iatiku, the breath of life, from Shipap; a tender feeling is kept for her, as well as respect."[10]

White also says that she is never represented in drawings or costume; however, there is at least one exception to the first part of the statement. It is derived from a sand-painting, but drawn by one of Stirling's Acoma informants. It represents Iyatiku as she appears on a Fire Society altar. The goddess is represented as a bird woman; she has wings, tail, and talon, but bears the head of a woman. Her body is yellow spotted to represent the earth. A red, arrow-shaped heart is the center of herself and of the world. Around her is a blue circle to represent the sky, while an inner arc represents the milky way; above it are symbols for sun, moon, and the stars.[11]

Possibly this representation of the goddess is unique, but Iyatiku

[9] Stevenson, "The Sia," *loc. cit.*, 37, 39.

[10] White, "The Acoma Indians," *loc. cit.*, 66.

[11] Stirling, *Origin Myth of Acoma*, Pl. 10, Fig. 2, and 121n.

is ubiquitously represented in the Keres towns by a corn-ear fetish which is called an Iarriko. It is basically a perfect ear of corn, with each kernel in place right down to the tip; or if not, kernels are glued on. It has a reed or grass base into which beautiful and symbolic feathers are set upright. The Iarriko is a personal fetish and accompanies one throughout his life; at death it is destroyed, or, among the Zuñis, the similar fetish is broken up and the seeds planted in the owner's fields.

The fetish is not peculiar to the Keres, nor is its import, but the goddess connected with it is Keresan. At Zuñi the fetish, "ĕt'tonĕ, a most sacred object of the A'shiwanni, symbolizes Earth Mother, rains, and vegetation, including all that supplies physical nourishment to man, the mi'li symbolizes the life-giving or soul power which comes from A'wonawil'ona, the supreme bisexual power, who is the breath of life and life itself."[12] The Zuñi mi'li is breathed upon and one inhales from it, both acts symbolizing an interchange of the breath of life between the supernatural forces and an individual man.

For the Keresan individual the similar feathered corn ear fetish is a most important object, representing at once the heart of his life, and at the same time the heart of his mother-goddess, Iyatiku. The object has very great power, since the goddess herself handed the original one to the first chief when she returned to the underworld.

" 'I, Ûtsĕt [Iyatiku] will soon leave you; I will return to the home whence I came. You will be to my people as myself; you will pass with them over the straight road, I will remain in my house below and will hear all that you say to me. I give to you all my wisdom, my thoughts, my heart, and all. I fill your head with my mind.' " The goddess then gave the chief a staff of office and bade him work for all things good.

"He replied: 'It is well, mother; I will do as you say.' She then instructed this ruler to make the Iärriko which was to represent herself, that they might have herself always with them and know her always."[13]

---

[12] Stevenson, "The Zuni Indians," *loc. cit.*, 416. See also R. F. Kirk, *Introduction to Zuñi Fetishism*, 18–19.

[13] Stevenson, "The Sia," *loc. cit.*, 40–41.

It is this mandate to the town chief that established his functioning on a supernatural basis; he is not primarily a secular ruler, but a high priest who must take care of his people by fasting and prayer. As a sign of his inheritance of power from her, he is called *yaya*, which means "mother," but the people of Cochití hastened to add:

"But he is accounted the father as well as the mother of all the people. He has to pray and fast for all, even for the Whites, that all may obtain *ianyi*, i.e., life, health and good harvest. He can enter into no social entanglements, he is a man of peace. Therefore is he relieved of all executive functions. He neither denounces nor punishes. He gives advice and counsels harmony. 'Let us be united as brothers. Thus our Mother will aid us and keep us in health. Thus from her breath we shall receive the health she is herself possessed of.' "[14]

The goddess and her fetish have thus another important function, that of curing. Demeter was held to cure the bellyache, and the association of a Corn-Mother with health and curing is easy enough to understand—an empty stomach was a common enough source of pain. Iyatiku adds to that simplest form of cure, a full stomach, the concept of life-giving power as embodied in a fetish which is a part of herself. As an important part of the treatment for any illness the fetish is placed, standing erect, beside the patient and these simple words are uttered: "We are content; since yesterday our Mother has been seated among us."[15]

[14] Dumarest, *Notes on Cochití*, 197.
[15] *Ibid.*, 159.

Chapter Five

GERMINATOR

Muingwu, or Germinator

THE HOPIS likewise have a fetish of a perfect corn ear, though it differs slightly in form from its Keresan and Zuñi counterpart by the fact that it has a wooden base. This tiponi is wrapped in layers of homespun cotton which hold the feathers in place. In function it differs as well, in that it is not a personal fetish, but one kept in the hands of the principal priests. There is no Corn-Mother figure standing behind these fetishes, nor sitting in the underworld as a source of food and life. Instead, we find among the Hopis a male fertility god who is referred to as "virgin of the earth."[1]

We immediately meet the problem of why the virgin of the earth should be a male. The tiponi is clearly enough a female image. Each chief brought one from the underworld. "It is the mother of the people; in the interior are the seeds of all edible vegetation, all garden products, piñon nuts, cedar berries, every kind known to the Hopi."[2] Before considering the problem, or the possible goddesses who may have preceded, let us look at the present male divinity.

In the first chapter something was said on the relationship between Masau'u and Muingwu, since they seem to be closely related, and it was suggested that the difference may have been in part due to different towns of origin for similar beings. Now we find that Germinator exists under the dual names of Muingwu and Alosaka, and a difference of clan origin may again be assumed. The relationship might be something like this: the Bear clan had an encounter with Masau'u near Walpi on the First Mesa, as we have already heard. One of Stephen's informants, during the Flute ceremony there in 1892, told him that it had been the "chief of the Bear that overthrew Masau.' "[3] The chief of the Bear clan impersonated Alosaka, who has an im-

[1] Stephen, *Hopi Journal*, I, 584.
[2] *Ibid.*, II, 781. [3] *Ibid.*, II, 813.

portant bit in the Flute ceremony. Muingwu also appears, but he is there as a figurine near the altar. He is there "because from him comes all our knowledge of seeds and cultivation."[4] Alosaka is there in a dramatic role; he meets a group coming into the pueblo and in an exchange welcomes them if they bring rain and health, then accepts the tiponi of the town chief.

When we meet Muingwu as an important personage in a Third Mesa ceremony, he will be there as a representative of the Badger clan. The relations of clans to society, ceremony, and office is volatile, as their number and power waxes and wanes; but without insisting on particular clan names, I think one can see that similar gods under separate names came close together. Parsons suggests that the overcoming of Masau'u by the Bear clan may represent the triumph of health over death; among the Keres and Zuñis Bear is the great curer. More evidently it represents a contest of divinities and a peaceful compromise. Alosaka, in this ceremony, is specialized as the holder of the tiponi, which represents corn and all other seeds. Like the Keresan chief, he is also the father of the town and guardian of its health. Muingwu, at Walpi, is reduced to a figurine, representing the source of knowledge about seeds and agriculture.

Perhaps, before continuing, we should glance at the physical appearance of Germinator, or Muingwu. He is an anthropomorphic god, but is not represented by masks. At Walpi he naturally enough, as a fertility god, wears a pair of horns on his head. These horns appear in drawings and I assume they adorn the helmet of the (Alosaka) impersonator. In Voth's photograph[5] of the impersonator during the Powamu, the head is bare and he wears the white robe over his shoulder, rather than the white kilt. At Oraibi he carries in his left hand a small netted gourd which is filled with water, and sometimes honey, four corn ears, and a wooden, knifelike implement which is a planting or cultivating stick. In his right hand he holds the crook which represents the stages of life, and to it are attached a corn ear and packets of cornmeal to be distributed. The

---

[4] *Ibid.*, II, 793.

[5] H. R. Voth, *The Oraibi Soyal Ceremony*, Pl. LVII.

crook is a literal "staff of life," curved at the end like any other cane. Since many of them were found at Pueblo Bonito, they must have been a part of ritual and altars from the earliest Pueblo times.

At Walpi, Alosaka uses a netted gourd, carries a staff adorned with feathers—but not the crook—and there are other fertility symbols in abundance. Prayer-sticks with the feathers of yellow birds, to represent the scattering of yellow pollen, are made, and of course the ear itself, and the packets of pollen. One very unique item appears: a water rattle, which consists of four gourd discs sewn together in pairs, and placed one after the other on a rod. To this is tied a pliant crook festooned with shells at the tip. The sound the rattle makes is said to represent the "roar and commotion of the waters (ocean) at the early si'papu."[6] The discs represent the four underworlds from which we have arisen, but as opposed to this lower world the rattle also has a series of curved thorns to "hook the clouds," and at their tip is an eagle feather.

The fertile underworld is linked, in a riverless and nearly streamless country, with the powers of the sky. In the murals on the walls of Oak Mound Kiva at Walpi there were two brief murals representing two-horned gods. They were associated with the Powamu ceremony, with Germinator, in this case Alosaka. Apparently the murals were rubbed out as soon as it began to rain and they had thus served their purpose. He is represented as without arms, and in their place are wings and two lightning bolts. The wings remind one of the Acoma drawing of Iyatiku; the eagle is the king or queen of the sky and fertility falls from on high. Lightning signifies the coming of rain, and fields which are struck by it are supposed to be especially fertile. A second mural represents a kilted figure, with the netted gourd in the left hand, and lightning in the right. In place of a head are cloud and lightning symbols.

On the basis of these figures, one is tempted to think of Alosaka as a representative of the fertility of the sky, and Muingwu as that of the earth, but one should remember that Zeus combined both aspects within himself. He is not only the Rainy Zeus, but at times

[6] Stephen, *Hopi Journal*, II, 772.

becomes Zeus Chthonios, "the power which dwells in the earth and sends out of it the fruits of the field."[7]

In actual ceremony the heavens and the earth are called upon to join their powers. At the Niman, or farewell to kachinas ceremony, which is held in spring when the serious work of the farmer is about to begin, a priest stomps on the plank drum which represents Shipapu, the entrance to the underworld, and cries: "I call with the thunder, the lightning, with these [pointing to the four lightning effigies] of the four directions, I call to Muingwu, to the chiefs at all the six places, to hasten the clouds here with rain."[8] He is addressing Muingwu as the god of the Nadir, or the "below."

As chief of the Nadir, "Below sits Muingwu on Sichomo, Flower mound. He wears a mask of clouds of all these five colors, and before it flutter all the sacred birds and all the butterflies. Speckled corn and sweet corn grow there and melons, cotton, beans, squash, etc. All the cloud deities have black legs, hence the Agaves paint their prayer-stick legs black."[9] The reversal of colors is interesting. Masau'u, it will be remembered, had shining black legs, and at Zuñi the below was a sooty depth represented by the black corn people, while the above was multicolored. Here the order is reversed and the parti-colored corn represents the below, possibly to disassociate the activity of Muingwu in the below from that of Masau'u.

Germinator appears most prominently in the Powamu ceremony which takes place in February. The Powamu has two conspicuous purposes: it is an iniation rite for children—one of two such rites— and an augury for the success of the year's crops. Kachina dolls are given to women who want children, and some of the old who suffer are treated like children, which is to say lashed with yucca whips. As this is a cure for rheumatism, it doubtless signifies that they are to become like the young again.

The second element of the ceremony, and one which is much more to our point, is the testing of prospects for the coming crop season, somewhat as a nurseryman tests his seeds for their power of germi-nation before he plants them. Botanomancy is Stephen's name for

[7] Martin P. Nilsson, *A History of Greek Religion*, 122.
[8] Stephen, *Hopi Journal*, I, 518.   [9] *Ibid.*, I, 333.

the process in which beans, and a little corn, are sprouted in the kivas. There is a broader magical scope to the ceremony as well: Powamu is called a cleansing ceremony, and the name is said to be derived from a word meaning "to put in order, in proper shape or condition, as by this ceremony the fields and gardens are put in proper shape or condition, symbolically, protected against destructive forces (sand storms, ants, etc.), and in every way consecrated, as it were, for the approaching planting season."[10]

The clearing of the fields is a very literal matter; old cornstalks, brush, sticks, and stones are removed, but there is also the related intent of putting the cosmic year in order. By February, when the bright days come along, it is joyfully evident that the Sun has turned back again, and the earthly year must be prepared once more.

In the Hopi winter, "Pyu'ukanhoya, his breath is ice cold, he understands the cold, hence appeals to him in the cold moons of *kya* and *pa* (December and January.) During these two moons it is especially desirable to have plenty of rain or snow to permeate the land, then cold to make plenty of ice. If there has been little winter moisture and ice, when summer comes the fields get dry too soon and little or no harvest is yielded." After these two months the next moon goes and takes the great cold with it. Powamu exorcises the cold and assesses the coming season. The judgment is possible because February is a sort of negative for the positive print of summer.

"When Powa'muriyawu" [crescent-moon horizontal, or our February] "shines in the Above, its counterpart, Nasha'muria'wu is shining in the Below, at the house of Muriyinwu [Muingwu]. Summer is yonder, winter is here. All vegetation mature, fruits all ripe in the Below . . . .

"All plants come from [Muingwu]; prayer-sticks are made and 'placed' for [Muingwu] and in exchange for these prayer-sticks he sends us vegetation."[11]

The central part of the Powamu is the germination of beans.[12] To keep the symbolism straight some corn is planted, but beans have

[10] Voth, *The Oraibi Soyal Ceremony*, 71.

[11] Stephen, *Hopi Journal*, I, 239.

[12] Voth, *The Oraibi Soyal Ceremony*, 99–102.

two advantages: they grow faster at this time of year and the results are edible. The kivas make excellent hot houses in which all sorts of containers full of dirt and bean seeds are placed, while the fires are kept up night and day.

On the fifth day of the ceremony Muingwu arrives. He is impersonated by the chief Powamu priest, who is supposed to have come to the Hopi town, from below, by a circuitous route. He stands in silence for a while, then some elder asks, "Now, where did you come from?" Muingwu answers that he has come from below, from Towanashabe. "Well, all right, for what purpose do you wander about, tell us!"

Muingwu's ensuing speech is surprisingly not the standard address to the directions, but varies and repeats them to indicate wanderings: "All right, those there at Towanashabe were all assembled making a ladder. They put up the ladder; with turquoise strands was it tied together. That way we came up and out."

Since the speeches to the directions and to various kachinas are similar, one example will give their tenor: "Westward we came. On a road marked with beautiful red corn seed we traveled. We beheld the house of the Hototo Katcina chief. A beautiful red mist enveloped the house. Thus we went in. The Hototo Katcina chief was there. He had beautiful red corn seeds, beans, watermelons, muskmelons, and thus he lived there. Here these Oraibi children, little girls, little boys, of different sizes, here at *sipapu* shall they know our ceremonies. Yes, they shall know them! Beautiful ladder beam, beautiful ladder rungs, tied with turquoise strands to the ladder. Thus we came out."

After a great deal in this vein, the priest says that the children will be flogged with the yucca whips to enlighten their hearts, and their hair will be washed in yucca suds to make the ceremonial cleansing. The Muingwu impersonator then concludes:

"And thus then follow to the white rising and to the yellow rising [the road of life stretches toward the dawn, which the people face, rather than to the sunset], this road marked with nice corn pollen and on which these four old age marks (crooks) are standing . . . . On them you will support yourselves, and over yonder, where the shortest one stands, may you fall asleep as old women and old men. But I am not wandering alone." With that last sentence he ushers in four clowns.

And what of the beans? "At about three o'clock in the morning the inhabitants of the village begin to stir. In all the kivas where beans have been planted they are pulled and taken to the houses before the smaller children are awake. Small bunches are often tied to the presents to be given to the children at sunrise."[13]

The ceremony, in so far as the priests are concerned, involves a great deal of placing of pine sprigs, the sprouted green corn, the beans, and the prayer-feathers in the traditional manner. Honey as well as water is placed in the netted gourd, since it is particularly potent for feeding the clouds and the sun.

The Germinator that emerges from these brief glimpses at the Flute and the Powamu ceremonies is a god of vegetation, but he is scarcely specialized as such, and whether we regard him as single, or think of Alosaka and Muingwu as separate deities, the role is not limited. Germinator is the guardian of the town, a role which among the Keres was delegated by the Corn-Mother to the town chief. He is also the preserver of health, as Iyatiku was, but in the Powamu ceremony health, except for the ritual cure for lameness, is a wish that the child-initiates should live a long life and at last fall asleep peacefully. Clearly Masau'u's position as the god of the good things of the earth has forced Germinator to shift somewhat in emphasis.

The question which arises next is, did the Hopis ever have a simple corn deity, and if so, was the deity a female? In either case, one asks, why is the present Germinator a male divinity? The answers to these questions are most tenuous, but the evidence can be assembled for the reader to judge.

The simplest assumption is that the Hopis never had an earth-goddess; it is possible that they thought of the tiponi fetish as "the mother of the people" who held within herself the seeds of all edible vegetation and yet failed to anthropomorphize that concept. Some of the ritual songs from the Powamu ceremony indicate that the

[13] *Ibid.,* 110.

power invoked was not simply the corn ear fetish, but mother earth as a greater, if not anthropomorphic, spirit.

> Ha-o, my mother!
> Ha-o, my mother!
> Due west, blue corn ear, my mother!
> Due eastward, blooming bluebird flower,
> Decorate our faces,
> Bless us with flowers!
> Thus being face decorated,
> Being blessed with flowers,
> We shall be delighted, we shall be delighted,
> Ha-o, my mother. [14]

A vegetation goddess more complex than a corn ear and more specifically vegetal than Hard Beings Woman would seem to lie, blooming, somewhere behind that song.

If we look for such an earth-mother we find two candidates. One is that kindly creature, Spider Grandmother, who knows the recesses and the recourses of the upper side of the crust of the underworld. She did not quite fit in the scheme of the great gods, which could mean that she had been displaced when beast-gods gave way to anthropomorphic gods. The only evidence comes from a question posed by Stephen to a Hopi: "When I ask him as to colour emblem of the Below, he says never mind it. Spider woman and [Muingwu] are together there, are the man and woman chiefs there. Spider woman, he says, is my mother, is all mother, the mother of all."[15]

Such a statement is no proof that there was once a Hopi "mother-of-all"; it may only indicate that one Hopi knew of the Keresan goddess and identified her with Spider Woman.

There is a second candidate for the role of the lost earth-mother; varied information points to such a conclusion. Before presenting the evidence, it should be noted that whatever the value of the assumption, the Hopis of today make no such identification. The spirit in question is Sand Altar Woman, or Tuwa'boñtumsi. The first thing to be said in favor of identifying her with a lost earth-mother rests

[14] *Ibid.*, 143.
[15] Stephen, *Hopi Journal*, I, 744–45.

in the name. "Tuwa" means brown sand of the valley, or sometimes sand of other colors; she is represented by ridges or mounds of sand, which indicate the earth. The suffix "tumsi" is applied to a young woman who has not yet borne a child. By combining the two meanings we certainly have a "virgin of the earth."

If one could accept the glossary to Stephen's *Hopi Journal* at face value, the case would be improved, for it is stated, under the name of Sand Altar Woman, that "She is the mother of all living things, i.e. of all human kind, all animals, and all vegetation; plants suck from her breast a nourishing liquid, it passes up from their roots to their flowers and fruit, and animals and man eat of this vegetation, hence Tuwa'pontum'si is mother of all life. This liquid the bees suck from the flowers and make into honey."[16]

While it is logical that the earth-mother should be the mother of animals, as well as of plants, the two can be separated. There is another spirit, Tih'kuyi, who is mother of wild game and patroness of the hunt. Tih'kuyi is also Childbirth Water Woman and has a shrine, which Stephen describes as "the phallic niche-cache"[17] in which an image is kept. She is thus a goddess of all animal and human generation.

Tih'kuyi, however, seems to have a hard time holding her own place and often she is identified with Tuwa'boñtumsi, the Sand Altar Woman, thus making the latter the mother of all.

There is another suggestive piece of evidence to link Sand Altar Woman with a previous earth-mother goddess. She is the wife of Masau'u and at the same time she is the sister of Muingwu, Germinator, thus closely linking the three spirits of the crops. A deity is often demoted by this process of becoming a sister or wife to the similar god who is rising in importance. Certainly none of these observations prove that Tuwa'boñtumsi was ever anything more than she now appears to be, nor do they affect the possibility that she is simply an adaptation of the Keresan Iyatiku. Both of them are the mothers of kachinas, and Parsons suggests some other evidence indicating a Keresan origin.[18]

Let us return to Germinator and consider the problem of his male

---

[16] *Ibid.*, II, 1313.   [17] *Ibid.*, I, 261.   [18] *Ibid.*, I, 261n.

sex. Parsons found a very simple answer: Muingwu is the directional chief of the Nadir, and since all of the other chiefs are male, his sex was changed to bring this god into conformity with them.[19] While that is logical enough, it leaves out of account the fact that Alosaka is a male, as is Masau'u, and they are not directional chiefs. Furthermore, there is a Father Corn as well as a Mother Corn, as we shall see in a moment.

One is tempted to see in the maleness of Germinator a decline in the importance of a matriarchy, since Thinking Woman has demonstrably changed from a female goddess to a deity who is thought of, at times at least, as a male. The Pueblos are matrilineal and matrilocal, but there seems to be no evidence to indicate that they were ever matriarchal, and there is certainly no present tendency toward a patriarchy. The men do, however, dominate the religious life of the community and they tend to its agricultural tasks. It is in these two hemispheres, which are often joined in a single sphere of work-and-rite, that the change must have taken place. In the time of the Basketmakers these Indians were seed-gatherers, an occupation in which women are of at least equal importance to men. But once a semi-settled agriculture developed the situation changed. The cornfields are often far from home—too far to bring babies—the work is heavy and often dangerous. As a result the women tended to the repairing of the house and to the cultivation of small gardens near the village, while the men tended the life-giving corn.

Something of the position of the sexes in relation to corn can be seen in the following account from Second Mesa of a semi-ritualistic practice which takes place when sweet corn is first ripe. When this matures, which is well ahead of the Indian corn, large gourd-shaped holes are hollowed out near the cornfields. Fires are built in the pits and then allowed to burn down to coals, at which time corn plants are spread over these, then: "The cultivator has previously made two bundles each consisting of a perfect ear of sweet corn wrapped first in the yellow-flowered medicine plant . . . good for stomach trouble, and then in the brush (Snakeweed). The bundles are tied with yucca fibre and called Father Corn and Mother Corn. The cultivator takes the

[19] *Ibid.,* I, xli.

Mother Corn bundle, points it about the mouth of the oven in the six directions and then tosses it into the mouth of the oven. The collected sweet corn is then thrown in, the Father Corn bundle is placed on top and the oven closed with large stones packed down with earth."

Before sunrise on the following day the oven is opened, Father Corn is set aside, and the roasted ears are taken out.

"Before eating any of the corn each worker takes a mouthful from the Father Corn cob, 'to keep the belly fresh and in good health.' The remains of this cob and the Mother Corn are taken back to the village that the household group may sample them in a similar manner and for the same reason."[20]

Thus the powers of a corn fetish, "to keep the belly fresh," have been bisexualized. In the field the men eat the male bundle, while at home the whole household group partakes of both the male and the female power, a concept which is closely related to the Keresan thought that the town chief is a mother as well as a father to his people. Probably some such idea about the necessity of both sexes lies behind much of the confusion about the sex of many Pueblo gods.

In one notable instance there is no confusion in the Pueblo mind. To them the sea is a woman and the earth may be either a man or a woman, but the Sun is a purely masculine power. He shines far above the confusions of mankind beneath him, and his nearly steady strength keeps all of our movements within his grasp, whether we are primitive, or as sophisticated as may be. To the Sun and his golden, pollen scattering rays, we now turn.

[20] Beaglehole, *Notes on Hopi Economic Life,* 44.

Chapter Six

THE DIVINE SUN

Pautiwa, Zuñi chief of the Council of the Gods,
in a Hopi version

A DIVINITY must establish and maintain his identity and the shape of his personality in the minds of his worshipers. In that struggle the Sun as a god has manifest advantages over other divinities. Disbelief in or ignorance of his presence and power is an impossibility; he withdraws and returns his presence every few hours throughout the life of every individual who lives, or has lived, beneath the cap of the world. In temperate zones he retires to a perilous distance each year, leaving barren fields behind him, but returns again bringing the seasons of joyous crops to sustain life.

While most gods are particular to one locale, in their origin, or peculiar to a tribe or a nation, the Sun's splendor shines, without the need of conquerors or missionaries, on all terrestrial beings and upon the plants by which they live. Yet, despite such an awe-inspiring universality, he is neither an abstract nor a philosophical deity; he appears directly to each individual with the self-evident message to the primitive farmer and the modern scientist alike: all life is dependent upon the beneficence of the Sun's rays. There is in addition a nearly magical quality in the power of the Sun, even to the scientist. The first stage of photosynthesis, which transforms the Sun's energy into the living matter of plants, is a process so instantaneous that it takes fourteen zeros on the right side of a decimal to express the time lapse involved.

Other planets too have powers. The Moon, even in death, exerts a great and visible pull upon the cycles of our life on earth, and she subdivides our seasons. The several planets who may in turn become the Morning Star are often worshiped, or acknowledged; but these have their power in that they are the harbinger of the Sun, and the Moon gains hers as the pale alternative to the Sun's light.

136

Each day as the Sun rises the Zuñis stand before their doors and toss an offering of cornmeal to greet their "father."

> Now this day,
> My sun father,
> Now that you have come out standing to your sacred place,
> That from which we draw the water of life,
> Prayer meal,
> Here I give to you.
>
> Your long life,
> Your old age,
> Your waters,
> Your seeds,
> Your riches,
> Your power,
> Your strong spirit,
> All these to me may you grant.

The Sun is an ancient god, both in human history and in the cosmos. "Yes, indeed," said a Zuñi. "In this world there was no one at all. Always the sun came up; always he went in. No one in the morning gave him sacred meal; no one gave him prayer sticks; it was very lonely."[1]

In the mind of the Zuñi, in the repetition of his "always," which is our eternity, the Sun is the farthest point of reference, the initial glowing spot in the universe. Historically the Sun has remained strong in the Pueblo pantheon, while some other gods have begun to blur and change their shapes. He is also a very public god; many gods are bound to special and strictly religious ceremonies, but the Sun is invoked at any time or place. In the *Hopi Hearings*, where the matter at hand was largely political, he is often called upon, generally with the intent of asking his aid in keeping the Hopi course straight. His symbolic value as the one who "keeps the ways" is coequal with his generative power: "Every mid-winter come together and offer a prayer and make prayer feathers the way we have done here so that this life

---

[1] Bunzel, "Zuñi Ritual Poetry," *loc. cit.*, 584.

will continue on forever, and in like manner do the same thing in summer so that the sun will be taken care of as it goes back and forth in its course of life. Never doubt it."

At another point in the *Hopi Hearings* he is invoked as the care-taker god: "We will look to our father the Sun who travels above us every day taking care of all of us, and it is he who is the highest, and in all of our religious ceremonies we take care of him in our own way, so that he will continue to perform his duty in taking care of our life on this land." In another place the Sun is not invoked, but used as an example for an officer of the people. "We are here gathered together as one people, and it is my duty to hold all people as my people, and like Father Sun who is above all of us, hold all people together as one people and giving us life."

I take a final quotation from Dan Katchongva, the chief at Hotevilla. "They [the Friendlies] have burned up their altars and beliefs and traditions of the Hopi and buried it in the ground saying that that was the end and that nothing will come out of it anymore." In the face of this crisis Katchongva feels that he must turn to the Sun. "Now I have also went through hard times, as you have heard from other people. I have spend many days in jail and now I am old so I look around, in order to save this life that seems to be coming to an end, because I have been told what to do in this time. I am Sun clan. I look to my sun whose light gives life. This life must go on."[2]

While it is common knowledge that the Sun is a most important god in both the Americas, it may be forgotten that this was once true over much of the earth. In one of the oldest prayers in the world, the Braham, as he lights a fire on his altar at sunrise prays, "May the Sun quicken our minds." Many centuries before the birth of Christianity the root *div* in Aryan languages, meaning "light," or to "shine," was beginning to take on the concepts of *deva*, which includes all the bright powers of the morning. In the first century before our era, the Essenes, close progenitors of Christianity, were, according to Josephus, praying to the sunrise: "And as for their piety towards god, it is very extraordinary, for before sun-rising they speak not a word about profane matters, but put up certain prayers which they

2 *Hopi Hearings*. The quotations in order are from pages 81, 26, 117, and 257–59.

have received from their forefathers, as if they made a supplication for its rising."

The sequence of Sun, light, and life is apparent to everyone. At Zuñi the word for life is *tekohanane,* daylight—*te,* time or space, and *kohana,* white. When the early Christian writers were seeking a symbol for their god they came to "God is light," and added that it was a light no man can approach unto, both of which are Sun images. While to the scientist the energy given off by the sun is based on the self-regenerative carbon nitrogen cycle, a most complex process, to the Pueblos the relationship of man to Sun is quite simple.

The Sun is the giver of life, so life must be presented to him in turn, but it is no blood or burnt sacrifice, even of a beast. All of the Pueblos present the newborn child to the Sun on either the fourth or eighth day of his life, holding the naked child up to his rays at sunrise.

> Now this is the day.
> Our child,
> Into the daylight
> You will go out standing.
> . . .
>
> Our fathers,
> Dawn priests,
> Have come out standing to their sacred place.
> Our sun father
> Having come out standing to his sacred place,
> Our child,
> It is your day.
>
> This day,
> The flesh of white corn,
> Prayer meal,
> To our sun father
> This prayer meal we offer.
>
> May your road be fulfilled
> Reaching to the road of your sun father,
> When your road is fulfilled.

> In your thoughts (may we live)
> May we be the ones whom your thoughts will embrace,
> For this, on this day
> To our sun father
> We offer prayer meal.

While the divinity of the Sun is a natural and simple idea, the elaborations of his godly personality are not. To begin with, he has a history, as any god has, but it is not certain where this begins. Did he always exist, or was he created by other gods, or even by men? Parsons states that at Zuñi and Acoma he always existed. With the Zuñis, whose religion is definitely heliocentric, that statement is probably true, but elsewhere we may have it either way.

We have already heard one account from Acoma in which the people emerged into a world of darkness in which there was as yet no sun. After the people were lined up facing east, "Then she [Iyatiku] had the sun come up."[3] In that statement it is not clear that Iyatiku created the Sun; she may merely have been responsible for making him rise.

At Cochití the issue is quite definite; the goddesses existed before the Sun, and the mother created him: "The sun was made by *uretsete*. It is a disc of shells behind which is hidden *payatyama*, Sun-man, who illumines the world in his flight through space."[4]

In the Pueblo of Sía it is the Two Sisters who are responsible for creating the Sun. They discuss the problem during a kiva conversation and conclude: " 'Now we will make light, that our people may see; we can not now tell the people, but to-morrow will be a good day and day after tomorrow will also be a good day,' meaning that their thoughts were good, and they spoke with one tongue, and that their future would be bright, and they added: 'Now all is covered with darkness, but after a while we will have light.' These two women, being inspired by Sus'sistinako, created the sun from white shell, turkis, red stone, and abalone shell. After making the sun they carried him to the east . . . . The next morning they ascended a high moun-

[3] White, "The Acoma Indians," *loc. cit.*, 142.
[4] Dumarest, *Notes on Cochití*, 299.

tain and dropped the sun down behind it, and after a time he began to ascend, and when the people saw the light their hearts rejoiced. When far off his face was blue; as he came nearer the face grew brighter. They, however, did not see the sun himself, but a mask so large that it covered his entire body."[5] The last statement is an image similar to that contained in "the light which no man can approach unto; whom no man hath seen, nor can see."

At Sía it is known rather exactly what the Sun looks like as an anthropomorphic figure. He wears a shirt and thigh length leggings of fringed deerskin, embroidered and beaded moccasins, and a deerskin kilt with a snake painted on it. He carries bow and arrows and a quiver of cougar skin. His mask has eagle plumes upon it and hair that is "red like fire," to represent the Sun's rays. This very handsome fellow who has been seen and whose rays are only red horse-hair is, of course, not the real Sun, but a masked kachina dancer who represents him on earth.

While the Keresan Sun may have been created, or may have simply been called upon to rise, the Zuñi Sun is from eternity. First among the celestial powers is: "The Sun Father, who is directly associated with the supreme power; he always was and always will be . . . . Whatever the Zuñis fail to account for by incidents in the early stages of their existence is attributed to the agency of the Sun Father."[6]

The Sun, whether he has always existed, or was the creation of greater goddesses, has a simple aspect and a simple history. He shines, possibly because he is made of turquoise and abalone shell, his daily course across the sky is not far and his duties are few. "Each night the sun passes by the house of Sûssïstinnako, who asks him: 'How are my children above, how many have died today, and how many have been born today?' He lingers with him (sic) only long enough to answer his questions. He then passes on to his house in the east."[7]

The Sun's simplicity applies only to the distant object in the sky. There are ceremonies to him, and there are kick-stick races to speed

---

[5] Stevenson, "The Sia," *loc. cit.*, 29.

[6] Stevenson, "The Zuñi Indians," *loc. cit.*, 22.

[7] Stevenson, "The Sia," *loc. cit.*, 35.

him on his way; but his effects upon mankind are many and are accounted for by demigods and lesser spirits who act directly upon the stage of the earth.

The Sun Father has children by mortal women, and some of his offspring can travel a rainbow from this world to the house of the Sun and back again at will. The Little War Twins are such spirits, but they are culture heroes rather than personified aspects of the Sun's power. Two important and very different demigods of the Sun are Paiyatemu and Pautiwa.

Paiyatemu and the Corn Maidens

Paiyatemu, or the same being under another name, exists in all the Keresan towns, and under the same name he is important to Zuñi mythology as well; among the Hopis, T'aiowa seems to be his counterpart. From his name it would be reasonable to assume a Keresan origin for this frivolous god, but the similarity of his nature among different tribes, particularly in relation to the clowns, points to a Pueblo-wide concept.

To understand the conceptualism behind Paiyatemu one must recall a persistent dualism that runs through Pueblo thinking. In place of the Greek mean of "nothing too much," we find a Pueblo concern for opposites—"everything both ways." They allow full place to alternatives. In Keresan mythology there are two sisters; one is rich and the other poor, and one is tall while the other is short. Instead of a single war god there are War Twins. As these two relate to the towns one is the peaceful, father-mother, of the people; the other is an "outside," or war chief. When we come to a consideration of the clowns we will find that the essence of their behavior lies in an exhibition of oppositeness to all normal human behavior.

The duality in Paiyatemu is expressed both as a companionship and as an opposition to the Sun. Most simply he is a handsome clown, who bears the shield of the Sun on his journey, and at times entertains him by playing music on his flute. In addition to his role as companion to the Sun, Paiyatemu's more important function is to serve that god as a foil. While the Sun is the epitome of august and divine

142

power, Paiyatemu is quite the opposite. In fact, he is funny, and so senseless that his father lets him do as he pleases. It is in the latter role that he becomes the original and patron of the clown societies.

If we leave out of account the recently developed Hopi emphasis on the Sun as a holder of ways *(wimi)* as well as of roads, which are an individual's life course, we find that the power of the Sun is two-fold: power for war, and power for fertility. The War Twins, sons of the Sun, represent an elaboration of the first aspect, and Paiyatemu the second. He is strictly the fertilizing and sexual power of the Sun molded into anthropomorphic shape, a force which, when pursued as far as it will go, ends in the phallic grossness of the clown societies.

Leave off all serious thought when you are about to meet Paiyate-mu, for he is an outrageous being. This son of the Sun was born of a mortal woman who conceived him when a beam of sunlight fell upon her as she slept. Being half divine and half human, he exhibits both the power of a god and the coarseness of humanity. As the latter qual-ities are more active in the young, he most frequently appears as a handsome rascal who has but two subjects of study: maidens and music, with music perhaps being a way to maidens. Like many other gods, he ages; and when old he stands as straight and erect as a pine tree shorn of its limbs, but we hear little of him in that guise. He is most often seen surrounded by myriads of butterflies, playing his seductive flute from which the butterflies emerge as objectified musi-cal notes.

Strangely enough Paiyatemu has lost his name at Sía and Acoma, or perhaps those towns never detached his fully anthropomorphised figure, for there they call what is unmistakably the same spirit simply by the name of one of the clown societies, Koshari.

At Sía: "The first man created was called Ko'shairi; he not only acts as courier between the sun and the kachina, but he is the com-panion, the jester and musician (the flute being his instrument) of the sun; he is also mediator between the people of the earth and sun; when acting as courier between the sun and the Kachina and vice versa and as mediator between the people of the earth and the sun he is chief for the sun; when accompanying the sun in his daily travels he furnishes him with music and entertainment; he is then the servant of the sun."[8] (There is a second clown society, the Queranna, which is said to be for the Moon.)

At Acoma a similar story is told. "Iatiku turned to Koshari and said, 'You have done your work faithfully but you are not acting normally enough to be here with the people.' He was different from the other people because he knew something about himself, so Iatiku told him to go and live at the house of the Sun. 'You are to be a help to the Sun. You will be called at times to help here. You are not going to be afraid of anything or to regard anything as sacred. You are to be allowed everywhere.' "[9]

These accounts of a single being called Koshari obviously refer to the same being we are considering, so we are left to wonder what became of Paiyatemu, particularly since his name has survived at Sía. There, we are told, the creations of Sus'sistinako were divided into three groups, the Kachina, the Kopishtaiya, and the Pai'a-ta-mo. The Kopishtaiya, is usually a collectivity of spirits and in this instance includes animal life. Pai'a-ta-mo includes: "All men of Ha'arts (the earth), the sun, moon, stars, Ko'shai-ri and Quer'ran-na."[10] While the connection of the clowns with the sun and moon and with mankind is maintained, it seems that Paiyatemu has there fallen back into the generality of spirits from which he has risen as an individual demigod.

The Sun is the presiding god of the seasons and Paiyatemu is his deputy. The seasons bring the crops which are the sustenance of life, or life itself—"my flesh is your flesh," is said of the corn. Thus man forms an aboriginal communion with the powers of the field. At Zuñi Paiyatemu usually appears with the Corn Maidens, or their negative counterparts, the evil sisters. The Corn Maidens are the eight sisters of the god. He falls in love with them, desires them, and thereby frightens them away from the land. The number of maidens varies, but the number seems to be accounted for in the following manner: six of them represent the corn of the colors of the six directions. The number becomes seven if sweet corn is added; when there are eight, which is usual now, the extra number includes one sister to represent

[8] *Ibid.*, 33.   [9] Stirling, *Origin Myth of Acoma*, 37.
[10] Stevenson, "The Sia," *loc. cit.*, 32.

144

squash. The less common numbers of nine and ten are based upon the inclusion of a sister for watermelons and for muskmelons. In short, the maidens represent the basic food crops and their flight is a myth of the seasons.

When their flight is prolonged, as during a drought, it is claimed that the neglect of the Zuñi people has caused them to flee, and the myth becomes an admonition to take every care of the seed of seeds; the ears must be stacked properly, kept free of destructive forces, and the proper rites which relate to them must be performed. Since a good myth seldom contains only a single idea, there is an analogy to human reproduction which presents itself. At times the intent in a Corn Maiden story is a flight of the shy virgin. The maid refuses to be taken by a man and flees.[11] Though they are maids, they must in the inevitable cycle become matrons; so they are often called maid-matrons.

The Corn Maidens are basically nothing but the multicolored seed kernels of corn, and their story on that level is but the Battle of the Seasons. When Paiyatemu beseeches them to return they are "scattering bright beads in the northland." Where the seed maidens breathe, we are told that "warmth, health, and fertility shall follow."[12] As a practical matter, corn was most certainly a shy maiden, and just as certainly fled each year and must needs be brought back again. In not infrequent times of famine, the maids refuse to come back and become the plump matrons they should be. Against this danger and as a special plea to the maids, the Zuñis held a special ceremony at the end of each year, in our December, just before the winter solstice. The *molawia* enacts their return, which at that season is rather an invocation for their return, even before the new year has begun.

The Pueblos thought, with considerable justice, that their bodies were basically composed of corn, and that as a result, both they and the grain shared a simple corn-essence. The god himself explains this relationship: "Paiyatemu said, 'The Corn Maidens left us because one man desired them and wished to lay hands on them. We are their flesh and they give us themselves to eat. If they give it to us again

[11] Boas, *Keresan Texts*, 1, 82. [12] Cushing, "Zuñi Creation Myths," *loc. cit.*, 442.

and we plant in the spring for the rain to water we shall be fed again with their flesh. They will be our mothers and we shall be their children. If at any time we think evil thoughts or are unhappy they will go away from us again and we shall have nothing. When we dance the Corn Dance we shall carry their flesh in our hands. We shall not see them but they will be there in spirit. They will be among us and when we speak to them they will hear us.' The people answered, 'It shall be as you have said.' Yellow corn (girl) said to the priests, 'At the end of the year send for us and we will come to Itiwana. Newekwe Youth will always lead us. Pekwin [chief Sun priest] will go first (make the road) and Pautiwa will follow Newekwe, and after him Father Koyemci. My flesh is your flesh. When you put my flesh in the ground it sprouts and does not die. It is like your bodies. When they are buried in the ground they do not die, our flesh is like your flesh.' It is so. The people went home."[13]

Several things in the passage illustrate how a myth is made specific to a ceremony and society. The ceremony the teller has in mind is the *molawia*. At that season of the year the Corn Maidens naturally cannot be seen and must only "be there in spirit." The man who tells the story probably belongs to the Newekwe clown society. Newekwe Youth is a masked kachina called Ne'paiyatemu, an interesting linguistic cross between the Zuñi and Keres languages, since *paiyatemu* means "youth" in Keresan.[14]

The passage quoted above is so definite on the theme of death and resurrection that it suggests consideration of the murder of Paiyatemu by his evil sisters and how it may fit into the other parts of his myth. To begin with, one remembers a number of Mediterranean gods who were killed and reborn. Perhaps the most famous was Adonis, a god of vegetation, principally of cereals; each year he was killed, only to return to life again. Dionysos and Zagreus, as well as Orpheus, were dismembered; not all were reborn. Among the Pueblos such figures as Salt Old Woman, giver of herself, are consumed —if continuously—and are thus not involved in a cycle of rebirth. While Paiyatemu is a god of the season, and hence must die as a

---

[13] Benedict, *Zuñi Mythology*, I, 24.

[14] *Ibid.*, 269–72. See this passage for some light on the overlay of names.

146

part of the Sun's annual progress, his sisters must also die under the rules of the same system. By a very simple equation—the same reasoning that says "if corn and man are the same essence and corn is reborn, then man is also reborn"—we find that the sisters not only share Paiyatemu's death, but are responsible for it.

The Corn Maidens of Zuñi, who are shy or buxom as the season varies, are not always simple spirits of growth. In so far as they become identified with the seasons themselves they may be quite ferocious. In that aspect they are capable of killing the god who desires and pursues them. But Pueblo feeling likes to put the best possible face on every idea. If the corn tender eats the corn, thus destroying it, the corn spirit may also want to destroy the tender; an evil must be accounted for, and yet that cannot be attributed to the Corn Maidens, since corn is obviously good.

The simple expedient is to transform the Corn Maidens, by introducing eight evil sisters. In the story Newekwe Youth again takes the part of the god. As the god was running, which is characteristic of him, he passed the eldest of the evil sisters and she at once challenged him to a hiding contest. A hiding contest is a transparent echo of the disappearance of the Corn Maidens, or in other words, a Battle of the Seasons.

The sister hid in a cloud and he failed to find her, but when he crouched down behind the sun she drew a drop of milk from her breast and saw the tip of his headdress reflected in it. There are many versions; sometimes she hides in a squash blossom and he in a sunflower. In any case, in such a mythical contest life is always the stake. As he has lost, Paiyatemu's heart and head are taken and hidden. Because of what he represents, the dismemberment of the god is a major calamity. At first, birds are sent to find the parts of him, but they fail. The dragonfly, who is air-borne like the birds, and is as well a water-hovering creature, appears cautiously toward spring, and at last discovers where the heart and head of the god are hidden.

The eldest sister of Paiyatemu had taken his flute. She blew into it and out came the butterflies of the directional colors; the fourth was a multicolored butterfly—the god himself—who went to lure the evil sisters. He entered the room where they were weaving baskets, and they wanted to copy the designs on his wings. They pursued him, throwing various articles of their clothing in an attempt to net him, until they were all naked and exhausted and fell asleep. He took off his butterfly disguise and blew upon his flute; whereupon each of the evil maidens came out as a crazily flying butterfly, which undoubtedly involves a pun, the second meaning of which is "nymphomania": flying without direction. Though condemned as abnormal, these evil sisters yet had some salvage value, in addition to the moral point of the story; they were sent to the four directions to bring rain, and there is never enough of that.

While these stories vary with the teller and the society to which he belongs, they all seem to be concerned with the maintainance of fertility, vegetal and human, over a long span of time. Seasons and people vary. The maidens were not only able to flee, but they could contract their flesh as well. After their original, mythological flight, there was left "plenty of corn, but it was not good. There was no meat on it." From his Sun Father, Paiyatemu must constantly carry the message, "Be neither exceedingly shy, if you are a plant, nor overly bold, if you are a human, and since we are the same essence, we must work together to produce the flesh of life."

Such a harmony is not easily achieved, and the uncertainty of success has made Paiyatemu raucous, laughing, laughable, and frequently obscene; he is the clown patron of mankind, to whom no human activity is beyond the pale. Perhaps the difficulty of his task may explain why "in the grey mists of morning Paiyatemu was hidden—and is seen no more of men."[15]

Pautiwa and the Sun Kachinas

Pautiwa is quite the opposite of the clown-god Paiyatemu; his behavior is solemn and the attitude toward him is reverent. He represents the dignified power of the Sun Father. "Pautiwa, chief of the masked gods at Ko'thluwala'wa, is a truly magnificent person. His prestige is enormous. He possesses in unlimited measure the three most admired qualities—beauty, dignity, and kindliness . . . . His two

[15] Cushing, "Zuñi Creation Myths," *loc. cit.*, 447.

brief appearances at Zuñi mark him as a prince of gods and men. The moment he appears in the plaza at the close of the solstice ceremonies, the hilarity which has prevailed subsides in an instant and is replaced by hushed reverence. The two gods who have been making merry on the housetop to the great delight of the populace suddenly pale into insignificance before the newly risen splendor of Pautiwa's beauty and stateliness."[16]

Pautiwa is much less directly connected with the Sun than is Paiyatemu. Conceptually he is simply the one who presides over the Council of the Gods. Nonetheless he appears only at the solstices—and in the *molawia* ceremony of the Corn Maidens. He belongs to the Sun clan, and during his appearances he is dressed and attended by men of the Sun clan, because, as the chief of this group explained, "He is our child. He belongs to the sun."[17] The last statement may refer more to the clan than to the Sun, but the facts just given, and the item that he brings in the Corn Maidens during the Shalako ceremony, point toward Pautiwa's close association with the Sun.

One distinction between these two gods should be kept in mind: Pautiwa is associated with the kachinas and Paiyatemu with the clowns, a distinction like that already noted from Keresan Sía. The former god is the most important of the masked dancers. Those associated with the latter, such as Bitsiti, the whistler who also leads in the maidens, are also unmasked. Newekwe Youth, the clown, wears a mask and the clowns do too, but it is doubtful if they should be considered kachinas.

Perhaps it is worth noting that Pautiwa has, in a small way, migrated to Hopi. The chief interest in the fact lies in the excellent illustration it affords of the manner in which a god may be imported from another religion. I repeat that we are dealing with three religions of separate origins, linked by common living and agricultural practices. The rites are basically similar, but seldom join in particular, while the gods are very slow to move about and most of them do not transplant at all.

Pautiwa did migrate. About the middle of the last century a group

[16] Bunzel, "Introduction to Zuñi Ceremonialism," *loc. cit.*, 522.
[17] Bunzel, "Zuñi Katcinas," *loc. cit.*, 919.

from the Mustard clan of Zuñi moved to the First Mesa and settled in the middle village, Sichomovi. They brought with them a memory of Pautiwa and of a number of ceremonies, but as a small group could not possibly perform more than a portion of the Zuñi calendar, the memories were compressed into one, the Pamurti rite. This takes place in January, and in it Pautiwa is said to be the sun god of the Tansy-Mustard and Badger clans. The impersonator goes to each kiva in the three villages on First Mesa, announcing that in eight days the ancients will return. At that time a motley group of kachinas led by Pautiwa come up the trail from Sun spring. Fewkes gives a vivid description of the event:

"The procession entered the pueblo about sunset, presenting a most barbaric appearance in the rays of light from the western sky. The numerous masked men walked in platoons, wearing painted helmets, those representing birds prancing backward and forward, raising their arms, to which feathers were attached to represent wings; there were also platoons of men with painted bodies, wearing horned knobbed helmets closely fitting their heads, singing songs and shaking rattles. Prominent among all was a naked boy, painted from head to food with spots of different colors. He was called Tcolawitze and carried in his hand a cedar bark torch, one end glowing with fire."[18] The naked boy is the Little Fire God, Shulawitsi, who is associated with the solstice ceremony at Zuñi.

The Hopi Sun Kachinas

Hopi kachinas are variable in that they are not the same for all villages. Two Sun kachinas, as they appear on First Mesa, Ahul and Ahulani, have names confusing, but also enlightening, in their similarity. Both derive from the word *ahulti*, meaning "return." Ahulani signifies the return of the kachinas, as he is the first to appear at the beginning of the kachina half of the year; but he also symbolizes the return of the sun, and in some pueblos Ahul stands in for him, showing how closely the two are related in the Hopi mind. Ahulani brings with him two Corn Maidens, a blue corn girl and a yellow corn

[18] Fewkes, "Hopi Katcinas," *loc. cit.*, 27.

girl; and one part of the ceremony for the return of the kachinas and the Sun consists in a twirling or gesturing with a feather-rayed sun disc, representing the beginning of the shield-bearing journey.

Ahulani does not, however, wear a mask representing the Sun; in fact his mask is not always the same. Ahul does wear a sun mask, but not the familiar, conventional visage of the Sun, a title reserved for a set of kachinas under the name of *Tawa*, which is the Hopi word for Sun. The important appearance of Ahul is not at the solstice, but in the Powamu ceremony of late winter which was mentioned in relation to Muingwu. Ahul appears there, not as an agent to bring back the Sun, but as one who proposes to prolong the summer.

On one night of the Powamu ceremony, "Towards daybreak the Ahul impersonator is dressed and masked. He lies down by the fire and as the singing proceeds he gradually arises until at day break, representing the Sun, he stands erect and gives his call, hu—u! Then he lowers his head to the ground to raise it slowly and bend it backwards, giving his call. He does this four times . . . . This is mimetic magic to make the summer long and the sun move slowly . . . . At each place of visitation *ahul* kachina repeats his motions to make the summer long . . . . [the] Kiva chief or housholder will also help himself from *ahul*'s sack of meal in order to rub the meal on the faces of the household 'for a long life.' "[19]

The Hopi Tawa kachina should be mentioned, if only because his name is the Hopi word for the Sun and his mask is a beautiful conventional sun disc, surrounded by rays of feathers to represent the perihelion. In his left hand he carries a flute, as befits a sun deity. The Tawa kachinas are numerous, but they seem to have no specific symbolic duties; they appear in various short dances called *Soyohims*.

Winter Solstice Ceremonies

So far this book has avoided detailed accounts of ceremonies; the aim has been to establish a *theologeo*, or a discourse on the gods and divine things. The rites are of course related to such a scheme, but they approach the subject though many labyrinths. Most of the

[19] E. C. Parsons, *A Pueblo Indian Journal*, 1920–21, 45–47.

rites contain many elements: curing, war, clan tales and tribal history, seasonal and occupational tasks, tribal initiation, and the like. For a variety of reasons, the most important of which may be the place of specific clans involved in each rite, the ceremonies seem to combine their elements in almost random manner.

The Winter Solstice is a ceremony which has a single core among the Hopis, Zuñis, and Keres. The rites of primitive peoples are to some extent centered upon the seasons and the agricultural duties which are based upon them. The most clearly observed phenomenon is, of course, the return of vegetation in the spring, and numberless rites have been built around that rebirth. Further reflection leads to the conclusion that it is not the vegetation itself, but the cause of it, the Sun, who brings in a new year, and his rebirth takes place in midwinter.

Some Romans must have remained doubtful about the shift long after their calendar changed, for Ovid questioned the god Janus about the new year: " 'Come, say, why doth the new year begin in the cold season? Better had it begun in spring. Then all things flower, then time renews his age.' " But the god replied tersely: "Midwinter is the beginning of the new sun and the end of the old one. Phoebus and the year takes their start from the same point.' " (*Fasti*, 11, 149–64.) The same doubt probably accounts for our fiscal years which begin in June. The Athenians began their calendar with the first moon after the summer solstice, but in other parts of Greece this was not the case.

To a farmer, the summer solstice can pass almost unnoticed, except for the work. At the other end of the year lies the spectacular length of darkness, which is a cause of fear, since it signifies the opposite of bounty, but is also a reason for hope, since the next year and its new possibilities are at hand. Not least in importance, it is a time of leisure during which one may contemplate the nature of the gods and their relationship to mankind.

Acoma Winter Solstice

The date for the Acoma Winter Solstice is announced eight days ahead by the town chief who has been watching the sun. At this time someone from each household descends from the town on the mesa top to gather herbs for an emetic brew, which is drunk for four mornings as a ceremonial purification. On the following day prayer-sticks are made and from then until the end of the ceremony there is a taboo on meat, salt, and sex. An altar is set up in the head kiva where the men go to dance at night, and medicine societies are active in curing, as they are at Zuñi.

On the third day before the solstice men take their prayer-sticks to their fields and plant (bury) them, while the women cast their prayer-sticks off the east edge of the mesa. The masks of the kachinas are renewed with paint and feathers. Seeds, shrubs, trees, and live rabbits are collected by the men.

One day ahead of the arrival of the kachinas (who are here called Kopishtaiya, because they are the collectivity of spirits—an arrangement which does not, of course, agree with the Sía division of spirits, kachinas, and clowns), a new set of "brave," or war prayer-sticks is made. On the final day boys who have been initiated into the Kachina cult, but who have not yet performed, go through a second rite, and a rather chilling one. The boys are naked, except for a feather or two and a bit of rabbit fur; they hide in the crevices of the rocky mesa, where they will be found later by the masked spirits. Fortunately they have a sheep skin to sit on and a blanket.

Those who impersonate the Kopishtaiya descend from the mesa very early on the day of the solstice, travel east to deposit the "brave" prayer-sticks, then scatter two by two and sing war songs, returning toward the town before sunrise. In the town the war chief has long since aroused the people, who assemble on the eastern edge of the mesa to greet the returning Kopishtaiya. Somewhat apart, the town chief and the medicine men go out to a point on the mesa called the Sun's House, which is located at the southernmost point of the Sun's rising during the year. There they bury a diminutive and complete set of clothes for the Sun.

The masked Kopishtaiya come into the town carrying fox-skin bags of seeds. On their way they pick up the shrubs and trees they have concealed behind the abandoned church. As a handful of cattail fuzz is thrown into a crevice, a naked boy is pulled out, and rabbits are released in such a way that they seem to spring from the ground where the cattail seed has been cast.

As the Sun rises he is greeted with meal offerings. The trees and shrubs are planted in fissures on the bare mesa; seeds and sometimes gifts are given to the people. For the next four days the Kopishtaiya dance in the kivas, and sometimes in the plaza.

When the masked dancers leave the pueblo on the fourth day, they must not look back, lest the spirits whom they represent, who are in part the collective dead, might not leave the village. After throwing the trees and shrubs off the cliff the impersonators take off their masks, raising them upward and eastward to speed the spirits, and doubtless the messages they carry, on their way. Then the road back is closed to these invisible spirits by making four lines on the ground against their trail.

The Hopi Soyal Ceremony

The Soyal is a ceremony to honor the Sun and to "turn him back," at the winter solstice. Since it lasts for nine days and nights, it generally covers the period of the exact solstice. The intent of the rite is to dramatize the career of the Sun, and like the Acoma ceremony it has war associations and includes the return of the kachinas. The Soyal is also tribal; every man must participate and in theory must return to his original village. Since the ceremony has been described in detail by Stephen, Voth, and Fewkes, I will merely sketch a few salient points in the long and complex set of rites.

Each day the men from the kiva in charge of the ceremony go about an hour before sunrise to a rock nearly halfway down the mesa (at Oraibi), and each sprinkles a pinch of cornmeal toward the east, whereupon two leaders touch each man, one with a spear point and the other with hawk wings; these are held by men who represent the Hawk priest and the elder of the War Twins, Pookong.

The eighth day of the ceremony is called Totoka, or "food providing." On the previous day a prayer device called by the sneeze provoking name, hihikwispi, is produced in great numbers. The name indicates an object to be breathed upon. The hihikwispi is another variant of the prayer-stick; corn husks are tied to it at intervals on

154

cotton string. Eagle feathers are fastened to the points of the husks, and from the final husk extends a string with the eagle breath feather and the feathers of the birds of the six directions.

"Just when the sun is rising, the men who have prepared the hihikwispi in the different kivas, take them and put some corn meal and corn pollen into the upper husk and then leave the kiva. Outside the messenger first holds the hihikwispi to the rising sun and says, 'I aohikvsuu' (Breathe on this)."[20] If the messenger is married he takes it to his own home; if he is not, then to his parents' house. From outside he shouts, "Breathe on this." They take it in, and all breathe on it and return it to him. He takes it to his godfather's house and then to the house of his godfather's clan women. From each of these he receives a gift of food, generally wafer bread. After a round of visits to his own and other clan relations, he returns to his kiva and hangs up the hihikwispi, letting the meal and the corn pollen tied in the husks drop on the floor near the wall.

Invocation of rain is practiced by blowing smoke into holes in the sand before the altar; the holes are then covered. The process indicates a "planting" of the smoke to produce clouds. The climax of the ceremony comes on the ninth day, which is almost entirely devoted to the Sun, and the entire population joins in the culmination at daybreak on the following morning.

In the kiva two priests dance in front of the altar; one of these is the Star Priest who wears a large four-pointed star on his head, probably to indicate the Morning Star, the Sun's harbinger. Suddenly the second priest hands him a Sun symbol which has been concealed up to that time. The symbol is a disc with an archetypal sun face, streaming hair, and a circle of long feathers for rays. This disc is affixed to a stick so that it may be twirled.

This the priest, now acting as Sun Priest, takes; holding the stick in both hands, he shakes it, and then, while dancing north of the fireplace sideways from east to west, and west to east, twirls the Sun symbol very fast in the same directions, symbolizing the going and coming of the Sun. Someone makes the Hawk scream by using a whistle concealed inside the mouth—the drum beats louder, a song is sung.

[20] Voth, *The Oraibi Soyal Ceremony*, 39.

According to Voth, "The dancing and jumping of the Sun priest was varied and extremely picturesque."

About four o'clock in the morning, the ceremony having continued, a messenger is sent from each kiva to Tawaki, Sun house, or shrine, about three miles distant. He carries prayer-feathers from all the kiva members and in addition, "the four small cakes, two wheels, two cylinders, one small crook, one long and one short baho, and with the green grass from the altar, all to be deposited on the sun shrine."[21]

Some time after this the men carry the prayer-sticks they have made, through the dark of the mid-December morning, to their houses where the people are soon astir. "Just at sunrise the inhabitants emerge from the houses and streets, the women . . . and children carrying armsful of bahos to the east edge of the mesas." Hundreds are thrust in the ground at places sacred to the several clans, and next: "Bahos and nakwakwosis are now being offered in many various ways. They are placed in the houses, tied to ladders to prevent accident, placed in the chicken houses 'that the hens may lay eggs,' into the beef and sheep corrals, and tied to horses' tails, dogs', goats' and sheeps' necks, etc., 'for increase;' tied to the peach trees as prayer for large crops, deposited in springs for an abundant water supply.... One man even came running to the mission and tied a few nakwakwosis to the missionary's watch, which was hanging on the wall, and which the Hopi consider as a symbol of the sun, also calling it *tawa* (sun)."[22]

Next we turn to Zuñi, where the rites are perhaps more elaborate and include a well developed New Fire ceremony within the other elements.

The Zuñi Winter Solstice Ceremony

At Zuñi the winter solstice is truly a ceremony of the "middle," not only in the sense that the sun has reached his mid-point on the journey from summer to summer, but also in that it is the day from which the ceremonial calendar for the following year is calculated. It is the one rite in which all the various fraternities join together in participation. Of the many days involved in the event, the actual solstice is the one on which everyone in the community, down to

[21] *Ibid.*, 55–56.   [22] *Ibid.*, 57.

the smallest of babies, plants prayer-plumes in his fields. That day is generally the twenty-second of December, if the Pekwin has been accurate in his calculations, which has not always been the case in modern times. As an aid for his calculations, the Pekwin has, like the Hopis of First Mesa, an excellent mountain range horizon, where the travels of the Sun-father can be figured by sighting the point, or indentation, at which he comes out standing each morning.

There are two lengthy accounts of the ceremonies at Zuñi, that of Stevenson from 1891, and that of Bunzel from the 1920's. In these versions the number of days involved—actually it is the nights that are counted—do not correspond with each other. Stevenson has the important part of the ceremony last for ten days, that have been preceded by five days of prayer-plume making; while Bunzel divides the time into two equal periods of ten days each, centered on making the New Fire on the tenth night.

First of all the Pekwin, who is deputy to the Sun at Zuñi and the chief priest there, watches the risings of the sun from a particular petrified stump for a number of days—actually he does this every clear day in the year—and when it reaches a certain point, he makes an announcement from the housetops that in ten days the sun will come to the end of his southward journey and turn north again; this day he will strike a point called the Middle Place. Bunzel records the announcement of the Pekwin for the summer solstice; and it is quoted as an example of the style, since I assume it would differ little from that for the winter solstice.

> Now that those who hold our roads,
> Dawn ancients,
> Youths,
> Matrons,
> Maidens,
> Over their sacred place,
> Have raised their curtain.
>
> Here on the corn priest's housetop
> I stand up.
> My fathers,

My sun father,
We have made your days.
Divine ones,
Remember your days.[23]

He continues by telling in how many days the ceremony will begin.

The crucial, if simple, part of the ceremony consists in kindling the New Fire, an act around which are grouped various taboos, rites of exorcism, and of fertility. Since the Sun has war associations, the war gods, as at Hopi, have an important place in the first part of the ceremony, although it is said, "The Gods of War are thus honored that they may intercede with the rain-makers for rains to fructify the earth."[24] Several other gods appear, of whom the most important is Pautiwa, who makes two of his three annual appearances at this time; he, as we have noted, is the chief of the Council of the Gods, and his impersonator is the head of all the masked kachina dancers.

A good deal of the ground work for this, as well as for all ceremonies, consists in making multitudes of prayer-plumes of different sorts; with the added complication that if one belongs to several fraternities, he must make them for each one of those. The Pekwin continues his daily visits to the petrified stump, to make his observations of the sun. He has remained continent from four days before the first planting of plumes, and will remain so for four days after the last are planted; he also fasts from animal food.

On the fourth day, as recorded by Stevenson, the ceremonies continue throughout the night until after sunrise, when the offerings are made. At noon of the fourth day, the New Fire maker gathers a fagot of cedar from each house in the village; the sticks are laid log-cabin–wise and lighted at sunset. On the fifth day, the plumes are planted by the officers at shrines and by the lay people in their fields. Among other pilgrimages that are made, one is most interesting. About nine o'clock, members of the order of Paiyatemu, of the Little Fire and Cimex fraternities, play their flutes while ascending Corn Mountain to To'mapa, a shrine on the west side, and there deposit offerings to that god.

[23] Bunzel, "Zuñi Ritual Poetry," *loc. cit.*, 636.
[24] Stevenson, "The Zuñi Indians," *loc. cit.*, 116.

158

Let us travel back to a plume planting day in 1891: "The sun rose in splendor on the morning of the fifth day, making brilliant the mantle of snow that covered the earth. The valley was sparkling white, and the mesa walls were white, with here and there a patch of dark blue, the pines veiled by the atmosphere. The snowy plain was a vast kaleidoscope from morning until evening, the devotees in their bright clothing going to and returning from their sacred mission."

When the people reach their own cultivated fields, they deposit the plumes in shallow excavations, and even "the tiny babies have their hands dipped into the meal and held over the plumes. These plumes remain uncovered until sunset the following day, that the Sun Father, in passing over the road of day, may receive the prayers breathed upon the meal and into the plumes, the spiritual essence of the plumes conveying the breath prayers to him."[25] These excavations are filled in so that the plumes may not be disturbed, which is quite the opposite of Hopi feeling toward offerings; there, once the sacred mission has been accomplished, the body of the prayer seems to be fair game for children.

After the plume planting there follows a period of taboo centered around fires and fats. No ashes or sweepings may be taken from the houses, and no artificial light may appear outside the houses, not even the distant flash of firearms. The New Fire is kept up during the day and banked while the fire tender sleeps at night.

On the tenth day the dance director of each kiva awaits the coming of Pautiwa at midnight—two or three o'clock in Bunzel's account. He keeps to dark corners to avoid the light, throws meal down each kiva hatchway to announce his presence, and makes four marks to indicate that in four days the fast will end. The headmen inhale from the meal and say, "Now he has brought in to us the warm breath of summer, so that we may have good crops." The fire burns on the altar day and night during the fourteenth day. The masked impersonators of the gods appear in the village and an all night ceremony is held during which no one is allowed to fall asleep.

"The songs and dancing of Shits'ukia and Kwe'lele continue until the rising of the Morning Star (warrior to Sun Father) which is care-

[25] *Ibid.,* 119–20.

fully watched for by men who keep ascending the kiva ladder. When the star has appeared Kwe'lele and the director of the order of Kok'ko thlan'na (great god) of the Great Fire fraternity take their seats near the fire altar. Kwe'lele places his horizontal fire stick on the floor and proceeds to produce fire by friction."[26] A spark is caught in cedar fiber and waved to bring it into flame. The breath must not be blown upon it; since breath is associated with clouds and rain, its use to bring fire would have an adverse mimetic effect, perhaps scorching drought.

A group of brand carriers and attendants leaves the kiva, one carrying a torch. The Pekwin carries a basket of meal and a blue corn ear in his left hand. Some members scatter meal ahead of the procession and others to the side. Four warrior kachinas carry bows in their left hands, and the bunches of yucca with which sleepers have been "whipped" awake. The party proceeds to a point east of Zuñi where two firebrands and many plumes are deposited. This is a sign to the village that the fire taboo is ended.

The fire keeper returns to the kiva to chant a long prayer, while the women take the sweepings they have saved to the nearest field belonging to them. They are deposited with the words, "I now deposit you as sweepings, but in one year you will return to me as corn." Over the live coals the same thing is said, except that the return will be as meal.

On the fifteenth day five Sun clan members are seen, coming over the plain to the south of the village. Behind them, a considerable distance and to the east, comes the long figure of Pautiwa, coming to make the new year. The impersonator carries a blue stick with a hoop to which are attached eagle plumes and the feathers of the birds of the six directions. He walks right through the water of the river, then circles the town four times, ending up on the east side of the village, where he plants prayer-plumes in a niche in the wall, which is then cemented over. The same is repeated for the other directions, and two prayer-plumes are planted in walls inside the town, for the Zenith and Nadir. At sunset he visits each kiva, casting meal and depositing plumes, while the Great Fire society sings to him. The three gods then depart for the west and the home of the council of the gods.

[26] *Ibid.*, 130.

When the impersonator returns, he tells what signs he has seen and from these gives auguries for the coming year.

Late that night there is a fire ceremony of gay character, with large fires in every house, and bonfires in the street. These the children are allowed to keep up. About eleven o'clock the thele'lele appear wearing bison robes, hair side in, over their heads. They are pelted with live coals as they run through the streets shouting, "More fire; give us more beautiful flowers." While this is going on the Salimobia kachinas visit each kiva with baskets of seeds, which are given to everyone. These have special virtue, and in the spring will be planted with particular care.

Every fourth night thereafter, for a series of four, special offerings are made. "Each member of the Ko'tikili carries a bowl of food to the road leading to Ko'thluwala'wa, praying as he goes that the gods will bless the A'shiwi with rain to fructify the earth, that she may bear to them the fruits of her being. The food is emptied into the river as offerings to the Kok'ko A'wa (all the gods)."[27]

The Calendar

The Sun is a power for war and a power for fertility; in addition he sets the seasons and with the help of the moon establishes the calendar. The Pueblo year is divided into two halves, based in part upon the sun, and in part upon ceremonies and the agricultural activities of the community. The moon provides a pair of six lunations, plus that odd one, which can be ignored, or simply left to drift at the end of the year. The summer solstice is recognized with minor ceremonies, because the Sun's turning is less crucial then, and the great urge is toward the summer work; even the gods leave during the growing half of the year, so that mankind may be free to attend to the mundane duties that support life. As a result of agricultural orientation, some of the Keres have a divided year which is based upon periods of growth and dormancy, at least in so far as the names of the months are concerned.

The turning back of the Sun in winter is primary and considered crucial in all three tribes. Among the Hopis our December is called

[27] *Ibid.*, 141.

"Dangerous moon." The extreme length of the dark is more notable than the length of light at the other solstice, because the dark
holds a complex of psychic fears. Even the ordinary affairs of men
become unseen; witches may be about, storms shroud even the daylight hours, and nothing grows in the dark. Growth and life are
synonymous; when things don't grow there is a suggestion of death.
The Zuñi New Fire ceremony is a mimetic suggestion that by re-
kindling hearth fires, and thence the Sun's divine fire, all life may
begin to warm again.

At Zuñi the duality of the solar year is strictly kept, even to the
anomalous extent of calling our July the "Limbs of trees broken by
snow moon," since it corresponds to January. Kroeber had a complaint against the Zuñis. In respect to a discrepancy between two
myths he said that it was "characteristic of Zuñi loose-endedness:
everything is systematically organized, but no system ever comes
out exactly."[28] To the student such a state of affairs is unsatisfactory,
but it is no more than the general human condition; and in the instance of the monthly calendar the Zuñis have leaned rather toward
rigidity, while the Hopis and Keres have not.

Everyone who studies the Hopi calendar notes that it has something of a ragged end at the second half of the year. The task of
fitting thirteen "moons" into the two halves of the solar year proved
more than difficult, so that toward the end there is uncertainty; and
consequently there are two names for October at Oraibi, and different
names on First Mesa for both September and October.

Since it is difficult to keep the various months in mind, I have
added a table which may be of some help to the reader.

ZUÑI[29]

December (Turning back moon), *I'kopu;* June, same name.
January (Limbs of trees broken by snow moon), *Taiyamchu;* July,
same name.
February (No snow in the road moon), *O'nanulakiakwame;* August, same name.

[28] Alfred L. Kroeber, *Zuñi Kin and Clan,* 101.
[29] Stevenson, "The Zuñi Indians," *loc. cit.,* 108.

March (Little wind moon), *tHli'tekwakia tsanna;* September, same name.

April (Big wind moon), *tHli'tekwakia thlan'na;* October, same name.

May (No name, "not nothing" moon), *Kwashi'amme;* November, same name.

ACOMA AND LAGUNA[30]

April (Sticky ground; wheat sowing time), *Pus-chuts-otes*

May (Ground soft like ashes; corn planting), *Sho-wats-otes*

June (Corn tassel), *A-chin*

July (First appearance of corn ear), *Hi-shin*

August (Beard of the corn), *Ya-mon*

September (Corn in the milk), *Ki-nut*

October (Mature corn), *Ki-ti-stchi-ta-ta*

November (Fall of the year), *Hai-a-tassi*

December (Middle of the winter), *Sin-ni-kok*

January (Moon when the little lizard's tail freezes off), *Me-yo sitch ta-watch*

February (Plant root; daughter of spring), *Yu-mun*

March (Same plant above ground), *Stchum-mu*

HOPI[31]

November (Initiate moon), *Kel-muya;* June (Plant moon), *Kel-muya*

December (Dangerous moon), *Kya-muya;* July (Go home kachina moon), *Kya-muya*

January (Play moon), *Pa-muya;* August (Play moon), *Pa-muya*

February (Exorcising moon), *Powa-muya;* September (Big feast moon), *Powa-muya*

March (Cactus blossom moon), *Isu-muya; October* (Harvest moon), *Isu-muya,* also *Angok-muya* and *Tuho'osh* (Basket)

April (Grease-wood fence moon), *Kwia-muya*

May (Too cold to plant moon), *Hakiton-muya*

---

[30] Gunn, *Schat-Chen,* 223.

[31] Titiev, *Old Oraibi,* 174; E. C. Parsons, *Hopi and Zuñi Ceremonialism,* 58–61; Stephen, *Hopi Journal,* II, 1037–41; Titiev, in Museum of Northern Arizona, Reprint Series, No. 5, 16–19. See also Parsons, "Time Keeping," in *Notes on Zuñi,* II, 296–301.

The Hopi calendar differs from the Zuñi in that it divides the year into two unequal halves, comprised of the five months of the growing season, with the other "half" beginning at the important Wuwuchim ceremony in November and lasting through May, the "Too cold to plant moon." This system, which roughly divides the year into winter and summer, is based on crops rather than the solstices. Parsons mentions a similar popular division of the year at Zuñi: "The Zuñi year is reckoned today at least from solstice to solstice (tepikwaiipa), although there seems to be a general idea that it might just as well be reckoned from *itiwonna* to *itiwonna* or from corn ripe to corn ripe."[32]

The reader may wonder what actually happens to the thirteenth moon, and the answer seems to be that she is of little importance, despite the fact that the Hopis call their months "moons." The Zuñis and Keres do not use even this pretense. The Pueblo year is at once agricultural and ceremonial. The Pueblos, like other farmers, know within a few days the proper time to plant and are likely to use their own judgment, particularly if the date was successful the past season. In so far as corn planting is a religious matter, at least some seed must be planted at the sacral time, even if much of it is planted earlier or later.

In the reckoning of ceremonial dates, the solar calendar can be resorted to in some detail, as the sun-watcher priest observes not only the solstices, but certain of the houses of the Sun between these ends of his journey. On the Oraibi horizon calendar, there were ten such points based upon a skyline horizon to the east.

A simple diurnal count fixes most ceremonies. Four days before the first ceremony is to begin, the organizers hold a smoke to announce it; then the rites occupy a certain number of days, the count of which is fixed. Thereafter, it will be announced that in so many days the smoke for the next ceremony will take place. Thus the lunations are of little importance in reckoning time for either crops or ceremony, and the paucity of ceremonies during summer may contribute to the ragged conclusion of the year.

Since the calendar does not appear in books on the eastern Keres,

[32] E. C. Parsons, *Notes on Zuñi*, 300.

I assume they have long since adopted our western system, as have other Río Grande pueblos. (The Tiwa town of Isleta has a dual ceremonial year, but it is based upon the Julian calendar, rather than upon sun observations.) However, from the two western Keres pueblos, Acoma and Laguna, a native calendar is given by Gunn, which may or may not be an indication of former Keres reckoning. The duality of the year is not stressed in relation to the winter solstice, despite the important ceremony at that time. Instead we have an agrarian division of the year—in names at least—in which the months of May through October are related to the growth stages of corn. Since Gunn arbitrarily began with our January, with equal liberty I have begun with April, on the list above, to emphasize the corn half of the year.

The duality of the year, however it is divided, has a strong influence upon man's view of the physical cosmos—or perhaps one should rather say, the physical appearances of the spiritual cosmos—since to the Pueblo mind all, except man, exists in a divine order which works perfectly, but antithetically. The course of man is to maintain the order by rites, to bring it closer to his needs, by rites, and thus to combine his uncertain path with the fixity of the cosmos.

Battle of the Seasons

Whatever the basis for division, the Pueblo year is most certainly cut in two—by ceremonies, by rites and myths, and, as is natural, in simple tales. Sometimes a rite and a tale are very close together, as when a Hopi youth is sent out at the summer solstice. After he has planted his prayer-stick, he must walk back to his village very slowly, picking flowers. His slowness indicates that "the Sun must not travel back too fast lest there be untimely frosts, therefore the messenger to Sun's house has to return very slowly, lingering to pick flowers, which he will give to the solstice chief to use as pigments for his winter solstice prayer-sticks, 'so there will be more flowers' the summer following."[33]

When there are no late frosts, the growing season is lengthened at the expense of the barren months, to the delight of all those who

[33] Parsons, *A Pueblo Indian Journal*, 95n.

tend fields. From such a feeling arises a common tale: the "Battle between Summer and Winter." One such tale comes from Acoma. It is set long ago, at White House, the mythical village in the north where the Keres first learned of their gods, met the real kachinas, and were instructed in the ways which they should follow.

The spirits in the story are Shakak, ruler of North Mountain, who is the spirit of winter, and his opponent is Miochin, of South Mountain, who represents summer. At Sía it is said that Shakak means spruce tree and Miochin a variety of oak. I do not think, however, that they are tree spirits, but merely one aspect among many—including animals, birds, butterflies, clouds, and the like, which are identified with the spirits or "chiefs" of the directions.

The Acoma chief's daughter, Yellow Woman, and Winter, her husband, long ago lived at White House. They never planted then, for it was always cold. In this reverse of Eden, Yellow Woman, who was the leader of Corn Maidens, was married to Shakak of violent temper, and so long as he stayed near his wife, the people found that their crops would not grow. In that condition they were forced to live on cactus—as the Pueblos did until recently in times of drought.

One day Yellow Woman had wandered a long way from home in search of cactus when she met Miochin, who asked her why she ate cactus instead of corn and melons. In one account this spirit wore a shirt of buckskin with squash blossom ornaments. According to what Gunn heard, he wore a shirt of yellow, woven from corn silk, a belt of green corn blades, a tall pointed hat of the same material, topped with a yellow corn tassel, and leggings of the moss that forms on ponds and springs. His moccasins were embroidered with flowers and butterflies. In his hand he carried an ear of green corn.

When he met the maiden he offered her the ear of corn; she asked if it grew nearby, but he said no, "it is from my home far away in the south, where the corn grows and the flowers bloom all the year." Would she like to go? She cannot; she is the wife of Shakak.

Versions of the romance diverge at this point. In one, when she reaches home with the corn, her parents recognize immediately that the man she has met is Miochin. They ask that she bring him home on the morrow to replace her miserable husband, Shakak. In another version the maid promotes the new affair. After eating the corn and melons she states: " 'It is good. Let us go, to my house I take you.' 'Is not your husband there?' 'No; he went hunting deer.' 'When will he be back?' 'Today at night he will come back.' Then there northward they went. Then they arrived there above in Acoma. 'There on the plaza in the middle on the north side above where I live.' Then there up they climbed, Summer and Yellow Woman. Then downwards they entered." She called the people and they ate corn and melons with thanksgiving.

In the evening Shakak returned home in a "blinding storm of snow and hail and sleet, for he was in a boisterous mood." He knew within his bones that Miochin was there.

"Thus spoke Winter, 'Who is here?' thus said winter. 'I,' said Summer, 'Downwards enter, Winter, it belongs to you. Climb down to me here!' thus said Summer. 'No,' said Winter. 'I cannot go in downwards,' thus said Winter. 'I shall melt entirely. To this my house I shall go.' "[34]

It seems that Winter wore a shirt of icicles and was covered with frost from head to foot. In one version he does approach Miochin and the frost melts away, exposing the bulrushes in which he is clad. Miochin returns to his home in the south to prepare for the battle to which he has been challenged by Shakak. He calls together all the birds and animals of summer, and selects the bat as his advance guard, as his tough wings will protect Miochin from the sleet and hail that will be thrown against him. He also sends Eagle to gather a kind of rock that becomes very hot in a fire. Shakak has meanwhile assembled all the birds and animals of winter, with a magpie for his van.

Miochin advanced from the south with all his forces. Fires of resinous wood were built on the special rocks and these sent up huge clouds of steam and smoke upon which Miochin rode toward White House in the north. Shakak came from the north on a black blizzard driven by freezing winds. Miochin fought with summer lightning, which singed the animals of the north, spotting them, or turning them white.

The clouds of smoke rushed onwards, melting the weapons of

[34] Boas, *Keresan Texts*, 34.

Shakak, who, finding himself defeated, called for an armistice. Miochin got Yellow Woman for himself and according to the treaty, "Then on my part summer will be mine; on your part, yours will be winter. To me will belong spring and from there seven months. On your part yours will be the fall and from there six months."[35] In this story summer not only won the battle, but arranged a proper lunar calendar with the extra moon to his credit.

A mere winter's tale to be sure, but these figures are represented on prayer-sticks and by kachinas, and thereby become a part of rites addressed to the world around the Pueblos. To that larger world, the cosmos, we next turn.

[35] *Ibid.*, 33–35.

Chapter Seven

THE COSMOS AND THE SYSTEM
OF THE SIX DIRECTIONS

One of the Zuñi Salimobias, warriors and seed gatherers of
the six directions; he is called Cipikne by the Hopis.

THE SPIRITS engaged in the battle between summer and winter represent more than the seasons; they also stand for the North direction and the South direction. The six directions permeate every phase of Pueblo thinking and activity. The directions give meaning to the concept that one's pueblo is the center of the universe, around which point days, seasons, life, and crops, and even the dead revolve.

The Zuñi A'shiwannis, have already been mentioned; six of these priests are associated with the six directions, the priest of the Zenith being the Pekwin, or deputy, to the Sun father. The important role of this priesthood comes during the summer when retreats and fasting are arranged in such order that one or another of the priests will be in continuous prayer from the end of June until the middle of September—the critical period for rain. Each group is responsible for rain during its period of fast. The chanting of the priests goes on in low tones throughout the night, sometimes to the accompaniment of a flute. These prayers are addressed to the dead members of the priesthood and ultimately to the clouds of the directions.

> Send forth your massed clouds to stay with us,
> Stretch out your watery hands,
> Let us embrace!
>
> To Itiwana you will come
> With all your people,
> Hiding behind your watery shield
> With all your people;
> With your fine rain caressing the earth,
> With your heavy rain caressing the earth,
> (Come to us!)
> Raise the sound of your thunders!
> At Itiwana

With your great pile of waters
May you pass me on my road.

. . .

Let your days be filled
With your waters
You will pass me on my road.
Those which all my ladder descending children
Have sown with magical rites,
All the different kinds of corn,
Yonder all over their earth mother,
They stand poor at the borders of our land.
With their hands a little burnt,
With their heads brown,
They stand poor at the borders of our land.
That these may be nourished with fresh water,
Thus runs the thought of my prayer.[1]

A prayer to the clouds of the directions does not establish the confines of one's world, since the clouds may arrive from directions as nebulous as themselves, but a sense of the importance of directions is so ingrained in the Pueblos that it has become almost instinctive; the whole community orients itself around a center with a rigidity which would be called compulsive if it were a question of individual behavior. Kroeber noted a very curious instance of this directional unfolding which is almost like a biological tropism.

The modern town of Zuñi had gathered into a very compact group of houses, for reasons of defense, but as that pressure began to relax, toward the end of the nineteenth century, and as an increase of population exerted another pressure, many people began to build houses outside the old town. The process sounds familiar enough, but there it took a specific direction.

"With the modern houses in the open, there is no reason why they should not be located at random. Yet such cases of centrifugal shift as have been observed and recorded on the map by arrows almost invariably involve mainly a radial extension from the center of town. Because a family has lived fifty or a hundred feet north of the east

___

[1] Bunzel, "Zuñi Ritual Poetry," *loc. cit.*, 662–63.

and west axis of the old pueblo, seems no reason why when they build a new house an eighth or a quarter of a mile out, they should quite regularly locate north of town. But the impulse is there. The force of this inclination is particularly marked for the former inhabitants of the southern blocks, since in most instances a southerly removal by them involves a settlement across the river, and particularly since all the houses on that side of the stream more than a very few years old were erected prior to the convenience of a permanent bridge."[2]

Kroeber felt that this deep rooted tendency to orient the house in a quarterly manner around the center must have been ancient, and he assumes the same tendency in other pueblos. Not only is the town oriented to the directions, but the fields are as well, and of course the world at large. When a Hopi goes to his field to plant he first builds a crude shrine, then he takes cornmeal and casts it about the shrine to the six directions. The purpose of this act is to put the field in the right relationship with the points of the Pueblo world.

The six directions are, of course, the four cardinal points, plus the Zenith and the Nadir. When one asks why these points should be all important, the answers are ready enough. As has been said, the system establishes the town and the individual at the center of the universe. The mythical content of the migrations shows that their goal was to find the "middle," a pilgrimage which is only vaguely connected with historical wanderings. Second, the system of directions places mankind in a right relationship to that all-important agricultural divinity, the Sun. He makes a daily journey from east to west, establishing two directions, and then he makes his annual trip from south to north and back again. On that journey are based both the religious and the agricultural calendars.

The question immediately arises: are the four directions actually the cardinal points? Naturally they are not, since they have, or at least had, nothing to do with a compass. Our N. E. S. W. may have overlaid the older conception, which was based upon the four extreme points of the rising and setting of the sun during the year. Stephen explains the directional gestures of a priest as follows: "He invariably begins his ceremonial circuit by pointing (1) to the place of sunset at

[2] Kroeber, *Zuñi Kin and Clan*, 122.

summer solstice, then to (2) the place of sunset at winter solstice, then to (3) the sunrise at winter solstice, and (4) the sunrise at summer solstice, next (5) the above, and (6) the below."[3]

The picture that derives from this scheme is that of a square—needless to say the earth is flat—rather than a cross, and the directional points are at the corners. This was probably once the concept of the Keres as well, but at the present time the corners are not the directions. Whether through some primitive geometry, or simply by adopting the cardinal points of the white man, their ceremonial points now approximate ours.

I mention the possibility of an origin of these points in simple geometry—using the word in its root sense of "earth measuring"—because it could very well have been worked out by the natives. At Santa Ana the square world is equally divided. "Midway between the four corners are the four cardinal points: Kikyami, north; Bunami, west; Koami, south; and Hanami, east. They are frequently referred to as 'middle (sina) north,' 'middle west,' etc., i.e., midway between the 'corners.' "[4] Considering the Pueblo preoccupation with the idea of the "middle," it is not impossible that these points were based on native thinking and only reinforced by our compass.

The Zenith and the Nadir are but two more points logically extending from the center. It has been said of the Aztecs, who also used a directional system, that the horizontal directions were associated with the divine powers of geography and climate, while the vertical directions had to do with the rank and order of a religious hierarchy.[5] However that may be for the Aztecs, it has nothing to do with the Pueblos, whose society is arranged horizontally, through clans, societies, and ceremonies, rather than layered in ranks.

The seasons, which are a configuration in time, and the calendar which marks off that passage in time, explain the need for a Zenith and a Nadir to complete a directional world. Most simply, the sun is seen above us once every day; and since he goes under the world, he must also shine up from below and brighten the underworld

[3] Stephen, *Hopi Journal*, II, 1190n.
[4] White, *The Pueblo of Santa Ana*, 83.
[5] G. C. Vaillant, *The Aztecs of Mexico*, 171–72.

mountain, "sichomo," the flower mound of the Hopis. When a longer time is involved there is the apparent alternation of the seasons, with the life and death of annual vegetation; if time is extended further, we observe the life and death of man. Whether corn, or man, is being considered, we find the same vertical opposites: man came from the underworld and in season returns there; the crop which grows on one side of the flat earth must be dormant on the opposite side. Time-wise the Pueblo world rolls like a hoop, literally "head over heels," and that gives great importance to the successions of "the Above" and "the Below."

A short passage from the *Hopi Journal* illustrates how literally that idea is taken: "When Powa'muriya shines in the Above [in February], its counterpart, Nasha'muriya [September] is shining in the Below, at the house of [Muingwu]. Summer is yonder, winter is here. All vegetation is mature, fruits all ripe in the Below. When the Nasha'n shining now in the Below comes to the Above, next September, it will bring just the same harvest as that it is now shining on in the Below."[6]

A similar duality carried into the everyday affairs of men can be very amusing, even if it is a somewhat less than cosmic. "When Oraibi flourishes, Taos declines. When it is well at Taos, it is ill at Oraibi. It has always been thus."[7]

The alternations of the season between the Below and the Above —in this case the surface of the earth, not the Zenith—is taken quite literally. Hence both prayer-sticks and seeds are planted as messages to the god in the underworld—to poke holes, as it were, into the Below. The prayer-stick indicates that the depositor wishes the fruit-ful season to return, and when seeds are planted in the ground, it is to indicate to the same god where the Hopi wishes the corn to come up.

The place of the Pueblo in his cosmos might be compared to that of a hoop-dancer in relation to his numerous hoops which he must keep circling around himself. Even historical time is centered closely upon one's self. Without written history the past very soon fades into a legendary and mythical era which is nearly timeless. History consists of those rather immediate ancestors whose doings one can

[6] Stephen, *Hopi Journal*, I, 239.   [7] Stephen, "Hopi Tales," *loc. cit.*, 3n.

remember: the middle, center, or self, and the children. The sun circles across the blue dome of the sky by day as at night the stars seem to travel with a smilar black dome.

> "Due above, black corn ear, my mother!
> Straight downward, blooming Sunflower."

Around one's self moves the clan, the societies, and the ceremonies. Around the Pueblo is the ceremonial circuit of the directions, each of which is controlled by a god, or a very powerful Spirit. Inside this square every object is animate, not only animals and trees, but often stones and the very pots one makes, and all of these things have some power. More will be said of animism in another chapter, but it is noted here to indicate the complex and delicate balance of the Pueblo world. All of these powers must be kept in order, so it becomes important that one should utter the exact words of the various prayers which will assure the continuance of the not perfect, but generally sufficient, relationships in all of the concentric realms.

Thus the function of Pueblo religion is not, as some anthropologists have claimed, to form "a supernatural buttress to support the weakest points of their social organization,"[8] nor is it true, as Parsons claims, that "Religion is less the antithesis to science than it is science gone astray."[9] There are large and meaningful areas of human experience which have little to do with either politics or science. After all, science can do no more to turn back the sun at the solstice than religion can, nor does it apply to initiation rites for adulthood. The function of Pueblo religion is psychic. You can clean your field after winter abates without rites, and you can hoe the corn because you have to; but there is undoubtedly more satisfaction, and ease, in tending the crops with rites as well as with a hoe.

Religion may sometimes buttress a social order; in general it tends to divide it. Western Europe and India have provided gloomy examples, and primitive religion is not immune. Titiev, who made the statement, was studying old Oraibi, a town which was torn in two by religion and nearly destroyed in the process which still goes on. Religion, I think, does not have a function so much as an intent. Pueblo religion

[8] Titiev, *Old Oraibi*, 3.　　　　　[9] Parsons, *Pueblo Indian Religion*, x–xi.

may have begun in compulsive magic calculated to keep spirits working in man's favor, but the extreme emphasis on ritual and ceremony indicates that its function is to enrich a sparse way of life, to establish psychic satisfactions where material ones are hard to come by. The method used is to insist upon man as the center and his importance in the role of one who *must* keep the divine hoops spinning, else they might fail and the world become meaningless chaos.

At the four corners of the world there are mountains, each of which is the home of a spirit. The wandering Navahos who adopted this system found it quite simple to identify these mountains with prominent peaks on the physical landscape. But the Pueblos with their separate centers were not so definite. The Hopi mountain of the Below is "flower mound." The first identification of these mountains is with the seasons: we have met Shakak, spirit of Winter and the North, and Miochin, spirit of the South and Summer. On West Mountain the Keres placed Morityema, the spirit of Spring, and on East Mountain, Shrui'sthia, the spirit of Fall. The latter did not like the smell of vegetation and was to "work to get rid of the smell by ridding the world of plants."[10] These spirits are represented by kachina masks.

The names given here are for the Keresan spirits of the directions and do not apply to the Hopis or Zuñis, but on the matter of colors associated with the directions the three tribes seem to be fairly consistent: North is represented by yellow, West by blue, South by red, and East by white. The Zenith and Nadir colors are not so settled, but black or "dark" represents one and "all colors" the other. The importance of the colors is closely identified with the colors of Indian corn and in many rituals the ears are set about the altar in their proper chromatic positions.

The identification of the colors of corn and the colors of the directions leads to a larger identification of corn with life and the gods. All of the supernaturals are invoked by the casting of cornmeal toward the directions. The offerings indicate the "roads" all of the spirits should use in coming toward the pueblo with their blessings, which may be not only crops, but curative powers, and the ultimate

[10] Stirling, *Origin Myth of Acoma*, 15.

blessing of finishing one's own "road" by attaining old age.

There are two sets of animals associated with the six directions and, although they have great power, they are not quite gods, nor are they totems. These animals use their power either for curing, or for hunting. At Zuñi, for example, the directional animals associated with curing are: panther (I assume mountain lion, as both *Felis hippolestes* and its variety, *aztecus*, are in the area), bear, badger, wolf, the eagle for the Zenith, and the shrew for the Nadir. In hunting rituals the list is changed to include only beasts of prey, thus dropping out bear and badger, who are pre-eminently the supernatural doctors of the Pueblos. The other hunting animals associated with the directions seem to be the lynx, or wildcat, and perhaps the jaguar.[11] Bear fills some of Frazer's qualifications, as an object "which a savage regards with superstitious respect, believing that there exists between him and every member of the class an intimate and altogether special relation." When the animal is killed the heart is cut open, the hunting fetish dipped in blood, and some blood is drunk. The Zuñis may also wear parts of the bearskin.[12]

The evidence seems to indicate that the animals are not at all ancestors, but gain their special treatment as a part of the powers of the directions. The Acoma hunter takes fetishes of the prey animals and swings them to the four directions with the song:

> It comes alive
> It comes alive, alive, alive.
> In the north mountain
> The lion comes alive
> In the north mountain, comes alive.
> With this the prey animal
> Will have power to attract deer, antelope;
> Will have power to be lucky.[13]

The hunters call one another by animal names, and the directions are used as a kind of gigantic magical trap to catch the game. "When the deer hunter sees the tracks of a deer he puts shells and precious stones into them. First a large piece of waki from the south, then

[11] *Ibid.*, 23.   [12] Kirk, *Introduction to Zuñi Fetishism*, 31.
[13] Stirling, *Origin Myth of Acoma*, 23.

turquoise from the east, white beads from the north, and pink beads from the west. Then, if the hunter goes eastward, the deer will soon be met."[14]

Boas refers to the spirits of the directions, under the names we have already given as the names for the seasons, as personified storm clouds, and as shiwannas that will probably do. However, as the name of the spirit of the North is said to mean spruce tree and that of the south a variety of oak, any personification must be quite loose and hold several elements together. Again, for the Hopis, both Stephen and Parsons refer to the animals of the directions as "pets" of the spirits or "chiefs" there, which seems like the wrong word. The power of the animals is not delegated by an objectified god at each of the four corners of the world. The directions are rather a source of supernatural power which flows from there to the Pueblo center. It has as its source a group: the storm clouds (and behind them the dead), the seasons, the various colored corn, the animals who bring in power for the hunt, for war, and for curing. There are trees, just as there are mountains, at the corners to fix the landscape of the Pueblo world.

There are also birds and butterflies for each of the directions. The birds are messengers of the gods; Motsni was the go-between for the Hopi chief and Masau'u, and at Zuñi the duck is not only a messenger, but the epiphany of a god. The butterflies are perhaps only an ornament added for the sake of consistency. Even stones fall into the pattern of the directions. The binding ingredient for all these influences on man's life is not so much a spirit, or "chief," as it is a color which links them all together.

At Zuñi stones are addressed by the chief of the Great Fire Society. At full moon in November the members of the society gather before sundown. At sunset the choir begins to chant a set of ritual songs; the chief priest speaks a prayer in a low voice:

> And furthermore, yonder in the north
> On all the mossy mountains,
> On the tops of the mountains,

[14] Boas, *Keresan Texts*, 297.

And along their slopes,
Where the ravines open out,
You hold the world in your keeping;
Ancient yellow stone,
You will make your road come hither
Where lies my white shell bowl,
Four times making your road come in,
You will sit down quietly.
Then with your living waters
Our young ones will nourish themselves;
Reaching to Dawn Lake
Their roads will be fulfilled.

Here the priest is addressing one direction and he follows with the other five, all identified by color, and he is most immediately addressing a stone of the color of the North set up before him, a yellow stone, and then he is speaking to his medicine bowl of white shell, which he regards as a spring of water in the center.

As this same Great Fire Society acts not only as the keeper of the solsticial new fire, but also as a curing group, we find another prayer, this one to the bear of the west:

And, furthermore, yonder in the west
You who are my father, bear,
You are life-giving society chief;
Bringing your medicine,
You will make your road come hither.
Where lies my white shell bowl,
Four times making your road come in,
Watch over my spring.
When you sit down quietly
We shall be one person.[15]

The priest has identified himself with the beast-god in order to gain his power for curing. Again one might see a totemistic association, if it were only bear, but it is equally addressed to "gopher" in the Below, who is also called father, and to "knife wing" in the Above. The prayer is thus not directed toward one animal ancestor, but to

[15] Bunzel, "Zuñi Ritual Poetry," *loc. cit.*, 784.

178

all of the directions equally and to the animals, mythical or real, who represent them.

The butterflies are not important enough to gain much of a place in ritual prayer, but they are of the air, and by their movements they suggest the passage of clouds, so that they too gain a place in the colored corners and the heights and depths of the world.

"At the north sits a chief wearing a yellow cloud as a mask, covering his head and resting upon his shoulders. Yellow butterflies flutter before him, and yellow corn grows unfailingly. At the west sits a chief wearing a blue-green cloud mask. Blue butterflies flutter, and blue corn grows. At the south sits a chief with a red cloud, red butterflies, and red corn. At the east sits a chief with a white cloud, white butterflies, and white corn. Above sits a black chief wearing a black cloud, with black butterflies and black corn. Below sits Muingwu wearing a mask of clouds of all colors, with butterflies and birds of all the colors, with speckled corn and sweet corn, with melons, squash, cotton, and beans."[16]

With this identification of the clouds with the ephemeral and the solid, of corn with butterflies, of health with the divine beasts of the sacred mountains that surround mankind, and the concept that the reality of death becomes a mist-like memory that clings to the mountains at the corners of the world and will return to the center in the reality of rain, we have concluded our sketch of the Pueblo cosmos.

[16] Stephen, *Hopi Journal*, I, 333.

Chapter Eight

THE GODLINESS OF PLACE

Alosaka, or Germinator

ANDREW HERMEQUAFTEWA, the Bluebird chief of the Second Mesa pueblo of Shongopovi, expressed simply an opinion that must be common to all Pueblo groups. "The Hopi land is," he said, "the Hopi religion. The Hopi religion is bound up in the Hopi land."[1] In Zuñi tales the Pueblo land is referred to as the "terraced plain," or as the "sacred terrace," and this design, derived from the visible mesas, is by analogy carried into the sky where there are "cloud terraces" that are often represented on altars.

In one tale a gambler suggests that the land is a kind of gaming table for the gods. "Forever upon the floor of his house there lay spread a great buffalo robe, the skin upward dressed soft and smooth, as white as corn-flour, and painted with the many-colored symbols of the game, even as our own. But he delighted to call it his sacred terraced plain, bethinking himself of the robe-spread of the gods, which is even the outspread earth itself, bordered by terraced horizons, and diversified by mountains, valleys, and bright places, which are the symbols and game marks whereby the gods themselves count up the score of their game."[2]

The thought that one's homeland is the playground of the gods is but a poetic statement of a relationship that is otherwise taken as a fact in divine cosmography. While the landscape as an entity may be regarded as sacred, there are always particular spots, whether mountains, lakes, rivers, springs, or groves, which have particular meaning and sacredness. These are often the haunts of gods and lesser spirits. The feeling is so strong that it persists long after people have forgotten magical or supernatural associations. One who has always lived within a metropolis will find himself drawn to certain places,

[1] Andrew Hermequaftewa, *The Hopi Way of Life Is the Way of Peace*, 8.
[2] Cushing, *Zuñi Folk Tales*, 386–87.

180

to one corner in a park, or a certain chair in a library, despite the fact that he knows there are many others equally as good. The hunter or the fisherman who returns inexorably to the same place time after time has added another element; he has not only established a place of comfort and security, but has as well established an area where environmental response is to some extent controlled by his knowledge of what can be expected to happen there.

In the Pueblo cosmos the village is the center, but to have meaning a center must have a number of points of reference outside the center. Most importantly there are mountains. We have already observed that mountains provided horizon calendars which served to orient a number of pueblos within the time span of the year. The value of the range in this instance is probably more sacred than practical, but very often the value attached to a particular place is an inextricable mixture of the practical and the divine.

Let us consider some of the sacred mountains which give one kind of structure to the Pueblo world. The world has to be particularized to some extent, since under mountains one may include whole ranges, notable peaks, certain hills, flat topped mesas, buttes, needles, cones, and particular rock formations which are identified with mythological characters, or serve as shrines. The peaks of the directions and their "chiefs" have already been mentioned. These are mythical mountains rather than real ones, and they are often represented by stone or clay objects set about altars, but they may also become identified with actual peaks. For example, to the people of Laguna the mountain of the west is the peak of Mt. Taylor, 11,334 feet high. Since it lies northeast of Zuñi and southeast of the Hopi mesas, it can hardly serve as a common directional point, but many people make pilgrimages there.

The Pueblo world is fairly well confined as an entity by the Sandía Mountains—the Keresan home of the War Twins—on the east, and the San Francisco Mountains—home of the Kachina—on the west. For north and south confines one may borrow from the Navaho account of the Pueblo War, and accept Hesperus Peak in Colorado for the north and Mogollon Baldy, in the White Mountains, for a south marker.

Some mountains had a very practical value in orienting the foot traveler in a rather confusing topographical world. To take one certain example, there is Cabazon Peak which lies on the trail between the Río Grande of the Keres and the western pueblos of Acoma and Zuñi to the south. Cabazon is called a neck by geologists, and a needle by others. The aptness of the latter is illustrated by the fact that it rises 2,160 feet from the floor of the valley, but has a diameter of only 1,400 feet. In historic times a path passed by this peak and down the Puerco on the east to Acoma; doubtless it was centuries old then. Another route probably went north of Mt. Taylor toward Hosta Butte, and thence to Zuñi, or pueblos farther west.

On the route between Acoma and Zuñi there is a rock of no great size, but of great fame: El Moro. The fame derives from the Spaniards, "paso por aqui," but for several centuries before they passed that way it must have been a refuge for those who journeyed between Acoma and the Zuñi area. At the foot of this cliff there is a water hole; and that it has long been there is attested by the fact that on the top of the mesa there is a ruined pueblo, not of historic time. The place was a refuge for travelers, and the idea of refuge is closely related to the divine. In ancient Greece one who took refuge in a temple was in theory safe, for if he were dragged forth and killed, the god to whom the temple was devoted would avenge him. The same idea persisted into the Middle Ages with the contention that a cathedral was a refuge, even for criminals. Probably this concept is based upon the root idea of water, and physical protection that certain sites afforded the traveler. In the Pueblo world most springs and dependable cisterns are in some way sacred. Many are associated with a particular society, or with an individual kachina. Some of these are a solace and refuge to everyone who treats them with proper respect, while others are so sacred that their comfort must be refused, except by specified individuals on ceremonial occasions.

There are some ranges and high peaks which are more closely related to the spirit world than to practical affairs; they are eternal and are nearer to the unknown reaches of the cosmos than man cares to go very often, unless he is prescribed to do so. A Hopi ritualist may run to the San Francisco Mountains and back again, as swiftly as possible, to complete a rite. His mission is practical only in the sense that it establishes and confirms a relationship between the Hopitu and the gods of those mountains.

At other times and to other places the speed may be less, and the goals may contain a larger practical element, but the trips, or pilgrimages, are nevertheless thoroughly involved with the spirit world. I shall describe two mountains—one being a mountain and a lake—in which the practical, the beautiful, and the divine are well mixed. These two places have an added interest in that they are pan-Pueblo in importance, and in that way tie the Pueblo world together in space. They also join the Pueblos in time, for trips were made to these places by the vanished peoples of Mesa Verde and Pueblo Bonito, and doubtless from a great number of other towns which are now in ruin, or level with the ground.

The earth is a goddess, and her most essential products belong to spirits representing aspects of her "flesh." Corn is of course the essence of that flesh, because mankind subsists upon it; its flesh becomes their flesh. Since man cannot live by corn alone, even when squash and beans are added, two other things must be found. Salt is necessary to season food, and jewelry is necessary both in rites and for personal adornment. Unusual objects, such as quartz crystals, often are used in connection with ritual. The Pueblos knew that by rubbing two of them together a glow would be produced in the dark: the so-called lightning stone. However, above all other objects in importance was the turquoise. Sometimes the turquoise is a gem of great beauty, but even when it is not, it has great value.

Castañeda mentioned that the Zuñis offered flowers, plumes, and turquoise of an inferior sort at their sacred springs. The superior stones, one may assume, went into fetishes, or into gems for personal adornment. Since the sources of turquoise are very limited, the mountains which bore them became the seat of extensive pilgrimages to gather the sones. The extraction of turquoise from the earth-mother was not as simple as picking up an occasional crystal on the surface; it involved extensive mining from prehistoric times.

The most notable mines were in the Cerrillos area, which is about fifteen miles southwest of Santa Fé and lies just beyond the present borders of the Santa Domingo Pueblo Grant. One of these mines, which has existed from prehistoric times, is on Mt. Chalchihuitl. The other, a few miles distant, is called Turquoise Hill. Chalchihuitl seems to be an Aztec word denoting not only turquoise but other blue-green, or green stones, such as jade. As no turquoise is found in quantity or quality south of the present border, it is assumed that the Aztecs and the Mayans drew on New Mexican mines.[3]

The amount of rock dug out in search for the gems on Mt. Chalchi-huitl was considerable; estimates of the dump area range from 2½ to 20 acres, and one open mine is said to be 200 feet in depth. In Pueblo history the mountain has a very special place, since pilgrimages were made there by the people of Mesa Verde and Pueblo Bonito. The first would have traveled some four hundred miles on foot to get the stones, the Bonitans less than half that distance; which may account for the fact that some fifty thousand pieces of turquoise were unearthed in excavating the pueblo. These gems belong to the period between A.D. 950 and 1150 and include two masterpieces: a cylindrical basket of inlaid turquoise mosaic, and a necklace of surpassing beauty.

Unfortunately no records of ritual in connection with a trip to Chalchihuitl are recorded. From information White gathered in Santa Ana[4] it seems likely that it was a directional mountain for the Keres: *Cuwimi Kai,* "a house inside which turquoise is found." Chalchihuitl was not only important as the prime source of turquoise, but it contained in its environs many other minerals as well, and the Spanish took over the area and mined it with Indian slaves.

Some writers report[5] that the prime cause of the Pueblo Revolt was a collapse of the mine, which killed a number of native slaves who were working on the mountain under the direction of priests. The event, which took place in 1680, was undoubtedly but one item of resentment, even if the question be limited to slavery in the mines. After the rebellion the Indians seem to have closed all mines, so

[3] S. A. Northrop, *Minerals of New Mexico,* 530.

[4] White, *The Pueblo of Santa Ana,* 81–82.

[5] Alan E. Disbrow and Walter C. Stoll, *Geology of the Cerrillos Area, Santa Fé County, New Mexico,* 43.

that the odd circumstance of a prehistoric mine being "discovered" in the latter years of the nineteenth century was possible. After American occupation Mt. Chalchihuitl became the seat of numerous patented mining claims. These effectively kept the Pueblos away from their source of turquoise, with at least one notable exception.

In 1910 a group of Santo Domingo Indians robbed the Tiffany mines on this mountain. Leaving a guard of about 16 warriors at the mouth of the mine, they descended the 125-foot shaft by means of a rope, ascending with some of the much-sought-for stone. Efforts were made by Santa Fé officials to capture some of the band: "The Indians still claim the turquoise mines from which their forefathers took turquoise centuries ago, but the title is in the American Turquoise Company of which the Tiffanys of New York are the principle stockholders."[6]

Under such adverse circumstance, it is not surprising that accounts of the religious nature of a pilgrimage to this mountain are not to be found. Fortunately the lack of information is made up, to some extent, by accounts of salt journeys to the Zuñi Salt Lake. At one end of this lake two cinder cones arise from the saline waters, and inside each of these craters, which are only about 150 feet high, lie two minute lakes which are the homes of the Twin Gods of War. The lake is closely associated, in mythology, with a Turquoise Mountain which is also of divine origin. The Salt Spirit is female and the Turquoise is male.

The presence of the War Gods here, when their more natural homes were Twin and Thunder Mountains, is not hard to account for after reading of the raid on Chalchihuitl. Salt may not be worth defending, but the salt gatherer must defend himself while gathering his burden in a spot which was attractive to many peoples. The craters could not command the lake, but they were good fortresses, and probably needful ones.

In a Zuñi myth the Salt Woman, Ma'we, like her later children, was making a pilgrimage in the company of the War Twins toward the south and with them went another spirit, Turquoise Man: "On reaching a beautiful lake, about 45 miles south of the present Zuñi,

[6] Northrop, *Minerals of New Mexico*, 535.

the Gods of War decided that they had gone far enough, and Ma'we agreed to stop with them, but 'Hli'akwa declared that he must go further. Though 'Hli'akwa endeavored to persuade Ma'we to journey on, she refused, and finally he said: 'You may stop here because you are not of so great value as myself; this is too near home for me.' So he journeyed on to the southwest and made his home in a high mountain protected by many angry white and black bears. Ma'we made her home in the lake, and the Gods of War selected a mountain rising from the lake for their home."[7]

Mrs. Stevenson adds in a note that plumes are offered to the angry bears which guard the home of Turquoise Man, and that meal is sprinkled upon these animals, whereupon they become friendly and allow the Zuñis to approach. The mountain alluded to was indeed far to the south and its whereabouts were a much better kept secret than Chalchihuitl, which was known to everyone. The Zuñi Mountain, which was "discovered" again at about the time the Stevensons were studying in New Mexico, is likely the one in the Burro Mountains about ten miles southwest of the present Silver City, but it may have been even farther south, in the Eureka district, some six miles west of the present hamlet of Hachita, where there is evidence of prehistoric working.

The place where Ma'we and the Gods of War stopped is of certain location. The Zuñi Salt Lake is in a contained basin, and in modern times the waters are less than a mile across. The Zuñi Salt Lake was described as early as 1598, when Captain Marcos Farfan wrote that the bed consists of "solid salt as white and coagulated and as good as that of the sea, and even better." At its center, he continued, the salt in the lake "is so thick that it must be as deep as a long lance . . . this witness believes it is true that in all Christianity, or outside it, there is nothing so magnificent, nor does our King have anything like it."[8]

That description indicates something of the special nature of this salt, and the place where it was found. While good salt was never as plentiful as the clay necessary for the making of pottery, there were

[7] Stevenson, "The Zuñi Indians," *loc. cit.,* 60.

[8] Northrop, *Minerals of New Mexico,* 11.

186

other sources, such as the salines east of the Manzano Mountains. The Hopis also had a good, if perilous, source of salt in the Havasupai branch of the Grand Canyon. The War Twins dwelt there too, but the Hopis also felt the particular pull of the Zuñi Salt Lake, as did many other Pueblo groups. This particular salt has been found in Mesa Verde, which is some 200 miles distant. Watson[9] estimates that the journey from the Mancos area to the Salt Lake and back took two weeks when the trip was direct. Since the salt had to be carried back in a buckskin bag, the return journey was probably slow, even when other Pueblos were not visited, and one can assume that some sociability—and probably permission from groups along the way—were mandatory. When the Zuñis took Stevenson to the lake, they spent the better part of three days covering the forty-odd miles to get there. From Talayesva's account, it seems that the return journey to Hopi took five days, and he had burros to carry the salt.

While the salt from this particular place was highly esteemed for its choice quality, the place had another value of equal importance: the journey was also a pilgrimage for rain. When Talayesva made the trip with his father, the decision to make the long trip was based, at least in good part, on the poor year from the farmer's standpoint and the desire to "try to bring rain to our drooping plants." The two of them performed the prescribed rites as they went along, including a foot race to a mesa top. This must have been hard on the old man, since Don played tortoise and hare with him until they got to the top, where they planted bread dough for the hawk deity.

The secondary importance of gathering salt for use was demonstrated shortly afterward when they met a Mexican who offered to sell them all the salt they needed for two or three dollars. The price was very reasonable, as they wanted hundreds of pounds, and if they had bought this they would have been spared many weary miles of travel. "But since we had prayer offerings for the Hopi gods, we had to go to the lake of course, make sacrifices, and gather salt in the prescribed manner; otherwise we would get no rain and run into a lot of bad luck."[10]

[9] Don Watson, *Indians of Mesa Verde*, 59–61.
[10] Talayesva, *Sun Chief*, 252–55.

For the Zuñis the trip is annual, in summer, and the members of the party are selected; no one goes without permission. There are various sacred places along the way, the most interesting of which is a corral that is both mythical and real. The guide who showed the actual place to Stevenson thought he must die within four days because his trespass had offended the gods. The corral is sacred to Ku'yapalitsa, whose Hopi counterpart is Tih'kuyi.

This goddess is a surpassingly beautiful virgin huntress and mother of game, much in the manner of Artemis. "Although a woman, she was wonderfully endowed by birth with the magic knowledge of the hunt and with the knowledge of all the animals who contribute to the sustenance of man,—game animals."[11] Like Artemis she has a dual nature; *Artemis Locheia*, "She of the Child-bed," was a goddess of childbirth. Stevenson describes her simply as "Ku'yapalitsa, a female warrior bearing the name of 'Cha'kwena."[12] Chakwena is a very important kachina at Zuñi, one who governs childbirth with such care that she must visit every house, even if the process takes more than a day.

If the Artemis pattern is to be followed, there is the question of a moon figure, which follows naturally on her connection with the life of women. I have found no such connection in Zuñi material, but there may be one among the Keres. Lummis[13] wrote: "There is a fragmentary Queres folk-story which bears internal evidence that its heroine was the mother of the Hero Twins—that is, the Moon." The Keres huntress is called Yellow Woman, and she is certainly as nebulous as the shadows cast by moonlight. Lummis was definitely thinking of Diana, since he puts her name in the title for the fragment, but he may have heard of direct moon associations with this goddess. The name itself may be suggestive. In one long Keres narrative she is killed at night and her brother, Arrow Youth, who is her male counterpart, starts in search of her after asking the aid of his friend Great Star.

The heart of Yellow Woman is eventually found after a confusing

11 Cushing, *Zuñi Folk Tales*, 104.
12 Stevenson, "The Zuñi Indians," *loc. cit.*, 356.
13 C. F. Lummis, *Pueblo Indian Folk-Stories*, 200.

list of places and events: "Then early in the morning he was expecting her. All day he waited for his sister Yellow Woman." A little later Arrow Youth says to the chief of spirits: "This I came to ask. I suppose you know something, how my sister Yellow Woman in the daytime may remain alive." After a passage saying that she will stay away four days, which suggests the dark of the moon with a Pueblo twist, we come to the following: "He wants her to be alive in the daytime, to be alive every day. That is what she wants . . . . Therefore you must come here and search for her all over here. Maybe among last year's water melon rinds and melon rinds and old corn cobs, there look for it." Perhaps the shape of melon rinds suggests the new moon? In time her heart is found. "They climbed up and went in (down). At that time Yellow-Woman's head was washed. Then daylight came in the morning. Yellow-Woman put on her dress, and so she was alive in the daytime."[14] These passages certainly sound as if they were based upon a myth explaining the phases of the moon and her occasional appearance during the day.

The other and more certain elements of the story involve the spirit of game, which in this instance is the brother. In some Keresan stories she is a huntress because her brother is too lazy to find game for them. He gathers them into corrals, the plaza, or box canyons. Eventually, after a few deer are killed, the others are released to Mount Taylor. Since we have been on something of a detour on the journey to the Zuñi Salt Lake, advantage may be taken of that to point out that the Acoma-Laguna stories concerning this spirit are located on or around Mount Taylor, while those of the Eastern Keres establish her adventures in the Sandía Mountains.

Among both the Zuñis and the Keres the virginity of this goddess is one of intent rather than fact, and it is not considered a virtue, but a sign of keeping everything to herself—not only her maidenly prerogative, but all of the game animals as well. She rejects all suitors, and sets them impossible tests, until the War Twins trick her into marriage. She is thus the wife of these gods. In the Keresan story just given she is referred to as "the mother of all of us." In Keresan mythology she is the mother of the War Twins.

[14] Boas, *Keresan Texts*, 56–76.

189

If we return to the topic of place, and to this specific corral, we will get a different view from Talayesva. He and his father passed the same spot, but as a Hopi he was not bound by the Zuñi mythology connected with it. To him it was a corral in which the Zuñis used to trap antelope. It does have some supernatural quality, however, for he admits that the antelopes were lured there by charm songs, which also made the walls rise up miraculously.

The Zuñi Salt Lake and the goddess who abides there are not taken with skepticism. She is pan-Pueblo. In the Hopi pantheon she is called Öng Wuhti, and is thought of as an old woman with the power to predict the seasons, as well as the giver of salt.[15] In Keresan myth she is called Tsi'ty'icots'a. That name, which looks so painfully Indian, is worth another slight detour. After writing it down I pronounced it to myself and was more than surprised to find the Greek word Ψιττακός which has come to us in the Latin, *psittacus*, meaning parrot. Ordinarily one dismisses such etymologies at once, but in this instance the story of the Salt Lake is also the story of the parrot clan. In Boas's summary he states: "They [the War Twins] throw the shuttlecock at the people of the village who are turned into stones. The Parrot people who have remained in their houses are spared. After the other people have been killed the parrot people come out and are told that they will be in charge of the salt."[16] I don't find a similar word as a name for parrot or macaw clans, nor anything similar in Spanish, so perhaps the name is something like the mysterious looking Tewa word *Pati*, which, without the aid of phonetics, can be freely spelled and translated back into English as just plain "polly." It would be interesting to know just which Latinate scientist loaned the word to the Keres, or if it is a representation of the bird's cry which in similar forms is valid in many lands.

However the goddess who lives there is named, she has an intense pull on Pueblo emotions, and one which goes far beyond the simple need for salt. Stevenson tells of the animation of their guide as they neared the lake. "After camping on the second evening, it was with difficulty that the Indian was prevented from continuing his journey to the lake. The old guide said: 'You are Americans and can follow

[15] Harold S. Colton, *Hopi Kachina Dolls*, 82. [16] Boas, *Keresan Texts*, 238.

190

in the morning, but I am a Zuñi, my mother (referring to the Salt Mother at the Lake) calls me, and I must go and sleep contentedly by her. Many years have passed since I have seen her, and I cannot rest until I have reached my mother.' "[17]

One source of the great emotion involved in the trip was simply peril, while the other was a vivid sense of communion with the earth as a goddess. The practice of ceremonial continence, both before leaving and upon return home, and the association of the site with the War Twins, indicates that salt gatherers were thought of as a war party. Doubtless there were those who did not return.

In addition to the peril, there was a sense of communion at the lake, and a feeling of a greater Pueblo community on the journey. The Zuñi guide mentioned above merely wanted to sleep beside his mother, the lake. Hopi visits to this earth goddess, whether in Havasupai Canyon or the Zuñi Lake, involve a brief rite of simulated copulation with "Salt Woman, giver of herself." Talayesva was considerably embarrassed, as there were Mexicans present, but boldly denoted two aunts as his presumed partners. Since, instead of laughing, they said he did what was proper, I assume the rite was common. The Zuñis have formalized the occasion, so that the pilgrim exchanges, with his aunts, bowls of salt in return for bowls of grain.

"Their father's sisters broke up soap-weed root and made suds to wash their hair. They said, 'You are our child. We are washing your hair who have been coming from Salt Lake so many days.' They brought in bowls of grain to give to their nephews and they washed their whole bodies. The head aunts filled up the bowls with salt and all of the father's sisters took them home. That is why we still bring in the salt in this fashion."[18]

I should add one ironic note on Don's trip. The salt is no longer as deep as when Farfan plunged his lance into the lake, and as the two pilgrims could not gather enough, they were forced to buy from the Mexican whom they had met on the way down; but this was not too much of a calamity, because when they arrived back in Hopi land with their laden burros—it was raining.

[17] Stevenson, "The Zuñi Indians," *loc. cit.,* 356.
[18] Benedict, *Zuñi Mythology,* I, 49.

While there was peril in these long trips, either to the Salt Mother, or to the Turquoise Mountain, those who returned to their aunts must have had a rich experience. The young would learn the physical confines of the Pueblo world, establish its geographical monuments in the mind, and discover that there were other small groups of friendly people, much like themselves, in the vast and nearly empty space surrounding their own town. If they stopped along the way they would see other religious ceremonies, hear many stories, and exchange legends and myths. The sum of the experiences would be a more general picture of Pueblo life than could be gained in the one village that was the isolated center of the world.

There is another kind of mountain and another kind of journey that takes one there, or to some sacred spring or shrine. These trips are usually made in great haste. A Hopi ritualist may be required to run to the San Francisco, plant prayer-plumes, and then run back again. The haste of the runner suggests that the spirits should hurry toward the village with their great powers. Snow, rain, and even hail are the visible benefits they bring, but a more nebulous power which might be summed up in the word "blessing" is also sought. The prayers often ask for fulfillment—"May their roads be fulfilled"—a wish which includes not only long life for the "children" of the priest, and their children, but the more general blessing of completing all of one's roles in the community with success and happiness.

The flat-topped mesa is yet another kind of mountain, and its importance is all too clear: the whole village fled to the mountain top when danger threatened. The Hopis and the Acomites made the system permanent by combining the mesa and the village, which has the advantage that the women and children can already be in or near the fortified mesa, and only the men will be exposed in distant fields. There are ruins of many Hopi villages in the flat, but they are ruins. Oraibi dates from the twelfth century, and Acoma may be even older, which shows that trouble is not altogether new. The other Hopi mesa-top villages were all founded in the period during, or just after, the Pueblo Revolt,[19] and I believe that fact explains itself.

[19] For the founding dates of each pueblo, see Stanley A. Stubbs, *Bird-Eye View of the Pueblos.*

Undoubtedly the most famous of mesas is the Zuñi To-yo-al-ana, or Thunder Mountain. That it was used as a defensive point by more than one Zuñi town in the distant past is evidenced by the statement of an anonymous writer in 1540: "On the XIX of the past month of July he went four leagues from the city to see a rock, where he had been told that the Indians used to fortify themselves."[20] The mesa was used for defense in historical times, even before the rebellion. In 1630 the Zuñis killed a priest sent there, and then immediately fled to Thunder Mountain in the expectation of retaliation. In mythologic times it was also used as a refuge from the great flood.

From the nature of its use it is natural that it is the seat of shrines and idols to one of the War Twins: the younger. The Elder Brother has his shrine on Twin Mountain nearby. Thunder Mountain is also the home of Paiyatemu. Cushing describes this shrine in its mythical coloration: "Some times the people saw over Thunder Mountain thick mists floating and lowering. At such times, near the Cave of the Rainbow, a beautiful halo would spring forth, amidst which the many-colored garments of the rainbow himself could be seen, and soft, sweet music, stranger than that of the whistling winds in a mountain of pines, floated fitfully down the valley." The war priests are sent up to discover the source of this music.

"No sooner had the warriors reached the cave entrance than the mists enshrouded them and the music ceased. They entered, and were received by a splendid group of beings bearing long, brightly-painted flutes amongst whom the leader was Pai'-a-tu-ma, the father of the Ne'we band [an order of clowns], and the God of Dew."[21]

While mountains are but one part of any study of the sacredness of place, they do in a way contain all of it. Later I will give a more detailed account of the mythological landscape of the Pueblos and the topography and ecology in which it finds meaning. Until then, that music may as well become silent in the mists that surround the shrine on Thunder Mountain.

[20] Adolph Bandelier, "An Outline of the Documentary History of the Zuñi Tribe," *Journal of American Ethnology and Archaeology*, Vol. III (1892), 29.

[21] Frank H. Cushing, *Zuñi Breadstuff*, 38–39.

Chapter Nine

CLOWNS AND GODS

A Hopi version of a Zuñi Koyemshi clown

IT MAY SEEM SURPRISING that clowns should enter into a book on the gods, and if they were merely clowns they would not find a place here. Unfortunately we have to leave out most of the pleasant and humorous manifestations of these figures, and consider other aspects, which are less pleasant, but which relate them to the supernatural.

The demigod Paiyatemu is both a supernatural and a clown. He has as a Keresan counterpart "Koshari," which is merely the name of the clown society, but it is singularized into a deity who is the patron and founder of the society. One group of the Zuñi clowns, the Koyemshis, are thought to have once been supernatural, and their name is said to have been derived from words meaning "god husband." The indication is thus clear that there is a close relationship between clowns and gods, despite whatever one may think of their behavior.

Many of their acts are simple pranks, everyday satire and jest. Since these are identical with our own clowns, we may reluctantly pass over this merriment. A second class of activity is not altogether foreign to our culture, but it is now rare. This consists in making fun—obscene fun—of all that is most respected and sacred.

At the beginning of the Shalako ceremony, which takes place at Zuñi in late November, a group of ten masked figures comes across the plain from the abiding place of the gods. These sacred clowns, the Koyemshis, whose original is one of the supernaturals, have come to announce that in four days the gods—actually the kok-kos, or kachinas, representing them—will return to the town, after their long summer absence, and that in eight days the Shalako will begin. The occasion is a stately one and most of the activity is solemn, despite the grotesque masks, and the covering of pink clay paint which has given these creatures the popular name of "mud-heads."

194

When the ten have drawn up in the plaza to make the announcement, all but the leader take the opportunity to make obscene or ridiculous speeches. The second Koyemshi may begin with words which sound like a prayer:

> Now that those who hold our roads
> Night priests,
> Have come out standing to their sacred place,
> We have passed you on your roads.
>
> Our daylight fathers,
> Our daylight mothers,
> After so many days,
> Eight days,
> On the ninth day you will copulate with rams.[1]

This travesty of a prayer, the ritual phrases of which are not only sacred, but are as well powerful instruments in the mouths of the priests of the societies to which they belong, indicates the extreme latitude allowed, or perhaps enjoined, upon the Pueblo clown.

Before we come to Christian parallels a similar practice might be mentioned from the Greeks. One of their most impressive rites was a pilgrimage along the Sacred Way from Athens to Eleusis. The route was lined with temples, and sacrifices were made and hymns sung. At one point along the way a man called a "bridger," because he sat on the bridge of the river Kephissos, hurled obscene jests and curses at the pilgrims. Like the Pueblo clowns, he was officially sanctioned, or one might say, required.

Among the Pueblos there is, or rather was, no rein on what Bunzel calls "bestiality" in the speech of the clowns. Unfortunately little of it is recorded. If Cushing suffered from too much empathy in not telling all he knew, Bunzel came to the same result by being overly nice and not repeating the detailed explanations the children gave her. It is not, after all, a matter of vulgar entertainment; and the content of the clowns' speech would be of value in interpreting their intent. The behavior of the clowns, it should be remembered, is socially approved and vicariously participated in by the whole group.

---

[1] Bunzel, "Zuñi Katcinas," *loc. cit.*, 952.

As such it has little in common with individual deviants with whom one tends to associate some of the acts.

Verbal obscenity and the travesty of religious rites have counterparts in many cultures. In medieval France a mass was celebrated, supposedly commemorating the flight of Mary into Egypt. In it a procession of asses was led into the cathedral, and at the conclusion of each part of the mass—Kyrie, Gloria, etc.—the congregation brayed like an ass. For several centuries "abominations," such as smutty jokes, were related at specified times, even in the cathedral of Notre Dame. The clergy themselves participated in electing the "Fools' Pope." "In the very midst of divine service masqueraders with grotesque faces, disguised as women, lions and mummers, performed their dances, sang indecent songs in the choir . . . burned stinking incense made of old shoe leather, and ran and hopped about all over the church."[2]

That kind of behavior differed from the Pueblo clown in that it was a temporary license, largely a triumph of lay people, and disapproved of by many of the religious authorities. In time it became a purely secular rite, such as our New Year's Eve. With any original intent lost, the acts become merely a vague individual drive toward chaos.

To understand the motivations, which were once considered permissible or mandatory, but are now repressed altogether in social behavior, we must examine the background of clown societies in general and then outline the formation and associations of the Pueblo clowns in particular. The generic figure behind the clown is often called the trickster. He is a familiar being in many cultures; he appears in such tales as "Reynard the Fox," or as the coyote in American Indian stories. He frequently is found in mythology and in epic cycles which are recounted aloud, or he may appear dramatically in person as the Pueblo clown. Sometimes he is a god, or an aspect of a god. The Greek God Hermes, in many of his miens, is of the type.[3] Masau'u, despite his other qualities, is at once said to be "a thief, a liar

[2] C. G. Jung, as quoted in Paul Radin, *The Trickster*, 197.

[3] On this point, see Norman O. Brown, *Hermes the Thief: The Evolution of a Myth*.

... also a persistent practical joker." His kachinas are funny, and they appear at the wrong time of the year. Paiyatemu is an archetypal trickster and, except for his role as shield bearer to the Sun, he is little else.

Trickster's name explains a part of his nature: he is always attempting tricks, but while he is cunning he is also silly, so that as often as not his tricks redound upon himself and he becomes a victim, a buffoon—our clown. He has extremely gross appetites for both food and sex, and often these are not simply a surfeit of normal diet, but also include the abnormal.

Kerenyi states that "The phallus is Trickster's double and alter ego," a fact which that author attributes to an association with the masculine origin of life. Such a statement, if applied to Pueblo clowns, is likely to lead one in a false direction—they are not simple fertility spirits, nor are they a part of a sexual rite, such as one finds in the Sioux Sun Dance. Their sexual activity is a mime only, and often they are enjoined to continence for several days at the time of their performance, as would be the priests in any other ceremony.

The prominence of scatophagous acts, particularly by the second group of Zuñi clowns, the Galaxy fraternity, also points to a role which is not identical with simple sexual fertility rites. Despite the unpromising background of the trickster, or the clown, he shows a surprising tendency to identify himself with a culture hero, or even with a god. According to Radin, the trickster was never a god to begin with, but was elevated by the priests, because "he is admittedly the oldest of all figures in American Indian mythology"[4] and thus his presence in the origin stories had to be accounted for. His presence among the immortals, however, was not always acceptable and Radin, referring to the Oglalas and the Dakotas, says that "a small, but important, number of tribes prefer to regard him as a deity who has been definitely displaced and reduced to the position of an evil-working semi-deity by a more powerful deity."[5] Paiyatemu was, to be sure, sent away from mankind, because he was too silly and because he knew something about himself. What he knew concerned not only the sexual drives in polymorphous array, but also the related activity

[4] Radin, *The Trickster*, 182–83.   [5] *Ibid.*, 164.

characteristic of infancy and childhood. The Pueblos accepted this material as objectified in the clowns.

To my mind, we are not here dealing so much with the primitive ages of mankind as with the early phases in the development of any human individual, either a long time ago, or today. It may be related to the history of human evolution, in the sense that each individual, to some extent, repeats the biological history of mankind—a kind of extension of the aphorism that ontogeny recapitulates phylogeny— into the early stages of individual human life.

The uncontrolled sexuality of the clown, or the god who in time may stand in for him, is like that of the natural world from which man has risen, like the millions of seeds scattered aimlessly by plants and by fish. As the Tsimshian myth has it, trickster is told to "scatter the various kinds of fruit all over the land; and also scatter the salmon roe in all the rivers and brooks." The fecundation of the world of nature, outside of man, is certainly senseless, as the primitive man, who watched the aimless drifting of thistledown, or the scattering of salmon roe, knew. But out of the aimlessness does come a basic kind of creation, and creation is ultimately a power belonging to gods.

The Zuñi Koyemshi clowns embrace this aspect of life quite literally. The bumps on their heads contain all kinds of seeds, and the mud with which they paint their bodies and heads comes from the slime of springs. While life in its origin is seemingly formless, man also shared this fate in his beginnings. The Winnebago trickster wears his intestines wrapped around his belly on the outside, and bears a giant and detachable—hence loseable—phallus. He often carries it in a box, a situation which has given the American burlesque theater one of its basic routines. The Zuñis in the age of the original Koyemshis were equally formless; their bodies had no vents, and as a signal stamp of bestiality the people had tails and their hands and feet were at that time webbed.

When man takes a backward glimpse at himself, he takes note of the simple animal to whom he is related. There is no budding theory of evolution involved; primitive men are very close to animals in their own estimation, and often they consider themselves inferior to them, but not too much should be made of the distant past. There is another aspect of trickster, "for he represents not only the undifferentiated and distant past, but likewise the undifferentiated present within every individual. This constitutes his universal and persistent attraction. And so he became and remained everything to every man —god, animal, human being, hero, buffoon, he was before good and evil, denier, affirmer, destroyer and creator. If we laugh at him, he grins at us. What happens to him happens to us."[6]

There is a transition implied in that statement, but before we consider the elements which might go into an "undifferentiated present" let us look at the clowns of Zuñi again. The Koyemshis, as we have heard, are expected to utter travesties—the word is based on its meaning as transvestite—of the usual sacred prayer, or they may defile normal religious forms in any way they can think of. Despite this their father ranks fourth in the Council of the Gods. Since the Zuñis created their gods not in the image of man, but rather modeled them upon their ceremonial officers, we often find two names, the second being the name of the priest. Stevenson[7] gives the first four in the Council as Pautiwa, who presides; Kiaklo is his deputy and the myth bearer; Shulawitsi is deputy to Sun father; Sa'yatasha is the fourth. The earthly counterpart of the latter is called Kia'kwemosi, or Ka'-wimosa. As a priest he is the rain priest for the north direction, but as a mythical figure he is an important father. His eldest son is Kiaklo, but it is with his youngest son and daughter that we are concerned here.

Kiaklo had been unable to find the middle, so the youngest, whose name is Si'wulutsiwa, is sent out. This is important in that he became the father of the Koyemshis. He is also called "father" in the sense of leader of the clowns. The events happened like this: he took his sister, whose similar name likewise indicates long-haired beauty, with him on the search. After they had reached a distant mountain he made his sister a bower of cedar branches in which to rest while he hunted for game. When he returned he sat with his chin on his hand, gazing at her beauty until he became enamoured. She was very angry when she awakened and recognized his desire, but as they lived when "all

[6] *Ibid.*, 169.
[7] Stevenson, "The Zuñi Indians," *loc. cit.*, 33.

things were *k'yaiyuna* or formative, when the world was new!" all things were possible. She has been seduced.

In protest against the disorder of his desire, she stamped her sandal and divided the mountain on which they were standing in two, and a great river flowed between them. Her eyes had grown great and glaring, and her face became spotted and drawn. She fled from her brother, but he pursued, and when he caught up with her the sight of her transformation drove him to madness.

"As she turned again back, he threw his arms aloft, and beat his head and temples and tore his hair and garments and clutched his eyes and mouth wildly, until great welts and knobs stood out on his head; his eyes puffed and goggled, his lips blubbered and puckered; tears and sweat with wet blood bedrenched his whole person, and he cast himself headlong and rolled in the dust, until coated with the dun earth of that plain. And when he staggered to his feet, the red soil adhered to him as skin cleaves to flesh, and his ugliness hardened."[8]

The sister alternately felt both horror and pity; she laughed and cried. "Now they were like silly children, playing on the ground; anon they were wise as priests and high beings." After a time—often said to be a very short time—a series of children were born to the pair, the first of whom was undistorted except that she was "a woman in fulness of contour, but a man in stature and brawn." The next eleven born were of the ugly shapes of the Koyemshis, and they likewise were undifferentiated sexually. According to Cushing, the brothers were "in semblance of males, yet like boys, the fruit of sex was not in them! For the fruit of mere lust comes to naught, even as corn, self-sown out of season, ripens not."[9] The myth carries the warning that incest, and probably in-clan breeding, will produce *'hlahmon* (hermaphrodites), but that is only a small part of the meaning of the clowns.

These clowns contain a pair of contradictions. "Silly they were, yet wise as the gods." That is, they were stupid louts; and yet, like mad people in many cultures, they are thought to be nearer the gods, and to bring their messages. The second pair of contradictions is

[8] Cushing, "Outlines of Zuñi Creation Myth," *loc. cit.*, 400. [9] *Ibid.*, 401.

sexual. On the one hand they are phallic spirits of fertility: they carry the seeds in their knobs and are covered with earth. They possess the most potent love magic, and in their play they often simulate sexual intercourse. On the other hand they are sexless and are considered to be impotent; in at least one ceremony the penis is tied down with a cotton string to indicate the impersonator's impotence at the time.

The Hopi clowns engage in a phallic game which enjoins ceremonial continence and draws its humor from a suggestion of impotence. In the game women attempt to pile four cones, one on top of the other, and walk a certain distance; if they succeed they win a prize of food items. While the attempts are being made, the clowns shake their rattles, sing, and cry out, "Don't fall! Don't fall!" After this all of the clowns lie down as if dead, a priest brings ashes, pulls aside the breechcloth, and casts a bit of ashes on the penis of each—an act which is a symbolic measure to preclude intercourse.[10] The frequent use of ashes—the fire is out—and the fact that Bunzel found that the Koyemshi impersonators were all past middle age, suggest an inclusion of a final possibility in human biology.

The fact that impotence is a part of Koyemshi nature is explained by Parsons[11] on the grounds that there are two types of phallicism, one emphasizing continence and the other incontinence. She feels that the Koyemshi represents the former mode, and relates it to the continency which the leaders practice with the intent of bringing rain during and after the ceremonies. The idea that sexual power can be translated, by abstinence, into some other kind of power, is by no means limited to primitive peoples. In our own day Gandhi was able to turn this and other negations toward political ends. The Pueblos, fortunately, limit the duration and frequency of their taboos.

The word "phallic" as used by most anthropologists is limited to the Greek meaning: the male organ, or a symbol taking its place; and they think of this symbol in its potentially fertile phase. In psychiatry the word has a different, if equally arbitrary meaning, and it throws enough light on the nature of the clowns to be worth considering. Physiologically the genitals are the last organs to reach even potentially effective use, yet mankind is not reborn from a void when

[10] Stephen, *Hopi Journal*, I, 176.   [11] *Notes on Zuñi*, 237.

he reaches puberty. The second birth is based upon a long series of experiences extending over many years, and related to the same, or closely identified, organs. It is this long course that the clowns celebrate.

The drenchings with buckets of urine, the eating of excrement, are a part of the infantile past. The simulated copulation is characteristically pregenital, or "phallic" in the psychiatric sense. Around all of these activities there is collected a mixture of excitement, curiosity, shame in some societies, and a confused pleasure which, as it has no goal, usually ends in childish merriment. Needless to say it is an essential phase in human development, during which exploration and learning take place at a rapid pace. The clown is as much an open recognition of these aspects of human development as he is a symbol of the sexual side of adults, including the diverse possibilities.

The foolishness of the child and that of the mad are easy to equate; both the child and the insane man act in unreasonable ways, but at times they seem to have special insight which penetrates beyond everyday reason. On the other hand, the hysterical wisdom of the clowns is also associated with simple insanity which has no use. A Zuñi told Bunzel that "The Koyemci are the most dangerous of all the kachinas. If anyone touches a Koyemci while he has his paint on he will surely go crazy. They carry the sacred butterfly, lahacoma, in their drum to make people follow them. That is why they are so dangerous. Anyone who follows lahacoma will go crazy."[12] Doubtless there is a pun involved, but however it is taken, the clown accounts for all of the possibilities of human behavior other than the normal.

The organization of the Koyemshi differs from other clown groups in that they are not a fraternity. The ten men who serve as the Koyemshi impersonators are appointed by the priests at the new year and serve for a full year. It is a most arduous year, since they participate in the retreats as well as in the ceremonies. Because the task is difficult, at least four societies provide groups of men, so that no one band will have to perform oftener than every fourth year. The groups tend to be the same since the impersonation is quite an art.

The other Zuñi clowns belong to the Newekwe, or Galaxy, fra-

[12] Bunzel, "Zuñi Katcinas," *loc. cit.*, 947.

ternity and differ from the Koyemshis in that they are not thought of as gods, or even as of divine origin. If that were altogether true they would hardly need to be included here, but they are basically the same creatures, though perhaps in an unpromoted stage of their history.

Recent students, like Bunzel, grant them "more adult and subtle satire" than that of the Koyemshis, and they are much given to mimicry, mummery, and burlesque. On this level their actions seem to be purely for entertainment, although in their private ceremonies some of the obscenities seem to have a serious intent. The costume of the Galaxy clown consists of a Hopi blanket as a skirt. He wears cotton leggings; he is bare to the waist, and painted with grey mud from "ashes spring." His hair is tied in two bunches on top of his head, somewhat like horns. On the mud of his back is engraved the figure of *Bitsiti*, who is a kachina associated with Paiyatemu. That god is not the patron of the society, a role which is taken by a rather beautiful kachina called the "Great God." He wears long hair, a long spade beard, and has long green horns in place of ears. On his head there is an elegant fan of feathers. He it is who administers excrement to the initiates and members.

The Galaxy is a curing society, but so drastic that no one wants to accept the services of the fraternity unless the need is very great, since those who are cured must join. Mrs. Stevenson was both horrified at the antics of the Galaxy and thankful that no other fraternity behaved in such a fashion, but, bless the great scholar, she recorded what she saw. The behavior is drastic enough, but the recording is valuable in that it gives an eyewitness account of a rite which usually comes to us only through literature.

"While the scenes at the closing of the initiatory ceremonies are disgusting, the acme of depravity is reached after the [Great-God kachina] takes his final departure from the plaza. The performances are now intended solely for amusement . . . . A large bowl of urine is handed by a Koyemshi, who receives it from a woman on the housetop, to a man of the fraternity, who, after drinking a portion, pours the remainder over himself by turning the bowl over his head. Women run to the edge of the roof and empty bowls of urine over the Newekwe and Koyemshi. Each man endeavors to excel his fellows in buffoonery and in eating repulsive things, such as bits of old blankets or splinters of wood. They bite off the heads of living mice and chew them, tear dogs limb from limb, eat the intestines and fight over the liver like hungry wolves. It is a pleasure to state that the Newekwe is the only fraternity that indulges in such practice."[13]

Enough has been said of the anal and oral aspects of the clowns, so we will devote some attention to the last part of her description. (Note that the Koyemshis are closely associated with the Galaxy clowns in this performance.) The rending of a live beast and the eating of his still warm vitals and steaming blood is by no means unique. The Greeks had two words for it: *sparagmos* for the tearing, and *omophagia* for the eating. As a rite it is most often thought of in connection with the worship of Dionysos, who was himself torn to pieces and eaten when he was an infant. Orpheus also comes to mind, and doubtless other gods had a similar rite, since it was known to be practiced on Crete at least as late as the third century B.C.

When Benedict wrote her *Patterns of Culture*, she used the Zuñis as the type of the Apollonian culture, as opposed to the Dionysiac; she made her picture clear by leaving out such strikingly Dionysiac traits. In Euripides's greatest play, *The Bacchae*, the subject is explored at great length; and at that stage of religion "it seems likely that the victim was felt to embody the vital powers of the god himself, which by the act ὠμοφαγία were transferred to the worshippers."[14] In other words, a type of Communion.

In the situation of the Zuñi clown the god is scarcely apparent. Even the Koyemshis are at best but proto-gods, so we have something more basic, unless the rite involves more than has been recorded, which is certainly possible. It could very well have been addressed to the Great-God kachina who has just departed from the plaza. However that may be, there is a simple idea behind the rite which in the beginning has little to do with gods. In relation to Dionysos as a victim, Dodds says: "He is the principle of animal life . . . the

---

[13] Stevenson, "The Zuñi Indians," *loc. cit.*, 437.
[14] E. R. Dodd, *Euripides Bacchae*, xviii.

hunted and the hunter—the unrestrained potency which man envies in the beasts and seeks to assimilate."[15]

In theory and in myth the animal is supposed to be a wild beast —in the tragedies it is a human—but that is hardly a practical matter, so we find that the Greeks used a goat and the Pueblos a dog. From the former fact we derive our word for tragedy, "goat-song," and the prize was actually a goat torn in pieces. The Greeks also rescued the clown and put him to dramatic use. Comedy began as a fertility rite in connection with Dionysos, and the humor was just as broad as that of Pueblo clowns. Bowra puts it delicately as "a fertility rite, in which a *komos*, or riotous company, performed mimetic gestures to stimulate the fertility of the earth, and was quite unashamed in its use of phallic symbols and its unreserved language."[16] Whether we call him *komos*, or *koyemshi*, or *koshari*, the clown is from the beginning, and protean in his possible development.

Needless to say the most drastic behavior has disappeared, at least in public, as it is as offensive to the Indian as to us. Leslie White tells of a man at San Felipe pueblo who blundered into a meeting of the Kosharis, an error which automatically made him a member. He went home sick and lay about for days not speaking or eating, in dread of the prospect.

Not all of clown behavior is extreme, and the Zuñis have borne the brunt in this account; I assume that not too long ago the clowns of the Hopis and the Keres were very similar. There are two societies of clowns among the Keres, the Querannas and the Kosharis, a situation that seems to have been based upon the moiety organization of those towns. The groups were once alternated to some extent, but the Querannas have died out in some villages, and seem to have given way in importance in others. The natives do not think they are as funny as the Kosharis, and their humor is tidy. Neither of the groups is in itself a curing society, though both have ties with such organizations.

The Kosharis are the familiar clowns painted white, with black horizontal stripes around their bodies and corn husks in their hair.

[15] *Ibid.*, xx.
[16] C. M. Bowra, *The Greek Experience*, 130.

They are spirits of divine origin living in the east at the house of the Sun. At Sía the Querannas are said to be for the Moon and live in a house slightly to the north of the Kosharis.

Clowns have certain important functions apart from fertility, weather control, and humor. They were once related to war and hunting groups, with which they acted as scouts, but as war and big game hunting are of the past, there is little information available. In Talayesva's dream twelve queer looking striped animals, who were clowns, accompanied him to the border of the underworld. On his return they saved him in rough and tumble fashion.

Today the Kosharis have another important function in addition to clowning. They are the producers and directors of the religious dances and in addition they act as policemen. White gives an account of the role of the Kosharis in preparing a dance at Santa Ana.[17] It happens to be a Saint's Day dance, but the process is probably similar at any dance.

A few days before the dance the town chief and the outside chief present themselves at the Koshari house in Tamaya—the old town which is only used for ceremonies during the summer, when the people are down by the river with their crops. Masewi asks the Koshari head if he will help with the dance. The Kosharis organize the dancers and then go to the village with them to practice.

The clown's care of the dancers is minute from then on and includes all the duties of any other stage-manager. They tie on the cornhusks and feathers, or arrange the masks if it is a masked dance. They select two men, send them off to the mountains to get the spruce-branches which are a part of the costume, and feed them when they get back. On the evening before the dance, the head Koshari selects two men in each kiva to paint the dancers, and he sees that everyone borrows the bits of costume he may lack.

When the time for the dance arrives the Kosharis come out first, circle the town, and enter both kivas where they dance for a short time. They also count the dancers to make sure that all of them are present. In the dance itself they see that the performers keep their line and that the spectators do not interfere. When the dance is over

[17] White, *The Pueblo of Santa Ana*, 248 ff.

the chiefs thank them, and they are dismissed to their house where the sun rises, with the hope that the spirits related to them will send rain.

The Hopi clowns are very similar, although some are spontaneous rather than organized. They may give the people food, as in the game of cones, or the people may throw them food. They are not only bountiful, but grateful. When they are given food the clowns go out and cut wood, which they then bring to the doors of the women who have treated them with gifts. They have functions that one always expects of clowns, such as playing "straight man" for kachinas who have dramatic parts to play, or, when nothing else is called for, they may simply perform acrobatics. "The clowns join in line one behind the other, each grasping the uplifted right foot of the man in front of him. They soon tumble pell mell over one another, shouting and laughing." So observed Stephen on a cold January day in 1893.

Parsons emphasizes the fun aspect of the clown in her study *The Pueblo of Jémez,* where she describes a clown whose function is the gluttonous eating of a watermelon. Like any other melon eating contest, its present intent is good fun, but that the watermelon is a surrogate is abundantly clear. The Zuñi clown who was smeared with the blood of the live dog is only a half century earlier than the Jémez clown with red pulp of the melon on his face, and both are using exaggerated gluttony.

She places heavy emphasis on the aphrodisiac value of clown behavior, in circumstances where sex expression is limited and sexual emotion is never openly manifested. She sees a deliberate intention to give as outright a representation of sex as possible, for fun.

But she considers clown behavior as primarily a war trait, particularly in the formal obscenity toward women, the eating or drinking of filth, and in stereotyped gluttony.

Backward speech, eating or drinking in excess of things ordinarily repugnant, and playing practical jokes on old women were all items in the behavior of certain Plains warrior societies. But while the obscenity is a war trait, it is not only a war trait. Men want many kinds of power from their gods, and wherever possible they compound these desires so that the one represents the many, a natural process which gives both art and order to the outside world.

Despite what has been said in this chapter, one must remember that the clowns are above all "delight-makers," a quality that will remain after their extremes have lapsed; and one must also remember that there is something to be said for all but their most drastic behavior. The trickster figure, or figures, not only recall the past of mankind and the infantile struggles of the individual toward adult life, but they also present him a release in the present. Usually this value is referred to as a safety valve, but the question can be stated much more exactly.

Material which is repressed in the conscious mind, including recollections of an animal past and an animal beginning, is dropped into the subconscious mind. If that part of the mind were a wastebasket, the contents of which could be taken out at times and burned, all would be well. Unfortunately nothing is ever lost, and the material which resides in the unconscious often contains considerable driving power; our century bears terrible witness to the force of some unacceptable impulses.

While the confused material in the unconscious mind is not lost, it is lost to intelligent appraisal. If the same material is allowed a place in the conscious mind, it is readily available for criticism and correction. In that light, these disorders lose much of their force, and there is some wisdom in their official accommodation.

Chapter Ten

THE LITTLE WAR GODS

Paluña, or Balonga hoya, the younger War Twin

PERHAPS IT IS FITTING that an account of the diminutive gods of war should follow closely on that of the clowns, for assuredly they resemble childish tricksters more than aggressive warriors. Many of the stories in which they are the chief actors are directed toward establishing them as powerful sons of the Sun; a second group establishes them as effective culture heroes who lead the people at the time of the emergence and protect them from outlandish and imaginary foes; a third element pictures them as hunting for large game, by the use of magic or trickery. From the last role I suspect that their earthly counterparts, the "outside chiefs," or war chiefs, were ordinarily hunt chiefs and that war was but an occasional duty. Nonetheless, they are gods of war, and the Bow Priests, or the War Captains, as they are alternately called, take their powers and their duties from these twin gods.

The fact that they are twins should be qualified, in that they are always spoken of as the "elder war god" and the "younger war god." They are a pair, not of identical spirits, but more often of opposites. In the stories there is often the theme of the elder brother who makes the first attempt, but fails, and the younger brother then succeeds. When the younger brother carries the disc of the Sun successfully, after the elder has failed, we see some correspondence to the two Keresan sisters, but the War Twins always stay together. It should be noted that the twins exist far beyond the confines of the Pueblo world, but only the Pueblo pair and their particularities are considered here.

Since these two spirits are to some extent gods of war, a brief account of Pueblo warcraft is in order. The Pueblos did take scalps and they also held war dances, but they were never highly organized

209

with the purpose of war in mind. Since they had one branch of the Apaches on the southern edge of their area, the Utes to the north, a combination of Apaches and Comanches to the east, and the Navahos in their midst, the fact at first seems surprising. Wars are one of the first things to be noted by historians of any caliber, so there is no lack of material.

In the year 1540 the Pueblos and the white men first met in military combat. Coronado sent a Captain Alvarado to Acoma and the battle is described: "These people came down to the plain to fight and would not listen to any arguments. They drew lines on the ground and determined to prevent our men from crossing these, but when they saw that they would have to fight they offered to make peace before any harm had been done . . . . They made a present of a large number of [turkey-] cocks with very big wattles, much bread, tanned deerskins, pine [piñon] nuts, flour [cornmeal], and corn."[1] In other words, the war chief made his marks to "close the road" to his pueblo. When that combination of admonition and magic failed the Acomites turned to a strategy which has usually been employed the other way around. Instead of giving the natives gifts, the natives gave the Spaniards gifts—and a rather rich offering it was; about the best of everything they had, except turquoise.

The gallant Captain responded to these gifts by reporting, "These people were robbers, feared by the whole country round about." Whoever was round about in the Acoma country of 1540 must have been very lonely indeed, and the cutpurse was probably the last thing he feared. While the Acomites won that skirmish, in that the Spanish did not attempt to take the pueblo, it marked the beginning of a long and bitter struggle. The events which followed were, however, too late to affect the mythology of Pueblo warfare.

The fate of the Zuñis was different. There was a skirmish before the pueblo of Hawikuh. Several Indians, but no Spanish, were killed. Next the Spaniards stormed the pueblo in a fight which lasted about an hour; no one seems to have been killed. These defensive "wars" were waged in front of the town, by whatever strategy seemed hope-

[1] F. W. Hodge, *Spanish Explorers in the Southern United States*, 312.

ful: threats, magic, gifts, or an actual fight. Thereafter the town itself was resorted to as a defensive citadel, to be defended with rocks and arrows.

The effectiveness of that kind of warfare was undoubtedly great in the formative years of Pueblo culture. There were no horses and the distances were vast; without food supplies or good water supplies, laying siege to a somewhat fortified town was hardly possible. The aliens who surrounded the Pueblo country were at this disadvantage. The Apaches, who become important at a later date, were not a threat. Bandelier states: "It is certain that they [the Apaches] never interfered with any of the Spanish explorers and armed bodies between 1539 and 1542; it appears, also, that they were not troublesome to the sedentary Indians of Sonora and Zuñi at that time."[2]

Pueblo groups and tribes were not much given to fighting among themselves, although they quarreled often enough and often split apart, but alien groups were readily accepted, despite linguistic differences. The most notable exception is, of course, the destruction of the Hopi town of Awatobi. The immediate excuse was that it had accepted white ways, and it did fall at a time when normal courses were interrupted by pressure from outside religions.

On the eastern border of the Pueblo country there was war, but little evidence of fighting, or even abrupt abandonment, in the towns. According to Lambert the Galisteo Basin area suffered from "Plains Apache." "In 1525 these towns were decimated by a great raid carried out by the face-painting Plains Teyas."[3] In the following century the Saline Pueblos on the eastern side of the Manzanos and most of those on the eastern side of the Sandías were abandoned. Most of these pueblos belonged to tribes outside the present study: Piro, Tompiro, Tewa, and Tiwa. At a later date the most famous Pueblo military campaign was the sortie of the Pecos against the Comanches; of one thousand who went out to fight, only messengers returned to tell of the disaster.

The warlike period of the Pueblos began with the great Revolt

[2] Bandelier, "Outline of the Documentary History of the Zuñi Tribe," *loc. cit*, 7.
[3] Marjorie F. Lambert, *Paa-ko*, 5.

of 1680. In the beginning they deployed themselves with some skill, and approached a degree of unity between the tribes and towns, in order to expel the Spaniards from New Mexico; but subsequent events showed how little they were organized for war. During the revolt and in the decades that followed they fought in succession the Spaniards, the Navahos, each other tribal-wise, and from town to town. In these struggles a particular pueblo might be allied with other Pueblos, with the Spaniards, or the Navahos, or any combination of these groups.

In the first move of the Pueblo Revolt 500 Indians from Pecos appeared near Santa Fé. One entered the town bringing two crosses —"one red, as a token of war, the other white, indicating peace; but if the Spaniards should choose the white flag they must immediately quit the country. They said they had killed God and Santa Maria and the king must yield." According to Spanish accounts there were about 3,000 Indians involved in the siege of Santa Fé. Otermin, with a force of 100 men, made a sortie on August 20, 1680, killed 300 natives, and captured 47. These, "after their testimony had been taken, were shot in the plaza."[4]

At that time the Pueblos won, but they had not the least idea of political federation, or of organized and prolonged warfare. The defense of the individual pueblo was always the aim, and it made for some unlikely unions and always for compromise. While such a policy is not attractive, the fact remains that the Pueblos are as strong today as they ever were, while the Apaches and Comanches are not.

Toward the end of the nineteenth century the Priests of the Bow were still functioning for the good of the town. According to Stevenson, the ceremony for the initiation of the Bow Priests, the leaders of whom represent the War Twins, is quite pacific. "The younger brother Bow priest now takes his seat to the right of the elder brother Bow priest, and the Pekwin offers a prayer to the Sun Father for the well-being and good heart of his people, which is followed by prayers by the elder brother Bow priest, who again invokes the Gods of War. Nothing is said in the entire ceremonial in connection with the enemy. When the writer inquired of the elder brother Bow priest why there

4 Hubert H. Bancroft, *History of Arizona and New Mexico, 1530–1888*, 179–80.

was no reference to war he was shocked, and replied: 'Only prayers for good and rains are offered,' no thought being given at such times to the enemy."[5]

With this background in mind we can look at the gods themselves. The Little War Twins have a mother whose role seems to be only that of keeping the record straight. More importantly, the Twins are wards of Spider Grandmother who constantly directs them, and saves them from the difficulties that beset them. While the Twins are culture heroes who save the people from all kinds of monsters, they often need help to save themselves, and Spider Woman supplies them with the best of advice.

The small size of these gods is doubtless due to their childlikeness; they are filled with all the mischief and wrongdoing—they deliberately violate any restraint or advice put upon them—of children, but they also have the tremendous potential for doing great things. Most of these great things are, of course, entirely in the realm of the imagination by any standards. The life of the Twins is compressed, since they mature in a very few days, as Hermes did, but even in maturity they do not lose their childlike exuberance and folly.

The parents of the Little War Gods are the Sun father and Yellow Woman of the North. Yellow Woman is largely a stock character, a peg on whom to hang the garments of necessity. While she does not figure in the stories, after she gives birth to these two, there are appropriate connections in imagery. The yellow North is the home of Mokiách, the lion god of the Keres and patron of their huntsmen, though in his yellow beastliness he is a rather small lion. The yellow North is also the seat of the powers of winter, which are notably more ferocious than those of other seasons.

The impregnation of the mother of these gods was miraculous. Often she conceives when a ray of the Sun falls on her as she sleeps, or when a drop of water splashes on her from a waterfall. Sometimes both events conspire, and one accounts for the elder brother, and the second for the younger twin. Sometimes the miracle is complete and they are born of the Sun's rays on mist, or again it may be mundane and due to piñon nuts. With such possibilities it is not surprising that

[5] Stevenson, *"The Zuñi Indians,"* loc. cit., 578.

they have a variety of mothers, and even grandmothers. Sometimes they are the grandsons of Salt Woman. The place of their birth is also a little doubtful. Despite the fact that they seem to have been conceived in the upper world they are the ones who led the people from the underworld.

Naturally their names differ with the several tribes. At Zuñi the elder is "Ahaiyuta," which also serves as the collective name for the pair, while the younger is "Matsailema." Sometimes the elder is given the Keresan name "U'yuyewi," which is a variant spelling of the younger brother of the Keres. The Zuñi pair are sired by the Sun and born of Laughing Waters. The Hopi names are even more varied, but we may take "Pookong" as the elder and "Balonga" as the younger. To each of these the suffix, *hoya*, youth, is added. The elder means son of the Sun, and the younger, water-dripping son. The Keresan names, which we will use, are fairly constant: "Masewi" (embraced by the Sun) is the elder, and "Oyoyewi" the younger.

At Zuñi their mother is not personified. "The earth was covered with mist. He [the Sun] threw his rays into the mist and there in the world his sons stood up. They were two (boys). Their hair was tangled, they had long noses, long cheeks. Next day they played together. The third day the younger brother said to the elder, 'Let us go and look for beautiful places' . . . . The younger looked over the world and he saw that nobody lived there. He said to himself, 'Tomorrow we shall be old enough to work.'" To his brother he then says, "'We are four days old and we are old enough to work. This is a good world and nobody lives in it. Let us go to the southwest. There below the people are living in the fourth world. They are our fathers and mothers, our sons and daughters.'"[6]

So the two place themselves squarely in the middle of the human race, which is where culture heroes should stand. At Sía they are more definitely sons and they are not born out of a mist, but to Yellow Woman. Ko'chinako, a virgin, was journeying toward the middle point of the earth. When she lay down to rest the Sun embraced her. In four days her pregnancy was visible and in twelve

[6] Benedict, *Zuñi Mythology*, I, 1.

days the twins were born. The precocious boys soon inquired about their father and were told that he lived away in the east.

The teller of the tale at Cochití has added a touch of human interest to Yellow Woman's story. " 'My mother,' said she, 'has had a child; I must have one also.' And she wandered about the mountains, tormented by the idea that, perhaps, unless she found a husband, she would not have the happiness of being a mother. Finally one day she noticed a ray of sunlight which entered through the top of the grotto, and she prayed to it to give her a son. She was soon assured that her prayers had been granted."[7]

The theme of the lonely virgin is elaborated at Acoma. In this case she is not only childless, but outcast, and it is not the Sun himself who impregnates her, but the demigod Paiyatemu. It happened that there was a girl and her mother who were despised by the people, but fortunately for them they were loved by the supernatural kachinas. The people were gathering yucca fruit and piñon nuts. The girl wanted to go along, but her mother worried because there was no one to take care of her; however, she took a lunch and followed the other people. "She came to where the people were camped; no one invited her in, so she camped alone. She passed the night and the next day went out picking piñons all alone. At noon [when the Sun is directly overhead] suddenly someone met her. He was Oshach Paiyatiuma, Sun Youth, spirit and ruler of the Sun. He spoke to the girl saying, 'Are you picking piñons?' 'Yes,' she said, 'but you frightened me.' Sun said, 'I will help you pick piñons, but I have brought you two piñons; I want you to eat them.' She asked who he was. He told her, 'I am Sun.' She asked where he lived. He said, 'Hakuoikuchaha (where the sun rises).' "[8] The two piñons, as the reader will have guessed, made her pregnant and she gave birth to the War Twins.

These Twins undergo a series of Herculean adventures which are somewhat similar from tribe to tribe. They first decide to go in search of their Sun father; they are tested by fire and by water, and are then acknowledged to be true sons. They are again tested by having

[7] Dumarest, *Notes on Cochití,* 217.   [8] Stirling, *Origin Myth of Acoma,* 92.

215

to bear the shield of the Sun across the sky; they steal lightning; they are swallowed by monstrous jaws and end in the underworld to lead the emergence of the people. Thereafter they kill various monsters that have been plaguing the human race. That group of stories is by no means integrated into an epic cycle, as it might have been.

The Twins even had a considerable part in the creation of the surface forms of the earth: "Twins made canyons with lightning; made mountains and rocks; everything that is finished."[9] In doing this work they often overdid what was necessary. In one account the world was flooded at the time of emergence and the people called upon vulture to fan away the waters. These flowed to the east and to the west and mountains began to appear. "Across these 'The Two' cut channels through which the waters rushed away, wearing their courses deeper and deeper, thus forming the great canyons and valleys of the world. The waters have kept on flowing for ages, until the world has grown and is still growing drier and drier."[10]

So much water is taken away, in fact, that nothing will grow and the people have to appeal to the Twins. In response they create trees and grass—but not cultivated vegetation—by pulling out their hairs and casting them to the winds. The lack of water was still a problem and the conclusion of the story shows the Twins advocating conservation with a mythological foundation. They advised, "when the people should become thirsty or should want water to use in quantity, they should pull up grass and in place of the roots water would come up. When they had used what water they needed, the grass should be put back in its place so that it would continue to grow and preserve the water from drying up."[11]

At some very early time in their lives, and doubtless before the mountain and canyon building that has just been recounted, the Twins were curious about their father and undertook a search for him. One day the little fellows inquired of their mother, "Where is our father?"

[9] Stephen, "Hopi Tales," loc. cit., 6.

[10] Frank H. Cushing, "Origin Myth from Oraibi," *Journal of American Folk-Lore*, Vol. XXXVI, No. 139 (1923), 166.

[11] Stephen, "Hopi Tales," loc. cit., 51.

She replied that he was a long way off, and told them not to ask; but they persisted and to the question put for the fourth time she was compelled to answer. She told them that their father lived away in the east and in order to find him they must go to the center of a great river. (Probably this is the same mythical river, which encircles the world, that we have heard of in Zuñi cosmology.) Spider Grandmother made bows and arrows for them, and when they at last came to the great river she spun a web bridge for them.

They "crossed the bridge and descended to the center of the river and there found their father's house. The wife of their father inquired of the boys, 'Who are you, and where did you come from?' 'We come to find our father.' The woman then asked, 'Who is your father?' and they answered, 'The Sun is our father!' and the wife was angry and said, 'You tell an untruth.'" Thus we have repeated the age-old problem of that other sky-god, Zeus, and his wife Hera. The wife in this instance was a little generous and gave the boys a bowl of scraps.

"His [the Sun's] wife was very indignant; 'I thought you traveled only for the world, but these children say you are their father.' The Sun replied, 'They are my children, because all people are my children under my arm.'" This rather general answer satisfied his wife, but the Sun must have suspected that the boys were his children in a more direct sense, for he put them through a series of tests, the first of which was to lock them in a heated sweat-house made of turquoise. Water was poured on hot stones, but the Twins cooled the house by the magic of spitting out bits of shell. (In an Acoma story it is from this house that the Sun gets his heat; the version given here is from Sía.)

"When the Sun ordered the door of the sweat-house opened he was surprised to find the children alive. He then had them cast into another house, which was very large and filled with elk, deer, antelope, and buffalo; he peeped through an opening in the wall and saw the boys riding on the backs of the elk and deer apparently very happy and contented."[12] Similar tests followed which involved the

[12] Stevenson, "The Sia," *loc. cit.*, 44–45.

bear, cougar, and rattlesnakes. After the tests the Sun accepted the Twins as his own and gave them magical bows and arrows and throwing sticks.

The Acoma version is simpler; the Twins are ideal hunters. They do not have to cross a river, but go directly to the Sun. They were energetic youths. "They had always gotten up early before sunrise. They always prayed early in the morning; they were well instructed in religious practices. So next morning they got up early and, after discussing it, they decided to start out to visit their father. When they saw the sun come up they said, 'It's not far, just on the other side of the mountain.' So they started that way, walking fast so as to get there quickly. They come to the top of the first range and saw another as far beyond as the first had been." Spider came to their aid and took the boys into her house. "She had just one boy in her family, so she asked this boy to collect webs from the other spiders, then to spin them into a ball so that it would reach to the house of Sun Man.

"At midnight Spider Woman awoke Masewi and Oyoyewi and told Spider Boy to take the small basket (web) and to put the two boys in it and take them to their father's house . . . . The woman held one end of the ball of spun web and Spider Boy dropped down with the other, unwinding as they went."[13]

Perhaps the most important test that the Twins had to undergo was that of carrying the disc of the Sun across the sky. The elder brother was not a success in this endeavor. "Sun said to him, 'When it is time for the first daybreak, put this downy feather on your forehead. When it is time to get lighter, take it off and tie on this parrot feather. Then start to come up. As you get halfway to noon, stop for a while and wait to see if anybody gives you sacred meal and pollen in Cochiti. As soon as you receive your sacred meal and pollen, go on again and wait at noon for somebody to come and give you food . . . . When you have come to setting, stop again and wait for food. As soon as you have stopped for a while, start off again and when you are getting near where Sun goes down, you will see two great monsters with long teeth lying down (on the horizon). Don't be afraid. Go right down." He was afraid to go, and waited. "The

---

[13] Sterling, *Origin Myth of Acoma*, 94–95.

monsters frightened him, and the sun didn't set that night. The younger brother watched; he was a long way off. He had great power, and he came fast. He pushed his brother down into the monster's jaws, and the sun set."[14]

While the exploits of the Twins are not invariably heroic, or even admirable, they stand for the War Captains of the Pueblos. Among the Keres the "inside chief" (generally called by the Spanish name *cacique*) is the spiritual ruler of the people; he is not an executive ruler. He does not till his own fields, and he acts as a judge only to admonish peace and harmony. The War Captains rank below him, but do the actual work of running the pueblo. They too have the responsibility for holding the old traditions intact, but their duties are for the most part administrative; they act as town criers, keep track of which children have been initiated, and are in charge of keeping secret ceremonials secret. The Captains serve for one year and must observe taboos—the War Chiefs at Acoma must not sleep with their wives during their year of service in office.

The War Twins also organized the Bow Priests at Zuñi and the elder and younger are supposed to have descended in a direct line from the original pair. The elder and the younger Priest of the Bow serve for their lifetime. While the Acoma society died out when warfare lost its importance, the Zuñis kept the importance of the war society by not requiring a scalp in hand for one to gain recognition. The scalp dance is celebrated every three or four years, even without a returning victor, but the ceremony of the Bow Priesthood takes place annually in October and is a harvest festival.[15]

The war dance was performed on First Mesa in 1893, after a lapse of thirty years, which is some indication of its necessity. The Twins, or their images, appear in certain ceremonials, but some of their force as gods of war has been absorbed by Masau'u and Sho'tokunungwa. The War Chief has simpler duties among the Hopis and seems to be most of all a policeman, while the Village Chief has active power, particularly in regard to land.[16]

[14] Benedict, *Tales of the Cochiti Indians*, 25.

[15] Stevenson, "The Zuñi Indians," *loc. cit.*, 578.

[16] Titiev, *Old Oraibi*, 64–66.

Since aspects of war gods will appear again in the next chapter, we may leave the Twins with the thought that they were divine heroes, great hunters, warriors of some note, but those who have inherited their powers no longer hunt big game, nor scalps. They engage in both religious and civil affairs, and along with certain kachinas and the clowns, are responsible for the ordered progression of Pueblo life.

Chapter Eleven

SNAKES AND
THE HORNED WATER SERPENT

Macibol, who dances while struggling with the Great Serpent

IN THE COURSE of this book, the nature of supernatural beings of many types has been considered, beginning with well defined deities of considerable power. The chapter which follows this one considers the world of animism, in which everything is believed to be living, and hence to have some positive power. In between the great and lesser gods, and the realm of scarcely or not at all individualized beings who possess some degree of *mana*, there exists another class of spirits who are greater than the latter, but who possess far less power than clearly defined gods. Among the middle group one finds some of the clowns, many of the kachinas, and the so-called "beast-gods." A few of the last group appeared in Chapter VI. In this chapter we meet the most powerful beast-god, the snake. Many animals have specialized powers; the shrew or the gopher for digging, for example, and these animals may become very helpful to mankind, or harmful to him.

A few animals are in a class slightly apart—a class which often includes the lion, the bear, and above all the snake. Other animals of especial power are not hard to find. In Mediterranean cultures the bull is a notable beast-god; he may be the form a god takes, or an actual god, such as a personified river spirit. Some special animals differ from the shrew and the gopher only in that the task with which they are associated is more important, as in the identification of the lion with hunting. A man may keep a simple lion fetish, which is a private object, but one which gives the individual extra power for hunting. The lion, however, is also "king of beasts," and in that thought lies a second symbol: that of a ruler as well as a hunter.

In Pueblo society the idea of lord or king was, of course, meaningless; but if they had needed a supernatural power to back such a concept the mountain lion would have been at hand. At Sía he is the "great father" of all game. "The Couger is appealed to, as he is the great father and master of all game; he draws game to him by simply sitting still, folding his arms, and mentally demanding the presence of the game; likewise when he wishes to send game to any particular people he controls it with his mind and not by spoken words. Though the cougar sends game it is the sun who gives power to the Sía to capture it."[1] Thus the lion takes his place in the hierarchy; he is a master, but is in turn a vassal to the great lord, the Sun.

The ability of an animal to become a god is in part due to his symbolic potential; which is to say, the number of ideas he can stand for, and the readiness with which one idea, or symbol, can be turned into another. That statement is not as complex as it sounds, and it is not intended to be in the least esoteric. The serpent is a lowly beast, and the fact that he so often tends to become a god needs some explanation.

A god, even the simplest god, is based upon a certain amount of abstraction in the human mind. Shakak, the god of the North and of Winter, is a very simple personification. The mind separates the qualities of winter, and then again separates these from another idea, the direction from which winter comes. As the number of symbols increases, and the possibility of interchange between them does likewise, so does the possibility that a simple figure may become a god. Simple personifications, or abstractions, are not so compelling, since they involve so little of the mind, particularly that part of the mind engaged in relating itself to the powers outside the skull. A Nike, Winged Victory, or Tyche, Fate, have a logical place in the scheme of things, and may even have cults, but they never have the power of an Apollo or a Dionysos. In Hopi culture the great strength of Masau'u is that he presents this great complexity of possibilities, partly logical and partly imaginative, which is lacking in even such a great figure as the Sun, and which would be wholly absent if he were only a symbol of death.

In this light the serpent may be examined more closely. He is not only a powerful beast, or a powerful, cunning beast, or a beast who combines power, cunning, and venom, but is as well one who has recourse to the underworld where the dead live. As such he may be

[1] Stevenson, "The Sia," loc. cit., 118.

an ancestor, and ancestors are likely to be benign and benevolent. In the latter capacity they may not have been benign, but may have been instead the protectors of the city, which at times leads to war. If they are killed in that role, they become heroes in the form of snakes; otherwise the snake, not altogether in the role of an ancestor, may simply become the tutelary guardian of the household. Since the snake can kill, it can also cure. In its role as communicator between the upper and the lower world, it knows of seeds and fertility, and the tilling of the soil. Agriculture involves weather control. Lightning controls rain. Lightning strikes swiftly, like a snake, and may kill; so the snake is again in the realm of the hero and war, and of curing for lightning shock or snakebite. Because there is so much power involved in these acts of gods, it is sufficient to spread to curing of a more general nature.

In the Biblical tradition the serpent got off to a very bad start indeed. Perhaps he was, as some have thought, a messenger sent from God to advise the parents of mankind to eat of the Tree of Life which would give them immortality. He advised, instead, that they eat of the Tree of Knowledge, so that he might save immortality for himself. The present text tells no such story, but there is no doubt as to the fate of the serpent: "Thou art cursed above all cattle, and above every beast of the field . . . . And I will put enmity between thee and the woman, and between thy seed and her seed."

The prophecy proved true, for when the Israelites were living in the desert many of them were bitten by poisonous snakes and died. Moses, at the Lord's command, caused a brass fetish of a snake to be erected on a pole; the snakebitten people who looked upon it were cured. In addition to simple enmity toward mankind, the snake gradually assumed another quality which was larger than mere venom. It was believed that the fallen angels were changed into serpents. At first the tradition was outside the Bible, but in the Book of Revelation the identification is complete. "And he laid hold on the dragon, that old serpent, which is the Devil, and Satan, and bound him a thousand years."

Since we have inherited that tradition directly, most people have but one attitude toward the serpent; and it is doubtless this single view which gives the fillip to the Hopi snake dances in the eyes of white spectators today. A mixed sensation of horror and awe draws thousands of spectators to the public parts of the ceremony. Most of these, I daresay, regard what they can see as utterly bizarre, as intriguing, but meaningless; extravaganzas, something like the Python-lady in a sideshow.

That this is not the only meaning of the serpent everyone knows, that is, everyone who has seen a doctor's automobile with the caduceus—a pair of snakes twined around the staff of Hermes—affixed to the bumper or license plate. To gain a different viewpoint from our common one, it will be worth the time to sketch, very briefly, the place of the serpent in Greek religion. Since we are on the topic of healing, we may as well begin with the god Aesculapius, son of Apollo. He was so skillful that he raised a man from the dead, but as that is not the prerogative of even divine doctors, he was himself struck dead by Zeus. The animal sacred to him was the snake. In time astrology took up the connection, and "the serpent [a constellation], which shines near the northern pole, was the author of medical cures, because it was the animal sacred to Aesculapius."[2] The connection with the stars as well as with healing will also be found to occur in the Pueblo account.

The wheat goddess, Demeter, is one of those deities who are attended by snakes. She is the bearer of fertility knowledge for both the field and the home; in the latter role she is the initiator of brides and grooms into the secrets of marriage. As a goddess of the field she supplied Triptolemus with seed grain, a wooden plow, and a chariot drawn by serpents, and sent him over the world to teach agriculture. The serpent was also a tutelary genius of the Greek household who protected its stores. That idea was very old, since the goddess worshiped in Minoan-Mycenaean domestic shrines was a snake-goddess.[3]

Serpents attended deities in part because the symbols were taken over from older religions. Zeus Ktesios appears in the likeness of a snake, as a protector of property. Zeus Meilichios was built on an

[2] Franz Cumont, *Oriental Religions in Roman Paganism*, 173.

[3] Nilsson, *History of Greek Religion*, 13.

underworld snake god. To him were addressed the *Diasia*, "ceremonies of imprecation and placation." He was the avenger of kindred blood, and the ceremony was addressed to whatever snakes, ghosts, and underworld beings were available. As vengence was closely related to war, that concept must be added. Athena is a goddess of war, or at least of protective war. She is either the mother, or foster mother, of Erichthonius, a serpent child who is often seen in archaic drawings peering from behind the aegis of the goddess.

Kindred, war, heroes, the dead, and ancestors are closely linked ideas; and they are also often linked with serpents, both by the Greeks and the Pueblos. Cadmus was the legendary founder and king of the great city of Thebes; around him gathered many myths: the slaying of the dragon, sowing its teeth, from which sprang the noble family heads of Thebes. The first of these was Echion, Snake-man. After the death of Cadmus, "he and his wife were turned into great harmless serpents."[4]

The warrior-hero, who is often an ancestor, or presumed to be one, by dying in battle becomes semi-divine and takes the form of a snake, in which form he is often figured on graves and altars. Plutarch states that when the body of Cleomenes was impaled, the people, seeing a great snake wind itself about his head, knew that he was more than mortal. Plutarch, being a rationalist of sorts, explains that when the moisture of the marrow evaporates it becomes thicker and produces serpents. Lest the marrow of this chapter likewise become too thick, the snake symbols of the ancients here give way to the present.

The Horned Water Serpent exists as a minor god among all the Pueblo tribes. He is described as "a gigantic serpent, also in the interior of the earth, nourishes the germs, supplies sap to those of vegetation, and life blood to those of animals. Specially, this deity is recognized as presiding over all the waters of the earth."[5]

In addition to the Horned Serpent god, the Pueblos took special account of living snakes, whether rattlesnakes or non-venomous kinds, and to these they attributed supernatural powers of one kind or another. Of those powers of the serpent mentioned in the résumé

[4] H. J. Rose, *Handbook of Greek Mythology*, 186.
[5] Stephen, "Hopi Indians of Arizona," loc. cit., 102.

of Greek symbolism, the only one which seems to be entirely missing is the connection of snakes with immortality. Because it sheds its skin and lives again, the snake has often been thought to be immortal. While the Pueblos had a number of gods who took human forms—though they do not die—they do not struggle with the idea of men becoming immortal spirits in a particular sense. Witches are possibly an exception, but for the most part at least, these seem to belong to the present generation. Other evil spirits may be of the recently dead, but these do not plague the living for long.

The Hebrew view of the serpent as the embodiement of unmitigated evil is never elaborated among the Pueblos; he is too often an ally for some desired end. It is evident, however, that the snake had such a potentiality, as the following note indicates: "While I was in the village, the large flat-bottomed boat that was used to ferry the Indians across the river to their farms on the other side was overturned on a stump in midstream. The next morning a red snake was seen coming out of the stump. The people told me this was probably the witch who had caused the disaster to the boat."[6]

Images both of actual snakes, which the Pueblos used in ceremonies, and of the Horned Serpent are very ancient in their culture. Archaeologists have found images of the rattlesnake in Pueblo Bonito in Chaco Canyon, an area which was abandoned about the year A.D. 1100. Judd illustrates an effigy of a rattlesnake which was contrived from a cottonwood root and still had the black paint on it; white paint indicates the markings and the tail.[7] While there is not proof that it was a ceremonial object, Pepper found in the same ruins a ceremonial staff with the rattles of a rattlesnake clearly indicated on it.[8] The Horned Serpent appears in a beautiful design from Sikyatki, a ruin about three miles north of First Mesa in Hopi country.[9] Since this town was abandoned before the Spaniards arrived in 1540, that god

[6] Esther S. Goldfrank, *The Social and Ceremonial Organization of Cochiti*, 94–95.

[7] N. M. Judd, *The Material Culture of Pueblo Bonito*, 278.

[8] George H. Pepper, *Pueblo Bonito*, 147.

[9] Fewkes, "Designs on Prehistoric Hopi Pottery," *loc. cit.*, 263.

obviously existed in prehistoric times. The design includes a shrine and is thus related to some religious ceremony.

While the far past is lost, some of the meanings attached to representations of snakes and the Horned Serpent god can be gained from comments by modern Pueblos. Ruth Kirk collected a number of Zuñi fetishes and the jars that contained them. They pertain to things great and small: to war, betting, curing, hunting, and the like. She also collected the native explanation for a number of these fetishes. "Many of the fetishes, especially those constructed of horn, suggest serpents and are said to be sea-serpents whose power is considered greater even than that of the Beast Gods. A few have a dragon-like appearance and many are animals."[10]

One of these kits was called a snake-jar. According to Kirk: "The fetishes were used for three purposes: control of weather, cure of snakebite, and treatment of tuberculosis . . . . They were the property of the North Priest, and used primarily during a severe winter to supplicate for warmer weather."[11]

The combination of curing and weather control is not hard to unravel if the Battle of the Seasons is recalled and the snake is taken as the center of the image. In the Keresan version Miochin, the spirit of Summer and summer-lightning, fought with these bolts. Snakes are identified with lightning, because of their zigzag course and their striking power, and lightning most often brings rain. The snakes fit into the image in another way. A Zuñi explained, "You see, snakes go to sleep in winter time, and in March when the snakes come out, at the same time they would take these fetishes out, and the sacred meals, and pray to the snakes not to bite any Zuñis during the summer."[12] The snake asleep is here taken as a symbol of winter; when he awakes it is a sign of summer coming on, and summer brings not only crops, but the possibility of snakebite and lightning shock which must be cured, often by the agent which caused them. If a man is bitten the North Priests must cure him. They use medicine, but there is also the implication that because they represent the time of

[10] Kirk, *Introduction to Zuñi Fetishism*, 24.   [11] *Ibid.*, 26.
[12] *Ibid.*, 26–27.

winter, when the snake is dormant, that the power of the season, or the direction, will prove helpful in the cure.

Another association joins at this season: war. The Bow Priests at Zuñi hold two ceremonies, one of which is in March and has to do with rainfall and the crops.[13] The snake is both a fertility spirit and a war spirit. If we look back to the Greek world the hero, who was primarily a warrior, although he too did duty as a curer, was often identified with a snake; since they lived in holes in the earth, they were thought fit to embody the spirits of the dead.[14]

The notable striking power of the snake after he has emerged, like the spring, from the cold sleep of winter—and the sometimes deadly effect of his strike—make him an excellent symbol for prowess in war. That power could be taken as magic: "The War Chiefs are only ones can take care of and have special ceremony . . . . The little fetish is supposed to be Snake Head. They scrape it off every time they go out to fight and put it on them; on their hands and legs and body. When they put it on something like that, they look fierce, scare you. They stand for snake, makes them like snake, quiet and strong and can kill anybody."[15]

Perhaps behind the scrapings of some such fetish lay a simpler and more realistic fact. In the early seventeenth century Fray Estevan de Perea speaks of "wooden pens in which the Zuñi kept rattle-snakes for arrow poisoning—rattlesnakes that hissed and leaped 'menacing as the fierce Bull in the arena.' "[16] I very much doubt that the venom would have more than a psychological effect, and that not on the victim, but upon the warrior who used the potent arrow. A similar result was gained, according to Stevenson,[17] by rubbing rattlesnake oil on each warrior.

According to one Hopi account the symbolic power of the snake is so great that the warriors did not even have to use the arrow—which

[13] Parsons, *The Scalp Ceremonial of Zuñi*, 33.

[14] H. J. Rose, *Religion in Greece and Rome*, 35.

[15] Kirk, *Introduction to Zuñi Fetishism*, 48–49.

[16] Judd, *The Material Culture of Pueblo Bonito*, 278.

[17] Stevenson, "The Zuni Indians," *loc. cit.*, 599.

is most often associated with the snake. In 1893 Ko'peli told Stephen that "In the old time the Snake society were actual warriors and when they went on the war trail they carried neither spear nor bow and arrow. They had the battle axe and the nodule club. They knew no fear and marched up to the enemy and seized him by the throat (as we seize a snake) and knocked him on the head with axe or club."[18]

That the same man was thinking in terms of symbols is shown when he states that the Antelope society had no real connection with the Snake ceremony—which is performed jointly by the two groups —but they were associated because they used rattles made from the scapulae of that animal. The two kinds of rattles form a natural link.

While on the subject of linkage, it may be useful to mention clan-pairs. The Hopis, Zuñis, and Keres all have, or had, Rattlesnake clans. The Hopis linked this clan with the Cactus clan, while among the Keres it is linked with the Panther clan. Kroeber suggests one reason for this kind of link between two clans. "Rattlesnake and Panther are both dangerous biting animals, and Cactus may be connected with them because its spine resembles a snake's tooth."[19] Perhaps the association of the rattlesnake and the mountain lion is based more on the general feeling that they are spirits of the hunt and of weather control, but the clan links are not often based on logical symbolism. Even at Hopi where the Snake clan still exists, it is not the clan, but the society, which holds the Snake ceremony.

Since the functions of the ceremony are broad, related to hunting, war, cure of snakebite, lightning shock and other ailments, as well as the inevitable plea for rain and crops, it could hardly be imagined that one clan could be given such a responsibility. The society is drawn from several clans.

The serpent as a fertility spirit has several aspects. Most obviously he communicates with the underworld, which is often thought of as a great system of waterways and lakes. The snakes are released after the ceremony to carry the message of desire to these waters. While this aspect of the snake is now uppermost, and the war connotations are dim, he does take on one aspect of the warrior. The enemy of the

[18] Stephen, *Hopi Journal*, I, 714. [19] Kroeber, *Zuñi Kin and Clan*, 143.

Hopis is no longer other Indians, but the possibility of losing the Hopi way of life. Against this vague opponent the snake stands as a guardian; he fights at one's side, so to speak, against the invisible enemy. Talayesva had a dream, or perhaps it was a vision, which was related in his mind to the attempt of a missionary to get those who had returned from boarding school to stay away from kachina dances.

"The old people and my Guardian Spirit had led me into the Wowochim and the Soyal [his ceremonies as Sun Chief] and I knew that I was spoiled for the Holy Ghost . . . .

"One day, while I was working in the field, it rained. Since it was nearly noon, I went to my father's field house and lay down to eat my lunch. Glancing to my left, I saw a snake coiled with raised head. He looked straight into my eyes and stuck out his tongue several times. I remained very still, thinking hard and prayerfully. When it stopped raining, the snake crawled to me, touched the toe of my shoe, and drew back. He returned, touched my ankle, came up to my knee, and drew back again. He seemed to think for a moment, came a third time, crawled up along my side to my chin, and licked my face and nose. I was frightened and sweating, but tried not to tremble. I spoke to the snake very quietly and in a pleasant voice: 'My Father, I am the son of the snake and the lizard. You have come to examine my heart and learn what kind of man I am. I am only a common man and not very good or wise. Please do me no harm.' Then the snake coiled partly around my neck and lay still for a moment. I thought to myself, 'If this sacred snake wants to harm me, what can I do?' Finally he moved away as if satisfied with me. I was glad that he had come to see me, for if my heart had been evil, he never would have been so gentle. I felt that this was the work of my Guardian Spirit, and that I was safe in his hands. I remembered how I had once raised a stone to kill a snake that almost choked me, and now I knew that it was my Spirit Guide that changed my mind just in time. I could also remember how when I dug a hole to die in, I was saved at the very edge of my grave. And, of course, I could never forget how the snakes dropped their heads when they saw me on the death journey and how my Guardian Spirit restored me to life and promised to protect me. All these things were proof to me that the ancestral spirits approved of my conduct and wanted me to stay on the Hopi Sun Trail."[20]

Don, in this passage, connects snakes with ancestral spirits, although just how they are related to the dead is not clear. It seems to me that the implication is that just as the snakes are man's messengers to the spirit world, so are they messengers from ancestral spirits to living men. In this one case they are rather powerful judges sent by the ancestors. Several problems are raised at this point. To what extent are snakes ancestors, and does the taboo on killing them represent a residue from a lost totemism? These questions are hard to answer with any degree of probability. Ruth Benedict has pointed out that Pueblo culture can have all the elements of a complex, without joining the elements into a pattern.[21] Her point was made in reference to the Guardian Spirit concept, which oddly enough appears in Don's account, although it is not a Pueblo theory.

For our purpose here, the pattern would be one of totemism and taboo. Among many cultures, the animal which is the clan symbol is assumed to be an actual ancestor, and thus he and all of his kind are sacred and inviolate. That there were snake clans is a historical fact, and that there were taboos on killing snakes is attested by the story just given. That the taboo extended to the Keres as well is illustrated by a short, and supposedly eyewitness story from Acomita, a summer village of Acoma.

"There were some Mexicans and Indians working on the section [of the railroad] near McCarty's. One day while working near the track a Mexican found a snake's nest. There were some little snakes and one or two eggs in it. The Mexican destroyed the nest, killing the little snakes and crushing the eggs. He did this in spite of the warnings of the Indians." The snake came into camp and inspected each man much as the snake had inspected Don. "When the snake had found the guilty one he crawled swiftly up the Mexican's body and wrapped himself firmly around his throat. The Mexican screamed

[20] Talayesva, *Sun Chief*, 206–207.
[21] See Ruth Benedict, *The Concept of the Guardian Spirit in North America.*

for help and tried to free himself, but the snake held on, tightening his grip. At last the Mexican dropped, strangled to death."[22]

Despite the assertion that this was an eyewitness account, there is no reality in the story in so far as it concerns killing a man. There are several species of constrictor snakes in the Southwest belonging to the genus *Lampropeltis,* the best known of which is the king snake. While they are certainly not dangerous to man, it would be common enough to have seen one crush another reptile or small rodent and thus provide the symbol. It is curious that the fear in both these accounts is not related to rattlesnake bite, which is such a ready image of death-dealing punishment by a snake. Instead, the snake examines the heart of each individual; if he has held to his traditions, including the taboo on killing snakes, he is passed by; if not, he may be strangled.

In the pattern of "totem and taboo," we have established the wide existence of Snake clans, and the taboo on killing snakes. There now remains the third element. Is the snake regarded as an ancestor? To begin with one should mention the use of the term "father." In ritual prayers snakes are often addressed as father, but this does not necessarily indicate any sort of direct kinship—it is rather a term of respect. There is, however, some direct evidence that snakes and ancestors were at times identified. Even the living, if they were defeated heroes, might become snakes; and these would in time become ancestors, but not the remote ancestors of classic totemism.

From Keresan Cochití comes a tale concerning the destruction of Pecos pueblo. The men, as we know, went out to fight the Comanches. Very few came back. The short fragment states only that "They fought and many were killed." Half of the remaining men, and those who stayed behind, planned to become snakes. They were evidently successful, since the women cried and a ceremony was held to restore the snakes to men.

"The women brought in pollen to feed to them. The medicine men tied feathers and hung them around the necks of the snakes praying that they should take the form of men and women again. For four days they prayed and sang, but they could not restore the

22 White, "The Acoma Indians," *loc. cit.,* 189.

232

snakes. They let them go and the rest of the Pecos Indians came down to Santo Domingo."[23]

There is, to be sure, no direct identification here of snakes and ancestors, but the idea is close at hand. Another instance of a near connection comes in the form of a denial. Stephen recorded in his *Hopi Journal* for August 7, 1885, an item entitled "Kiki Talks." "We never call the Snake father. The Antelope is called father by the Snake men. The father of Snake maiden is the father of the Antelopes, and the Antelopes are fathers of the Snakes."[24] Both the groups mentioned are societies, not clans, and the sense of "father" is that of "ceremonial father." Hence it is probably safe to assume that the idea of the snake as a totem does not exist among the Pueblos and probably did not, a point which is strengthened by the fact that the symbols of other clans are definitely non-totemic.

The existence of Snake clans was not special; clans were named after familiar animals and plants, and after important natural phenomena, such as Cloud, Water, Snow, Fire, Earth, and Sun. Even an important man-made object, the arrow, could serve. There could be no taboo on either killing or eating the object behind most of these symbols, so we must look elsewhere for the strong taboo against killing snakes.

It is as an agency for fertility that the snake gains his immunity from death, and it is the fertility of the fields that is uppermost in his symbolism in this respect. The snake does not appear as a strongly phallic spirit, except in a negative way. We will shortly examine the connection of snakes with warriors. Women weaken warriors, which leads to the widespread continence rule applied to those about to do battle, and the extension of this ban to the ceremonies of warrior societies, such as the Snakes. Indeed, at this time women should be shunned altogether.

"The smell of a woman attaches to a man who has any communication with her. The smell of a woman is most offensive to the rattlesnake, it makes him angry and he will bite. A man who has been

[23] Benedict, *Tales of the Cochiti Indians*, 16.
[24] Stephen, *Hopi Journal*, I, 718.

233

speaking with a woman on coming into kiva causes the rattlesnakes to become excited and angry. They will bite the men who handle them."[25]

The prominence of this aspect of the snake, or at least of the rattlesnake, tends to inhibit the use of the snake as a fertility symbol in human procreation, although it does not exclude it. Water snakes may impregnate women who violate their sacred springs, and the Horned Water Serpent may at times be invoked to overcome sterility.

It is, however, as messengers to the watery realms of the world and the spirits who control these waters that the snake is seen as the representative of fertility. Underneath the earth is a vast reservoir of water which rises to the surface in springs and lakes and rivers. The Horned Water Serpent is god of these lower waters, and he at times becomes as well the god of floods which can be either devastating or perilously useful to floodwater farmers. Actual water snakes of course join their spirits to the greater god. The other realm of water lies above the earth. While one does not ordinarily think of snakes in connection with the sky, they do have several means of access to it. Perhaps the most simple one is illustrated by the conclusion of the Hopi Snake ceremonies. At that time the snakes are released to the directions from which they have been gathered, with the prayer to the spirits of the four directions that they send clouds and rain over the pueblo.

"No sooner has the last reptile been thrown down than each Snake dancer, except a few of the older men, grab from the pile of snakes with both hands as many as they can get and then dash with their handfuls of writhing reptiles from the village and north, west, south, and east, those running to the last three points down the mesa, where they release the snakes."[26]

While these snakes carry the message to hasten the clouds home, a snake may have an even more direct contact with the waters above. Most importantly, it is by analogy with lightning; but before that is considered, let us look at a short statement from Acoma which illustrates how closely a mere idea may become associated with reality.

[25] *Ibid.*, I, 709.   [26] Voth, *The Oraibi Summer Snake Ceremony*, 347.

The possibility is so firmly fixed in the mind that the reality is readily adapted.

"Some men were seeking shelter from a hailstorm under some large cottonwood trees. The clouds were low and the wind was strong. Rain and hail were falling in torrents. While standing under the tree the men noticed a dark snake with red on his sides climbing up one of the cottonwood trees. He was climbing very swiftly. Soon he reached the top of the tree. But he did not stop; he went on, out into the air. He was seen for some time traveling swiftly through the air and clouds, until he finally disappeared."[27]

In this instance the snake was joining the torrents pouring down from the sky, which is a reversal of a commonly observed occurrence: the zigzag strikes of lightning which herald and accompany a storm. Lightning, by analogy, is a kind of celestial water snake. Often lightning becomes disassociated from the rain and holds fertility in just the blast. Probably the most famous instance of this is the story of the Theban earth-goddess Semele who was struck with a lightning bolt by the sky god Zeus; from her ashes was rescued the god of the flowing things that the earth produces, whether milk, or wine, or sap: Dionysos. In the picture writing of middle America a field struck by lightning is represented as being especially fertile.

The Pueblo Indians abstracted lightning; it could be either good or bad, and the good lightning could be either male or female. Since the latter distinction is closely related to the Horned Water Serpent, let us consider it first. In the sand paintings in front of the altar in the Walpi Snake ceremony, in the Antelope kiva, the same design is used for both snakes and lightning.[28] There is a zigzag body, a triangular head with dots to indicate eyes and mouth. Most importantly, two of these figures represent males. On the west is "yellow snake lightning, *Ti'yo Ta'lawi'piki,* Youth Lightning." Next to him is Maiden lightning. These and a similar pair spring from cloud symbols.

From the neck of the male "snake lightning" protrudes a horn;

[27] White, "The Acoma Indians," *loc. cit.,* 189–90.
[28] Stephen, *Hopi Journal,* I, 594, Fig. 330; pl. XVII; 672, Fig. 565.

on it is hung, or laid, a cylinder of willow wood. On the female figures is placed an annulet made of willow bark, or, I think, sometimes of rushes or flags. In any case, the small ring is made of plants that grow by water.

The second distinction is made between the lightning which blasts and that which fertilizes. In the Snake ceremony a whizzer is used. The whizzer is much simpler than a "lightning frame," and consists only of a flat board with a lightning design. It may be twirled about at the end of a string. The purpose of this is to divert the influence of "bad clouds; it is to call the good lightning to strike a place that has been blasted by bad clouds . . . a place made barren by them. When the good lightning strikes such a spot in the valley it drives away the bad cloud's influence. Afterwards this place is planted and becomes very fertile."[29]

Uppermost in the mind of the Indian who gave that explanation was the evil of lightning shock, or of death by lightning. Since the farmer is most likely to be killed in his field, the good lightning, the friend of man, must come and strike the field again, lest that field remain barren.

At this point we are poised between the snake and the lightning symbol. Before continuing with the deadly side of lightning, which becomes very closely associated with war, the war associations of the Snake society, and the lightning and star god who presided over this aspect of life, let us take a cursory glance at the Snake ceremony in its subterranean aspect. The snake is to the underworld waters much the same potent being as the lightning is to the waters of the sky. Since the Hopi Snake ceremony, particularly in its public aspects, has been fully recounted, only a few points need to be made here. No one village gives the Snake ceremony two years in a row; on the alternate year a Flute ceremony is given. Its symbolism is very similar, but the concentration is perhaps more definitely directed skyward.

One brief segment of the private part of the Snake-Antelope ceremony will suffice to give an indication of its underworld orientation. A variety of animals and insects, of which the snake is the chief,

[29] *Ibid.*, 637–38.

all of them closely connected with the earth and burrows in it, are related in this ceremony. On the standard rising above the kiva are "Skunk, weasel, and coonskins . . . . They all have the same smell, the same as snakes; they have the same ancestors. These are hung there as a signal to the Snake ancestors, the early Snake people of the underworld, who understand from them that the Hopi want rain."[30]

In one of the rites, that of bathing the recently captured snakes, the priest sits at the center with a large bowl in which he prepares a broth. Around him are placed objects representing the six directions, and beyond them stand six jars filled with living snakes. The directional objects are a portion of a bear's skull, and stone representations of lion, wolf, and wildcat. At the southeast, representing the Nadir, is placed a large quartz crystal. On the northwest an eagle is assumed for the Zenith, but no object is there; he is instead represented by the song the priest chants. The song well describes the intent and the activity going on:

> Listen to us, the blind beetle, blind beetle!
> The blind beetle calls to eat, calls to drink.
> The hunters watch, the Spider-Woman winks.
> The Ants, the Bees, all the Snakes sleep.
> Observe us, that now our water prepare,
> Like mother's milk it brings us strength and wisdom;
> The dove sings, all are doing, all is done, it is ready, it is ready.
> . . .
>
> All the waters make the one.
> Now the grasses, herbs, and roots,
> Gathered from the 'opposite points,' my hands bruise them.
> Intu calls us to eat our West element.
> Now our garments are cast off, we stand naked,
> We are ready to drink with the snakes.
> Come reverently, all the people
> . . .

The beetle is invoked here because he is one of the ingredients of the snake-medicine, and because the particular family is associated with

[30] *Ibid.*, 638.

"sleep sleep sleep sleep," as a short Hopi lullaby puts it. The sleep is the dormancy of the earth. The ceremony is held in the first part of our August, and a complementary one is held in January. At the time of the major ceremony the snakes are wide-awake—if at times subdued by their captive role.

Shortly after this point in the song, there is a kind of communion celebrated between the snakes and the members of the Snake society. The reptiles are poured into the medicine in the center basin, and they and the members all drink from the same bowl. The priest continues his song:

> Old man, old man, bring the vessel of fluid.
> The snakes are sucking our tongues, for which we are glad.
> Now all the elements are in, stir it well and drink
> The fluid of the spider; observe us.
> Come, let all of the men stand up
> And once let the vessel go round
> The old men first, now the youths!
>
> *I-ya-oha-e! i-ya-oha-a-ha-o.*
> The Blind beetle! *i-hi-el-o-a.*
> The Spider-Woman! *i-ya-a-ha-e.*
> The Snake-Virgin! *o—o-elo-a.*
> The warriors have found her children,
> Crawling, crawling, crawling here.
> Now we are ready to bathe them.[31]

In the final stanza a new being appears: the Snake-Virgin. We will meet this mother-of-snakes presently, when the Snake myth which stands behind the ceremony is considered. The snakes themselves need but little more comment. Their ceremony begins with a number of prayers by a crier addressing the cloud-gods of the directions. A fragment of one will give the tenor of many: "Therefore, being provided with these [prayer feathers], do not delay anywhere, but quickly have pity on us with rain . . . . You who live north, loom up, please!"[32] During the ceremony races are held to stress the

---

[31] Stephen, "Hopi Indians of Arizona," *loc. cit.*, 207–208.

[32] Voth, *The Oraibi Summer Snake Ceremony*, 276–77.

urgency of this plea for haste, and on the final day when all is ended, society members grab up handfuls of the snakes and speed with them in the four directions from the villages. The snakes are then released to speed the prayers on to the gods. Their messages seem, however, to be more symbolic than real, for the confused creatures tend to linger near the mesa for some time, making the area hazardous for the unwary.

At the present time, only the Hopis have the Snake ceremony in its well known form, but similar concepts exist elsewhere; in fact many of the prayers of the Hopi Snake priests are in Keresan, which points to a close connection in some earlier time. In Keresan Sía there is a Snake society which holds four snake hunts a year. The society seems to have been divided into six for the directions, and probably the hunts were divided into at least four parts; as it is said that the serpents of the north and south have special influence with the cloud-people, while those of the east and west have great influence with the sun and moon. The serpent of the Zenith, "Hu'waka (Serpent of the Heavens) has a body like crystal, and it is so brilliant that one's eyes can not rest upon him; he is very closely allied to the sun."[33] The serpent of the Nadir is our own lowly friend who is closely associated with *Ha'arts*, the earth.

The snake order of the Sía Snake society practices curing in ceremonials which involve snake-handling, and lightning is again closely associated with the snake; but whether this is confined to the weather aspect of the bolt, as it seems to be now, or whether it once included war functions, is not clear. At present, there are only two societies from which women are excluded: the Snake and the Cougar, the latter being for hunting and war. The prayers of this Sía Snake society are very similar, whether they are intended for curing or for weather control. The rain song is addressed to the trees of the cardinal points, while that for curing invokes the animals of the six directions, that they may be present.

Stevenson translates the Snake prayer for rain as follows: "Hennati, white floating masks, behind which the cloud people pass about over ti'ni'a for recreation; He'ash, masks like the plains, behind

[33] Stevenson, "The Sia," *loc. cit.*, 69.

which the cloud people pass over ti'ni'a to water the earth; Purtu-wishta, lightning people; Kowmots, thunder people; Kashtiarts, rainbow people; Ka-chard, rain."[34] The last word, she adds, is an emphatic invocation to the rulers of the cloud-people.

The Snake Myth

The Hopi Snake myth is presumed to be told as an explanation for their ceremony, but it is a much broader myth. A very similar story is told at Zuñi—and also by the Navahos. Seemingly, it is a broad mosaic, or perhaps one should say the beginning of an epic, in which many stories are combined, a fact which explains the overlapping of this myth with some others, particularly those concerning the War Twins.

The myth centers on a youth of high standing who is skeptical of the care of the gods for mankind. Let us call this youth by his Hopi name, Ti'yo. He is standing on the banks of a great river (often the Grand Canyon) wondering where all the water goes. Ti'yo assumes that it flows into the great underworld pool of water. One will remember at this point that Shipapu was often thought of as brimming with water. A part of the youth's wonder about the care of the gods, and as to where the water goes, involves a search for the sources of life and the dangerous passage to discover the truth. He will return as a hero, bringing confirmation of the gods' care, and authentication for the sacred ceremonies.

At the end of his journey he meets the Sun god and a goddess. The latter may be either Huruing Wuhti, Hard Beings Woman, or Spider Grandmother. The reason for the variance is that the Spider Woman is the ancient of the Flute society—which joins with the Snake in the ceremony under discussion—and when a member of that society tells the story he uses his own patroness.

Water is one of the sources of life, and its source is something of a mystery. Sometimes the issue is that simple. The people had just emerged, there was little rain, the corn was poor; in that condition they watched all that water going away and none coming back and so

[34] *Ibid.,* 123.

Ti'yo must find out. Sometimes he is presented as something of a Hamlet: "He seemed to be always melancholy and thoughtful, and was wont to haunt the edge of the cliffs. All day he would sit there, gazing down in the deep gorge, and wondering where the ever-flowing water went."[35]

The youth makes the trip down the great river in a hollow cottonwood log which is sealed with pitch. After passing numerous hazards his log runs aground and he is freed by the Snake Virgin. His experience at the end of the river varies, except that he always sleeps with the goddess there, or with the Snake Virgin.

"After a while he came to a place where the river widened very much. His boat ran ashore and he could not get it afloat anymore. So he opened it, got out, and saw that there was land, and also much water—the ocean. He also found many people living there. At one place he saw a hill out in the water. That was the House of Huruing Wuhti, the deity of such hard substances as beads, shells, coral, turquoise, etc. Presently a maiden approached him that was very pretty." She took him to a transparent island in the sea where there was a kiva in which there were Snake men. He gave them some prayer-feathers. That night he slept with the maiden and in the morning all the men had turned into rattlesnakes. They told him not to be afraid and all went out to drink the morning light. "When they returned to the kiva they were men again."[36]

Sometimes Hard Beings Woman calls him to the island and rolls a ball of cornmeal across the water for him to walk on; he meets the Sun, takes a journey around the world with him, and then sleeps the night with the earth goddess, in return for which he gets a bag containing all kinds of beads and shells. Naturally there are often monsters to be overcome, such as bears or lions which guard the island kiva and must be overcome with the aid of Spider Woman's magic. The most interesting of these is himself a snake, an unfriendly monster called Gatoya. "This mythic snake is also said to exist at the present time in far-off mountains, and is described as being not quite

[35] Jesse W. Fewkes, "The Snake Ceremonials at Walpi," *Journal of American Ethnology and Archaeology*, Vol. IV (1894), 107.

[36] Voth, *The Oraibi Summer Snake Ceremony*, 349.

so long as a Man's body. It has large eyes and great teeth, which can pierce the thickest buckskin; its body is gray and its head of all colors, and it can breathe death to a man at a distance. It is spoken of as the angry guardian of all snakes."[37] The most curious thing about this dragon is his name; it is simply the Keresan name for the Horned Water Serpent. All the monsters are overcome.

Hard Beings Woman has two natures: she is a withered hag by day and a beautiful maid at night. (The Sun outshines her beauty during the day, and her charms are only beads and shell and turquoise, which do not compare). "At sundown she went into a side chamber and returned a very pretty maiden with fine buffalo and wildcat robes, of which she made a bed, and after having fed him, invited him to sleep with her on the bed. Then Spider Woman whispered he should comply with her request, then he would win her favor and get the beads."[38]

Ti'yo's return journey is not the one of triumph one might expect. He has discovered that the Sun does count the prayer-sticks offered to him and has won the favor of the goddess, but the water motif is lost. He is given a snake virgin for a wife, and a sack of beads which will multiply so long as he obeys two proscriptions: not to open the sack, nor to sleep with his wife. When the bag is full he opens the sack despite his wife's warning (snakes are guardians) and loses all but the original beads—which accounts for the poverty of the Hopis in jewelry. When he sleeps with his wife, the offspring are actual serpents who bite the children of the Hopis, and are thus unwanted.

Into this scant outline may be placed almost any story the teller wishes to insert. Some are logical—the danger of the snake offspring causes the first Hopi migrations, or the supernatural derivation of the Snake society from those who could actually turn into snakes and back into men again—but many are scarcely related bits from general mythology.

At Zuñi the same mechanism is used, but the story is heliocentric. In the Hopi accounts just given, the role of the sun was not em-

[37] Fewkes, "The Snake Ceremonials at Walpi," *loc. cit.*, 110n.
[38] Voth, *The Traditions of the Hopi*, 33.

phasized, as it is in the role he plays with Hard Beings Woman, both in creation and in his daily journey. The Zuñi myth relates to the village of Hawikuh, where Coronado opened the historic age of the Pueblos. The young man, a mortal son of the Sun, wants to know if the Sun picks up the prayer-feathers offered to him. His journey to the west must have been long, for he would have to go down the Zuñi River to the Little Colorado, and then down that river to the junction of the Colorado.

The youth's log runs aground, and he is trapped inside for several days. Then a rattlesnake girl who was gathering pollen nearby rescues him and takes him to her people. They make him a snakeskin boat and he reaches his destination. The old woman here is called the Sun's grandmother. His trip through the sky is rather like Hardy's Dynasts, since they look down upon battles and those about to die. The narrative may be skipped to the point where the youth marries Rattlesnake Girl: "He went back to his home. Rattlesnake Girl hung her shirt on the wall. She was a beautiful young woman. He had intercourse with her and her snake skin dropped off and hit the floor. It made itself two heads and hung itself up again. In a year she had two snake babies. She swelled and was sick. She did not recover. They said, 'She must join the Rattlesnake Society.' So she was cured."

The youth in this version fares quite well in that he is made Pekwin, or deputy to the Sun father, but the maid is again expelled. Her snake babies played with the Zuñi children and bit them. "People in too great numbers became sick and the Sun said, 'It is best for the rattlesnake children not to live in Zuñi' . . . and they sent Rattlesnake Girl and the two rattlesnake children out of the village." The sister of the youth went to the Snake Place and lived there four years, after which she returned to Zuñi and cured sick people.

The snakes themselves are particularly adept at curing people dying of witchery. As this story ends the sister is in that predicament. "From Snake Place Rattlesnake Chief came. He came down the ladder and crawled across the heads of all the people who were dancing there. He came to the sick girl. She was hardly breathing. He sucked the sickness out of her heart. He started back across the heads of the people. The witch who had used her power to kill the sick girl hid her head, but the snake coiled about her neck and killed her."[39]

The Horned Water Serpent

The snakes that have been considered so far have varying degrees of supernatural power, but never a fixed personality. Horned Water Serpent is based upon many of the same associations of snakes, but has in addition a definable personality as a god. To begin with, he is not an ordinary snake, but a monster with bulging eyes and a horn, to say nothing of a fan of feathers or fur. He is also specialized as the god of waters, which, among the Hopis, Zuñis, and most of the Keres, is not associated with disastrous floods, but with fertility and longevity. Hence we find that the Horned Water Serpent is a kindly and often even a comic god.

The Plumed Serpent of Mexico, *Quetzalcoátl*, is so well known that the possible relationship between the two snake gods must be settled, lest the reader carry a false image in his mind. At most the two gods were distantly related by belonging to the general family of snake gods. The Plumed Serpent, at least in his final form, was a god of civilization, or wisdom, or culture, while the Pueblo Horned Water Serpent is not even a culture-hero, which is a likely first step toward becoming the symbol of a whole culture.

It should also be remembered that there was no one Great Snake god in the Mexican cultures; behind, or beside, *Quetzalcoátl* were other serpent divinities. There was *Xiuhcoátl*, or Fire Snake, who had a cult and a feather. Among earth goddesses there was Serpent Woman, *Cihuacoátl*, ruler of childbirth and death, and *Coatlicue*, Serpent Skirt, associated with spring—an association familiar to the Pueblos. *Chicomecoátl*, or Seven Snake, is obscure to me; but it is not surprising to find Cloud Serpent, *Mixcoátl*, God of Stars and numbers, and a war god, under the synonym *Camaxtli*. Out of these possibilities of snake symbolism, the Mexican Plumed Serpent rose to great place in the pantheon.

The Horned Water Serpent was neither mighty nor dreadful.

[39] Benedict, *Zuñi Mythology*, II, 66–67.

There is a delightful tale concerning the size of the Serpent. He and Coyote lived nearby. "They were still young, but the Water Serpent was already very long so that when he visited the Coyote and coiled up in his kiva he filled the entire kiva."[40] The Coyote freezes while the two talk. For vengeance, he builds himself a long tail of cedar bark, and invites the Serpent to visit him. The Serpent sees the ruse and kicks the tail over the fireplace. On his way home Coyote sees a fire behind him, and assumes the Hopis are burning grass. As he gets to the timber he sees another fire raging, and assumes that they are pursuing him; he flees to the Little Colorado, jumps in, and drowns.

That fable is hardly justified in a discourse on the gods, except that it illustrates how little of the awesome dragon there is in the Horned Water Serpent. There is an exception, however. As the god of waters, he is the god of floods and landslides, if not of the earthquakes and volcanoes that occur to the south. Floods are not a problem to most of the villages studied in this book, since only three Keres towns are directly on the Río Grande, but other Pueblo groups have stronger associations of the Horned Water Serpent with damaging floods and a punitive nature. It will be recalled that the monster who guarded the mouth of the river in one Snake myth was called Gatoya (the Keresan name for Water Serpent), and it was added that he still lives in some far away hills, which is to say the Río Grande. The northern Tewas, as well as the Tiawas of Isleta, are subject to ugly floods; their name for the Serpent is Avaiyo. The First Mesa Hopis, who are not only in no danger from floods, but are dependent on floodwater farming from small washes, invoke Avaiyo for flooding rains.[41]

The Hopi name for the Horned Water Serpent is Palulukong and his counterpart at Zuñi is Kolowisi. Under either name he is celebrated in a most unusual way. While most gods are represented by masks, the Horned Water Serpent is represented by an effigy, a mechanical contrivance reminding one somewhat of a small-sized Chinese dragon. Among the Hopis a special fertility ceremony, called the Palulukonti, is held in February-March, in which these effigies

[40] Voth, *The Traditions of the Hopi*, 184ff.
[41] Parsons, *A Pueblo Indian Journal*, 56–57.

play a major part. The kivas are filled with imitation cornfields sprouted from clay pedestals.

The relevant part of the ceremony, as described by Fewkes, is as follows: "A hoarse roar made by a concealed actor blowing through an empty gourd resounded from behind the screen, and immediately the circular discs swung open upward, and were seen to be flap hinged above [the discs are Sun symbols], covering orifices through which simultaneously protruded six artificial heads of serpents, realistically painted. Each head had protruberant goggle-eyes and bore a curved horn and a fan-like crest of hawk feathers. A mouth with teeth was cut in one end, and from this orifice there hung a strip of leather painted red, representing the tongue.

"Slowly at first, but afterwards more rapidly, these effigies were thrust farther into view, each revealing a body four or five feet long, painted like the head, black on the back and white on the belly. When they were fully extended, the song grew louder, and the effigies moved back and forth, raising and depressing their heads in time, wagging them to one side or the other in unison. They seemed to bite ferociously at each other . . . . It was observed that the largest effigy, that in the middle, had several udders on each side of the belly, and that she apparently suckled the others."[42]

The central and largest serpent is equipped with eight mammae which are made of skin stuffed with all seeds. "Cotton, melon, watermelon, gourd, sweet corn, seeds of all these and corn kernels are in the paps of the effigy of the mother Pa'lulukonuh."[43]

Thus the largest effigy of the Horned Water Serpent is female. On either side of her are two small ones which are referred to as babies, and beyond them are three effigies of male serpents. The fertility mimetically invoked here seems to be that of the earth. There is an extension of rites, both among Hopis and Zuñis, which consists in the "nursing" of the snakes by a woman, or more precisely by a man imitating a woman. The Hopi figure is Hahai Wuhti, who is the mother of all kachinas, and obviously of serpent representations as well.

"When all is ready, those in front begin another Pa'lulukon song

[42] Fewkes, "Hopi Katcinas," *loc. cit.*, 41.   [43] Stephen, *Hopi Journal*, I, 300.

and at the first note all the six serpents are thrust through the six circular sun designs . . . . Then Hahai'wuqti who stands with a basket of prayer-meal . . . passes along in front of the projecting, moving serpents and stooping down holds her breast to each, and each serpent in turn lays its lips against the mammae, imitating the action of a mother suckling a child, for she is their mother. She is the mother (maternal ancestor) of all kachina . . . .

"Hahai'wuqti, having passed across the curtain suckling the serpents, once or twice, passes across again, holding the basket of meal before each serpent, and each of them dips its head in the basket as if eating the meal offered. This is the food offering; during it she blesses the serpents in her customary shrill falsetto."[44]

Thereafter a smoke is held to ask Cloud to send lightning. Palulukong is effective since he is the pet animal of Cloud. It may be noted that the altar and screen used in this ceremony have representations of the war god, but lightning and the snakes are predominantly directed toward fertility.

At Zuñi the effigies are less complex mechanically, but Kolowisi is also attended by a female kachina whose name this time is Ahe'a. The rite is even more abstracted from any phallic magic than is the Hopi ceremony just described. In the former the emergence of the snakes from Sun symbols, and their presumed entry into the underworld with all the seeds to make the earth fertile, is certainly a lightly emphasized phallic parallel, comparable perhaps to the many creation myths which tell of the coupling of sky and water. To be sure Kolowisi is at times purely a simple sexual symbol. For example, a girl who dips too deeply in the spring, which is a hallowed place, will be magically impregnated by the Serpent and will be taken off by him.[45] The story is largely an excuse for a necessary taboo.

In the rite where the Serpent is nursed by Ahe'a, the emphasis is all on the desire for long life for one's children, which is a considerable extension of simple potency. With the Zuñi flare for the dramatic, the rite has been made into a complex tableau on the misery and grandness of old age. There are two initiations at Zuñi, and Kolowisi and Ahe'a do not appear in the one pertaining to adulthood, but in a

[44] *Ibid.*, I, 306.   [45] Benedict, *Zuñi Mythology*, I, 312.

very early one when the child is from three to six years old.

The drama begins out in the open. Instead of a screen there is a large portable tablet with a hole for Kolowisi's head and a crown of cloud terraces. This tablet is carried by two men who bring it into town. Beside them walk two men carrying spruce trees, doubtless symbolizing evergreen life, but as stage props they conceal the manipulator of the Serpent effigy and hide the shell trumpet which is blown at intervals. Several of the gods accompany the procession, including the great god Pautiwa, and the Salimobias who are the warriors and seed-gatherers of the six directions. They carry yucca whips of both symbolic and practical value. A Hopi woman explained them to me with candor as "policeman kachina."

The gods drink spring water, after which they indulge in a brief war ceremony; they break a great deal of pottery, crying "death to the Navaho" and setting fire to baskets, mimetically burning the Navaho camp.

Kolowisi's coming is announced by a trick bird fetish manipulated by a cord, so that he seems to run back and forth on a pole projecting from the kiva, while a shrill whistle, concealed, makes the chirps and warbles that announce the event. The Serpent is a single figure, about five feet long. The child's initiation has two phases, one of which is the ceremonial whipping that is a part of all initiations.

"The child, who is carried on the back of his godfather, wears a cotton shirt and two blankets, and is held on the back by two additional blankets and a piece of canvas which takes the place of the bison robes used in olden times. As the godfathers pass before the gods the children are struck four times by each god with bunches of giant yucca."[46]

While Kolowisi is simpler mechanically than his Hopi counterpart, he has more realistic touches. Water from the sacred spring is poured into him from a gourd and spurts from his mouth; seeds also are poured through him and children are given the impression that grass from the spring likewise comes from him. A portion of these talismans are collected in a bowl and given to the initiate by the godfather. The water is drunk at home by his family and sprinkled on

[46] Stevenson, "*The Zuñi Indians,*" loc. cit., 99.

248

their stacked corn, and the grasses are laid there. The seeds are planted apart in the fields, as they have a special power.

The central theme of the ceremony is long life for the children, to which the Serpent brings his special, life-giving powers. The young are whipped on to maturity and old age. In this process the nurse of Kolowisi plays as important a part as he does. She belongs in the realm of the dead; she is an old hag who cooks for the gods, but since she is a careful nurse to the Serpent, she will not stay behind when he is carried into Zuñi.

Because she is valuable as a cook, the gods do not want her to leave the Lake of the Dead: "They never let her come to Itiwana [Zuñi], and so she just stays there and cooks for them. She is very poor looking, she has no pretty dress and her hair is all tangled, and so they never want her to come. Still she wants to come. So this time Kaklo said, 'No, you must not go. You cannot go there. You are too old. And all our young ones look so pretty. You will disgrace them. We do not want you to go with all the pretty young ones.' But she did not want her child to go without her. She is the nurse of Kolowisi, and so she wanted to go with him." Though she is left behind, she escapes, and Pautiwa relents. "She will go there and give my people long life, so that they may grow old as she is."[47]

As this tragicomic figure walks along with buckling knees and tufts of white goat's wool for hair she constantly cries out, "Ahe'a, Ahe'a—Oh dear! Oh dear!" The less pleasant side of age is faced squarely, but one wants, nonetheless, a long life for the children and this the Horned Water Serpent and his nurse can provide. Since she has escaped from the Lake of the Dead, there is nearly a suggestion of the Serpent as a symbol of immortality, but that far the Pueblos did not go.

[47] Bunzel, "Zuñi Katcinas," *loc. cit.*, 968–88.

Chapter Twelve

THE FACE OF ANIMISM

Shulawitsi, the Zuñi firebrand-youth

ACCORDING TO the dictionary definition, animism is the belief that all objects possess a natural life or vitality, or are endowed with indwelling souls. To this it adds the possibilities that each object may have a conscious life and that the soul may be capable of a life outside the object. To that classic picture one may add the popular conviction that the world of animism is pantheistic. In order to face Pueblo animism honestly we must qualify and particularize general views. Since this book is concerned with gods—or rather with supernatural powers—it is necessary to distinguish between such powers, however small, and mere consciousness. It is also necessary to examine again man's place in the cosmos—world order, or harmony.

Let us begin with a simple statement of Pueblo animism: "To the Zuñi the whole world appears animate. Not only are night and day, wind, clouds and trees possessed of personality, but even articles of human manufacture, such as houses, pots, and clothing, are alive and sentient. All matter has its inseparable spiritual essence. For the most part this spiritual aspect of things is vague and impersonal."[1]

While that statement is true, it leaves out a number of concepts. To begin with, everyone will agree that living things are alive and that they, along with non-organic phenomena, possess "personality," which is to say, changing conformation, response to stimuli, and the like, and changes, including dissolution, which are easily equated in the human mind with one's own vital element. There is also a contemporary scientific point of view that grants considerable life to inorganic matter. The biologist Sir Charles Sherrington wrote: "Natural science has studied life to the extent of explaining away life as any radically separate category of phenomena. The categories of living

[1] Bunzel, "Introductions to Zuñi Ceremonialism," *loc. cit.*, 483.

and lifeless as regards science disappear." Or again: "The distinction between them is convention. This deletes 'life' as a scientific category; or, if you will, carries it down to embrace the atom. The vanishing point of life is lost."[2]

In this sense all matter has an inseparable scientific essence, if not a spiritual one. In the Pueblo universe there is a harmony of the whole, which will appear often in this chapter, and toward the end of this chapter Pueblo views will be considered in relation to various contemporary attitudes in Western thought. First, however, we need to understand the Pueblo view. Pueblos are not pantheists in either a mystical or in a scientific sense; their gods stand apart from the physical and biological world and have considerable, if variable, power to influence the course of events.

A related, if lesser, power resides in many insensate things, as well as in animals and men, but it by no means has an equal distribution throughout the world. Some things have special power, otherwise any object would do for a fetish; not every mountain is equally powerful. To learn of this supernatural power, and it limitations, let us examine a tree, an artifact, a stone, and an animal.

When a dance is to be held, one of the most frequent essentials for the dancers is a collar of spruce twigs, whether the dancers be masked or not. The spruce, which is actually Douglas fir, is the directional tree of the north for all three tribes. That is the region from which winter storms come, and the tree hence has a rain bringing potential at any season. The Zuñi name for this tree is translated "water comes out arms." "The breath from the gods of the undermost world is supposed to ascend through the trunks of these trees and form clouds behind which the rain-makers work."[3]

When the branches of this tree are to be gathered its blessing, or

---

[2] William K. C. Guthrie, *In the Beginning*, 19, 46.

[3] See M. C. Stevenson, "Ethnobotany of the Zuñi Indians," B.A.E. *Thirteenth Annual Report* (1908–1909), 97. According to Stephen, *Hopi Journal*, I, 395, "The spruce boughs gathered for kachina purposes in the spring of the year, if of glossy green, betoken absence of bad winds and that rains will prevail in the summer. If the spruce is dull (ma'si), it is an evil prognostication."

power, must be sought. When the people of Keresan Santa Ana and San Felipe need spruce boughs, men are selected to ride up into the Jémez or the Sandía Mountains. (Hopis go to the San Francisco Mountains.) They take with them prayer-feather bunches, one of which is to be planted for the spirits of the mountains, since there they are losing a part of themselves. These spirits do not seem to be particularized, or even localized. It is not surprising to learn that one Acomite opined that even an airplane could be considered as belonging to this friendly group of spirits. Not just any tree, but a suitable tree must be found. The gatherers from San Felipe carry turkey feathers wrapped in corn husks, and when the right tree has been located, "the feather-bearer approaches. After praying, he climbs as high as he can and ties one of the feathers to the highest point: 'that brings out the rain and the Shiwannas from the mountains.' " After this rite the feather bearer and the other gatherers take as many branches as are needed.

The one who "plants" the feathers on the tree top is the war priest's helper. An idea of the content of his prayer comes from the pueblo of Santa Ana. When he alone approaches the spruce tree: "He says, in effect, 'Let the ianyi (power, blessing) of the spirits go to the pueblo with the spruce boughs; let them send rain on the 26th to the growing crops all over the world.'"[4] Other feathers are planted in the ground with their tips facing back toward the village.

Ianyi, somewhat similar to the word mana, which has become general in our language, is interestingly translated as both power and blessing. Blessing implies that the power has to some extent separated itself from that in which it resides and tends toward the pueblo. The branches here seem to be the bearers of the power, and they are special, because they have been selected as a medium of communication between the spirits and man. There is no concept of the tree as an independent, personified, spirit, such as a Dryad who can slip out of the form of the tree which incases it. As a qualification, there are personifications in the Pueblo spirit world: "Salt Old Woman, giver of herself," and the Hopi *chama'hia* or Stone people. These are celts

[4] Leslie A. White, *The Pueblo of San Felipe*, 37, and White, *The Pueblo of Santa Ana*, 248.

said to have been left from the days when stones had speech, and life, and traveled about the world.

Stones have a particular power. In the first chapter the boundary stone was discussed in relation to Masau'u. The Zuñis, who have no such god, likewise set up crudely sculptured columnar stones to mark the fields they have cleared. Even after the field is abandoned, and after the death of one who has cleared it, these stones protect and assert the right of his clan to the land. The protective power of this stone may be personified in the form of an animal, in which case it indicates the reverse value of the stone fetish carried by a hunter.

Another type of stone, which is to become a household utensil, is cut out of the mother rock in secrecy, and apparently with more elaborate ritual and taboo than in the cutting of spruce boughs. The grinding-stone is the central piece of household equipment and making one is not to be taken lightly. A special priest supervises the work in the field. It is likely that cooking stones are made at the same time, since one reaction of a stone to improper procedure is to crack upon first heating. Not only must the newly made artifact be treated properly to appease its spirit, but the rock from which it was cut has to be considered. "When cutting out mealing-stones they make prayers and cast meal to the 'flesh of the rock.' "[5] The prayer is not to the soul or spirit, but to the substance; the harmony—or perhaps one should say the *status quo*—of the Pueblo world has been disturbed, and amends must be made lest this small change effect greater changes.

The power involved in both the boundary stone and in cutting the rock might be called negative power, since the wish is to maintain things as they are, or restore them to what they had been but a short time before. On the other hand, an artifact, or even a part of one, may also have positive power, as this note from Keresan Laguna shows. "To cure childhood illnesses, a reliable medicine consists of potsherds gathered from old ruins, ground fine, and drunk in water. The sherds are impregnated with power because they were made in one of the four epochs of the distant past, in each of which people were created by 'Our Mother' but later destroyed (not having proved entirely satisfactory), and replaced by a presumably better group.

[5] Cushing, *Zuñi Breadstuff*, 328.

This series of creations, incidentally, explains the presence of many old ruins scattered throughout the Southwest."[6]

Like the spruce tree, the broken pottery seems to be but the vehicle by means of which the power, in this case of "Our Mother" Iyatiku, is brought to the people.

The powers of animals and insects have been alluded to in previous chapters, but their special tie with breath in both animate and inanimate objects is worth a further note. The Zuñi word *pinnanne* means "breath," or "life." The breath of life is a very general concept and the act of inhaling or exhaling, no matter what the object consists of, transfers some of its *ianyi*, to use the Keresan word, to the recipient. How broadly the word can be used is shown in a Zuñi chant addressed by a "long horn bow priest." After asking for the expected life-giving breath and the breath of age the priest goes on to beseech:

> his water breath
> his seed breath
> his clothing breath
> his offspring breath
> his power breath
> his spirit strong breath
> his everything good luck breath.[7]

If the object is an animal, his breath is literally inhaled. Cushing, when describing a rabbit hunt in which he took part, describes the mortal event this way: "Before he was fairly dead, the Indians drew his face up to their own and breathed from his nostrils the last faint sighs of his expiring breath."[8] The rabbits involved were not mighty symbols, like the lion of the north, nor the spruce tree of the same direction, but lowly, indiscriminate victims of the most commonplace hunt, and yet each one of them has a power worth preserving and incorporating into one's self.

[6] F. H. Ellis, "The Woman's Page: Laguna Pueblo," *El Palacio*, Vol. LXVI, No. 1 (1959), 18–19.

[7] Bunzel, "Zuni Ritual Poetry," *loc. cit.*, 755. See also S. Newman, *A Practical Zuñi Orthography*, 167.

[8] Cushing, *Zuñi Breadstuff*, 592.

Likewise one breathes in from prayer-feathers, but the process may also be reversed, and the participant then breathes upon the meal which is about to be cast, or upon the sacrosant corn ear. Sometimes the breath is made visible by the blowing of tobacco smoke. The exhaling of one's vital element often signifies not only a wish, or a prayer that this power should be returned in kind, but it may also indicate an expectation that the power will be magnified. When a child is sick the Pueblo doctor gives it an herb broth, but he also breathes toward it, and on a feather which he waves toward the sick one. As a doctor, he has special powers on which he can call, and these are related to the general fund of supernatural power which abounds in the world. Before considering these powers as they exist in mankind, let us take another glance at the relationship between men and animals, in this case large game.

For the hunter of large game—deer, elk, mountain sheep, bear, and at one time buffalo—one necessity is a stone fetish which gives him special power. Although he may carve this himself, it gets its power (at Acoma) by standing near greater fetishes which are in the charge of the hunt society.[9] Presumably these in turn get their particular virtue from the animals themselves. It is interesting that the fetish may represent either the beasts of prey or the intended victim. I have in front of me a turquoise crudely carved to represent a mountain sheep. The implication seems to be that the consent of both the hunters and the hunted are necessary.

When an Acomite kills a deer, he first takes out the heart, and the fetish is made to drink the blood from that organ. The animal is cut up so that the head, backbone, and skin are all of one piece. On this the hunter sprinkles cornmeal, bits of bead, and shell, and prays that the animal be reborn. When the deer is brought home there are further ceremonies. They welcome him, and say that they are glad he has come and has "not been ashamed of our people." Meal is placed nearby and all visitors feed a little to the dead animal. His spirit is supposed to leave in about an hour.

The rebirth of the animal refers both to his spirit and to his physical body. The townspeople want him to come again and bring his or her

[9] Stirling, *Origin Myth of Acoma*, 22–25.

body to feed them. He came because he was not ashamed to visit these people. The spirit side must also be placated. Somewhere in the mountains, there is a greater deer spirit whose power has been damaged to some extent, and an element of disorder thus introduced into the world. Beads are hung about the deer's neck; they make the dead body beautiful, and as they are similar to the horn of his hooves, they will lead him back. After his spirit has left, the beads are blown into another room, and the men begin to skin the animal.

Again, as in the case of the mealing stone, the power which has been disturbed must be considered, but it is not an angry power, and when treated well it will give itself again and again. Because of this concept the prayer is addressed to the flesh of the rock, rather than to a spirit behind it; and the same deer may be born many times over and still bring his flesh to the pueblo.

While the Pueblos have been successful in civilizing the supernatural powers which lie outside of their communities—by agreeing that men and the infinitude of lesser spirits can live together happily on terms of mutual respect and gratitude, without undue anxiety, so long as the rules are observed—there is another realm of minor supernatural power that is more difficult to control. Men, or at least some men and women, are possessed by or possessed with supernatural power. Either of these phrases suggests that what we are calling supernatural power or spirit is capable of transitory behavior. The power, or part of it, may leave its normal seat and take up residence elsewhere. A few examples from more familiar cultures may clarify the phenomena.

In the Christian Eucharist the assumption is that the participant has taken unto himself not only the blood and flesh of Christ, but something of his divine power as well. He does this of his own volition, or he may refuse the bread and the cup for any of a number of reasons. In certain cases, the same idea is expressed, but the voluntary element is lost. The person is said to be possessed by the spirit of Christ, to the point where his own vital element has been put out. He may "speak in tongues," roll on the floor, dance, or merely shake. Whatever the psychological implications, the individual and his associates believe that he has been completely possessed by the god. In Greece the same experience gave rise to mantic prophets and to the earlier Dionysiac rites.

In all of these instances the individual, or group, is possessed by the supernatural spirit. The logical alternative to possession of the body by a supernatural is the abandonment of the body by its spirit, which seeks to join some divinity, or the collectivity of supernatural powers.

The Pueblos recognized all of these possibilities, but held their expression to an admirable mean: nothing too much. The pendulum of their thinking passed twice across the middle before it tended to either extreme. The impulse to abandon one's own body and join the individual spirit with a larger spirit world is recognized. It has been mentioned that the living were attracted toward their kindred dead, but that is an impulse to be allayed, not sought.

On the other hand, one may ask divine power to join with one. The most familiar example is that of the masked kachina dancer. During the time in which the mask is worn, it is thought that the god or spirit whom the mask represents actually dwells within the dancer. That power is extremely transitory since, once the mask is set aside, the man who wore it loses that specific power.

At Santo Domingo the question of transitory powers is neatly distinguished by the words *gainat*, *crutsi*, and *sicti*. The *gainat* have supernatural power; their number is made up of medicine men, the clowns, and all the officers of the pueblo. It is notable, however, that the officers have power only so long as they hold office, which in most cases is one of limited or at least interrupted tenure, so that the indwelling virtue actually pertains to the office rather than to the individual. It is illustrative of Pueblo equalitarianism that *all* officers are *gainat*; not only the medicine man, who obviously needs supernatural power for his work, but also the ditch-boss (whom one might think would only need a crew with shovels), since he is working with the sources of life. The *crutsi* are ordinary people in whom power is not lodged continuously, but only upon special occasions, such as a rite in which they have particular functions.

The *sicti*, or *hanno sicti*, are the common people who neither possess nor are ordinarily possessed by supernatural power. The common man of Pueblo society is a lesser reflection of the lot of his society as a whole. The physical world which surrounds the handful of people is intractable, and the spirit world with which he must also come to terms is powerful. To make his way, and in the past this way was very short, perhaps thirty-five years, within his physical world and the spirits who stand within or beyond it, he has a minimum of supernatural power at his disposal. There were fetishes to aid him in hunting and war. There were also the officers, priests, and doctors who were ready to intervene between either divine powers or simple spirits and the individual who weakly faced the world. Even the common man also had available the power, however small, possessed by a ritual prayer, the casting of meal and the important corn ear fetish, the Iarriko, which represented the heart of his own life.

There is another kind of supernatural power which may be possessed by a number of people; it is a negative power exercised for malevolent ends. Witches and Two-Hearts have such a power. They and their power are transitory, first in that they may take the form of an animal to conceal their evil work, and second, they may possess their prey. Most often, this possession by the witch takes the form of illness in the victim, as in the story of the snake's revenge in the last chapter. Another common type of possession is the production of sexual passion in the unwilling victim of the witch, who may be of either sex.

It has been argued that these witches may have been of European origin, but I doubt that. They are an almost inevitable alternative to those supernatural powers that work for man's good. One signal difference between European-American witchcraft and that of the Pueblos is that the supernatural power in the latter instance is not derived from daemons or a devil. Of European witchcraft Kittredge says: "The idea of a formal compact with Satan, which plays so important a part in the history of witchcraft, was supported by great fathers of the church."[10] The Pueblos had no evil god, although the Zuñis' Knife-Wing is nominated by some students for such a role.

[10] G. L. Kittredge, *Witchcraft in Old and New England*, 239.

258

Knife-Wing is a beast of prey, an eagle, and a war spirit and as such will certainly take a scalp—of the enemy. He will also steal a maiden, but in neither case is he an objectified enemy of mankind.

The power a Pueblo witch uses is very simple personal magic and may even be used for a kind of good in hunting or war. "A handsome boy caught more rabbits than his friend, who was a witch. The latter was jealous and asked the hunter to divide his catch. He refused, giving him only one rabbit. Next day the false friend bewitched him, taking away his luck in hunting, and then suggested a plan by which they might get many rabbits. He made a magic hoop of a pine bough and when they passed through it they became coyotes and caught many rabbits."[11] The evil lies in the fact that the witch then jumped back through the hoop and became a man again while his companion remained a coyote and was chased by the dogs.

Neither are the Pueblo witches disassociated evil sprites like the Greek Erynies who may swarm up from the underworld to plague or avenge men; they are simply ordinary humans who possess a special degree of supernatural power and direct it toward antisocial ends.

By this point in the book I think the supernatural world of the Pueblos has been surveyed at least roughly, sometimes by compass only, but at other times the chains went rod by rod. In the second half of this chapter, the Pueblo world will be faced toward several different strains of thinking in the Western world of this century. First, however, a short résumé of the animistic and god-filled Pueblo world may be useful as a threshold for that discussion. The first writer on Pueblo religion, Castañeda, said that "what they most worship is rain." I think it would be safe to rephrase his words to read, "What they most worship is a rough harmony in their universe." As we have just seen, they did not deny the existence of evil which has a supernatural force, nor did they objectify it to the point where their world was torn by factions of the gods. They were never the warrior children of any great god. Strife on a large scale was recognized, and they fought; but it was disturbing to the normal order, and the first recourse was to various gods who might settle the problems in their

[11] Benedict, *Zuñi Mythology*, II, 286.

own way, notably not by the destruction of the enemy, but by a return to normal order. The war chief referred to in Chapter I asked the American cavalry to retire and not disturb the normal social processes of Hopi life. A Zuñi war chief, with less success, used a whistle—a clarion call to the supernaturals—which was supposed to disperse the Spanish military.

The great gods scarcely intervene in human affairs, or in the processes of nature on which man depends, in any way other than to assure the *status quo*. Masau'u merely told the Hopis that if they wished a meager life they could join him on his land. The prayers to the great Sun god are to the effect that the Sun continue his usual course; one wants a normal life span for his children and himself, and crops sufficient to maintain the family and the race. Thinking Woman of the Keres is a creatrix who is remote from living men.

In the animistic world the same situation pertains. Bunzel wrote of the Zuñis that, "In so far as all are harmonious parts of the whole, the surrounding forces sustain and preserve humanity in the status quo."[12] Abundance is not to be thought of, but the frugal relationship between man and nature must be preserved. The stripped tree, the cut stone, the slain deer, or the slain enemy are all disturbing events in an orderly world. Many rites and prayers are directed toward mending such interference on the part of men.

Many of the fertility gods and goddesses are likewise directed to the same end: normal crops, normal reproduction, and normal seasons. The divinities provide the first seeds, and then smile over the efforts of mankind. Even in what would seem to be the most notable exception, the rain dances, the bounty sought from the cloud spirits is not in contravention to the normal path of nature. The feeling seems to be that man has performed the rites and duties expected of him, and the cloud spirits should now do likewise.

The lesser gods do intervene in human affairs, or at least they did in mythical times. Spider Grandmother has enough cunning to influence even the will of the Sun, if need be. The War Twins are ever ready to help mankind. A beast-god can be taken either way. Bear has the power to cure, and it is hard to say whether this is stop-

[12] Bunzel, "Introduction to Zuñi Ceremonialism," *loc. cit.*, 486.

ping the normal course of nature which would result in recovery or death, or whether it is simply the restoration of the human body to its normal state.

Man is indeed the center of a supernatural universe in which all of the fragments are interrelated, but this anthropocentric arrangement is not a position of strength, but one of concern; hence most of the year is devoted to rites and ceremonies which protect mankind from any radical change in circumstances. That feeling exactly duplicates the physical situation of each individual town, which is but a minute dot in a vast and dangerous environment. Under such circumstances man is not likely to develop a grandiose view of himself and his position in the cosmos. He does not dominate the world around him; he is demonstrably weak, a huddle of a few families—and these may easily disappear, as he knows from the ruins of hundreds of vacant pueblos that dot the cliffs and mesas. In that world man is likely to regard himself as one of the least of beings, and his pueblo as comparable to an anthill scurrying with busy life.

"In this system the starting point is man, who is the lowest because the most dependent and the least mysterious. In just so far as an organism resembles man is it related to him. Insofar as it is mysterious, is it believed removed from man, further advanced and more holy.

"Thus animals, being mortal, are more nearly related to man than are gods, but the animal is more closely associated with deity than is man because the animal is mysterious and has powers not possessed by man. Dogs are less holy than snakes, because dogs are better understood by man and have more understanding of man, than do serpents. Elements and the phenomena of nature, because still more mysterious and powerful, are closer to the supreme beings than are either men or animals."[13]

Probably that statement could be modified to some extent, since Pueblo gods are not, or at least were not until recently, supreme in either the root sense of being "above"—except, of course, spirits of the Zenith—nor in the sense of holding power that can not be overruled. The gods are even capable of war among themselves, but most

[13] Kirk, *Introduction to Zuñi Fetishism*, 7–8.

commonly they are a part of an universal order. Man is not at the bottom of column, or ladder, as the least of all things, for the simple reason that the Pueblo world is multidimensional and extends in at least six directions. Animals are farther away than one's fellow human beings, and gods are more distant still; but all of these, and the phenomena of nature, are closely linked together. Man is neither the denizen of the lowest realm, nor an outcast, but one who resides in a center where down is as important as up and out; in every direction, there is a sounding board for the spiritual universe.

Posed at the beginning of this book was the question, "What is all this dancing about?" In seeking the answer, the point of view of the Pueblo Indian was the central focus. If the previous chapters have explained in interpretation based upon authentic Pueblo behavior, something of why and for whom the Pueblos dance, there still remains a question for those of us who are not Indians, and who at the same time do not choose to look upon these events and beliefs as mere pageantry.

Pueblo religion is very much alive in the twentieth century, as it will be in the next, which raises a second question: what does it mean to us? The most surprising thing is to discover that these cultures still exist in our midst; there is no chance for us to conjure up a golden age or a tropic paradise, nor is there any longer a possibility of wishing them brushed aside in a quest for land, minerals, oil, or any other sign of technological change. We must look a living culture in the face and ask, what does it mean to us?

The living Pueblo religion touches us on several intellectual levels. The concern of sociology and anthropology with this field is apparent from the titles in the bibliography. Much of the concern is merely descriptive, but sometimes it reaches the realm of speculative thought. Religious thought is active on a number of levels, from the ridiculous to the sublime. One religious approach will be of no concern here. The Pueblo world is ringed with those who by various methods would convert them to their own faiths. The Sunshine Baptists ask their converts to move down from the Mesa and abandon all elements of Hopi religion. The Catholic church has settled for only a most nominal allegiance from the Keres, although it has thoroughly absorbed the Tewa towns which are not many miles up river. The non-Christian Ba'hai advise the Hopis to keep their own religion, but to add a new prophet and his teachings to the foundation.

The Catholic Workers group has had some influence on the Hopis. Pueblos are good listeners, and up to a point very compliant, particularly when they already agree. A number of the Hopi Traditionalists are pacifists, and many others would be happy to cut any ties with "Washington." All of these alien religious groups will have some effect on Pueblo religion, either by attrition, by forcing a shift to secrecy, or by calling up a strong negative response.

The interrelationship of religious bodies on such a level is a matter of some interest, but of limited concern, since the dogmatist on any side is certain of his answer and that those who differ err. Consequently I will consider instead the views of a religious philosopher of great fame who may never have heard of the Pueblos: Martin Buber. Buber regarded animism as a most important step of mankind in a search for one God. As a counterbalance to that view, we will look at some of the opinions of Sigmund Freud, who was an atheist, although not a noisy one. To his mind animism was and is the infancy of mankind, a period of growth comparable to that of the individual life cycle, which man leaves behind as he matures. Both Freud and Buber were good students of ethnology, and based their conclusions on standard texts as well as upon their more personal views of man.

A third point of view on animism and its unfolding, and one which is certainly more widespread, holds that it reflects a stage in the development of society. At one time such a view was called "economic determinism," but I think the more comfortable and inclusive name would now be social determinism. Unfortunately no one writer embodies the social approach so neatly as Buber does the religious, and Freud the psychic, view of the place of animism in the life of men and man. Paul Radin is used here, since his book is readily available, and he presents his case schematically. Titiev's words that "the main purpose of Pueblo religion is to buttress the weakest part of their social system," and the viewpoint of Parsons, that it is science gone astray, are both part of the same attitude, even though they do not elaborate stages.

These three approaches to animism—religious, phychic, and social —(if I were a Pueblo I am sure I could find a fourth direction) are all based upon the same material. They agree in some respects, they overlap in others, and in some ways they are in hopeless contradiction. As a student rather than a teacher, I will only try to set the problems as clearly as I can grasp them. The question has shifted from "What is all this dancing about?" to "What is this thinking all about?" I have neither a choice among them, nor a synthesis of the three views. Any observations made along the way, even when presented as statements, should be taken as questions, not as conclusions.

All of these attitudes relate to man's relationship with the supernatural world, which stretches from minor spirits to gods both great and small. There is no doubt that mankind has had such a relationship, and that it is most often of primary importance, whether the phenomena be taken as a religious reality, a psychic reality, a social reality, or some combination of these.

A second point these views hold in common is a firm belief in some sort of evolutionary process tending toward a goal. With Buber the process, at times historical and at times individual, is the gradual unfolding of man's thorough perception of one God. To Freud the goal was the unfolding of a mature adult who recognizes and to some extent controls the fetters of his past. Many who uphold social determinism are committed to the goal of a more perfect society.

Possibly the evolutionary bias will prove to be the weakest point in all these views. (Some ancient philosophy and much of modern physics work from a different base than that which is made by analogy from biology.) The evolution assumed postulates a growth from the belief in scarcely differentiated spirits to belief in a number of well defined gods, and possibly the concentration of these into a single source and supreme power.

Let us first look at a few of Radin's statements. These from *Primitive Religion*—published in 1937—may reflect an extreme view of social determinism, deriving from the climate of the times in which they were written; and they are at odds with earlier works, such as *Monotheism Among Primitive Peoples*, where social causation is explicitly rejected. Nevertheless, these statements make a convenient

264

frame in which to place one picture of the relationship between animism and highly developed gods.

Put most baldly, his view states: "We cannot, in fact, insist too strongly upon the fact that totemic society had a broad, cooperative, and egalitarian base which militated very strongly against the type of individualism favorable to the development of clearcut deities. Only when special economic conditions developed—such as trade and a definite unit of exchange as found, for instance, among the Melanesian Trobriand Islanders and related tribes or on the northwest coast of Canada, with the attendant appearance of classes and castes—did the situation alter."[14]

Below this level of totemic beast-gods Radin recognizes animism, but not as a religion. Do not "all aboriginal peoples share the belief in an animated world? Is not animism their basic religion? To this we must reply that animism is not a religion at all; it is a philosophy. The belief in the general animation of nature has nothing to do with the supernatural." (I must say here that the last statement is too big a nut for this chipmunk to conceal in his cheek with any intent to swallow it.) "An object, animate or inanimate, derives its supernatural quality from its association with a number of distinct elements and from the transference to it of certain ideas, concepts and activities."[15]

When objects function as spirits, it is because the actor has acted upon them, through magic first, and also through the bond between the living and the dead, which sets up tensions which must be resolved. The fusion of these desires with the object—often through the catalyzing agency of the shaman—gives, through interaction, the quality of spirit to the object. This view is closely parallel to Freud's "omnipotence of thought" and to Buber's "Thou," and it seems to be innate in mankind rather than socially determined.

These spirits may combine with totemic gods and become "true gods," but not in a totemic society with its "emphasis on democracy." Radin postulates "the cult of the ancestors" as the most important at Zuñi, and to it all may belong, which makes it democratic and of "the

[14] Paul Radin, *Primitive Religion*, 215.
[15] *Ibid.*, 198.

most archaic stratum of beliefs." He then notes that the continuing existence of these ceremonies poses a political, if not economic, problem: "It was certainly not in the interests of these priests to allow a ceremony to flourish unhampered where individuals were permitted to establish a direct relationship with the supernatural world without priestly intermediation. It is not reasonable to suppose that even priests who, as Bunzel states, regarded themselves as 'too sacred to contaminate themselves with dispute or wrangling' would calmly allow so direct a challenge to their power and prestige." He believes that they must have compromised due to special economic-environmental causes or to some special and possibly some recent historical event.[16]

Radin grants the Zuñis clearly outlined deities, but not, I gather, "true deities." Of the Zuñi pantheon he states: "Where we find such a tremendous development of ritual, one would naturally expect the deities worshipped to be clearly outlined. This is precisely what one does find. The delineation, however, is not in terms of idols but in terms of masks, and principally in connexion with the *katchinas*." These he believes to be of late origin, and subject to strong Catholic influence. The Pueblo religion, he feels, was one of infinite complexity, "but one which had no conception or delineation of deities higher than that generally encountered in the normal totemistic cultures."[17]

Fortunately he defines "true deities and gods." Only "where supernatural spirits are fashioned into idols, and housed in special sacred structures, and have true theogonic myths connected with them, can it be claimed that they are true gods in the ordinarily accepted meaning of the word."[18]

In order to round out his conceptions, it is necessary to mention monotheism and the tendency to monotheism. For this one must fall back on early works. In his view monotheism is the product of exceptional thinkers who may appear in any age or society; it is the speculation of individuals who are not determined by either economic or social necessity, or even by historical progression, and yet both society and history play some part.

"It is true that the factors concerned in the complete credal triumph

[16] *Ibid.*, 236. [17] *Ibid.*, 238. [18] *Ibid.*, 246.

of monotheism in Judaism, Christianity, and Mohamedanism have never been satisfactorily explained, but they are emphatically of an individual, historical, and psychological nature. For myself, I am inclined to believe that the spread of monotheism is far more definitely a reflection of certain facts of a general sociological order than has hitherto been recognized. Certainly it has not been the triumph of the unifying principle over the disruptive, of abstract over concrete thought. Yet, on the other hand, there must be something subtly appealing in monotheism, for wherever it is found a definite influence is seen to be exercised over the thought of those who are stubborn polytheists and animists."[19]

I have not done justice to Radin's theories in this area, and it is unfair to extract bits from books written a decade or more apart, but they do set the stage. At its broadest reach the question is one of man's relationship with the supernatural world. All of history attests to the indubitable fact that there has been such a relationship, and that it is often intense, either in individuals or in a society as a unit. The reality or non-reality of any supernatural world is not a valid question in this study.

While Radin frequently disclaims evolutionary theories, he seems to have one. He postulates for Zuñi an archaic strata of ancestor worship, then perhaps an egalitarian phase where deities, like people, were not clearly defined, and then projects a stage when the priests become dominant and true deities develop. There are a great many difficulties in the way of such a view. Most important, perhaps, is the fact that if we consider the Pueblos as a group, we find that all the possibilities from the simplest spirits to highly defined deities exist simultaneously. Admittedly all the evidence has been gathered within the last one hundred years, and there may have been earlier and simpler stages, the concepts of which were retained in later developments.

The economic and social base for all of the Pueblo groups is similar, and yet on that base the three tribes we have considered have built three quite different pantheons. The Zuñis have very nearly confined theirs to a small council of male spirits represented by masks. Beyond these an otiose, sexless divinity is responsible for creation.

[19] Paul Radin, *Primitive Man as Philosopher*, 372.

He certainly represents a "monotheistic tendency," at least in the minds of some of his formulators. The Keres pantheon rests essentially on two Great Mothers, one subterranean and otiose, the other the earthly mother of mankind. Their kachina cult differs from Zuñis' in that it is scarcely related to the pantheon at all, whereas some of the Zuñi masks may well be considered idols of the gods.

Among the Hopis the divinities are clearly outlined, and male for the most part. It would not be possible to confuse Masau'u and Muingwu in their present delineations, nor to confuse either with Sho'tokunungwa. The Hopi kachina cult is not strongly orientated towards the major pantheon—one could almost say that the Masau'u kachina represented a separate being from the god himself. If we assume an identical economic base for the three tribes, which I think is justified, it would then be difficult to connect that base with these gods in the form of a necessity.

If we take social organization as a determining factor, the problem differs slightly. Let us take the priestly class. In Keres Santo Domingo "clans do not control offices, membership in societies, nor ceremonies."[20] Among the Hopis and Zuñis they often do, at least in theory. The question here is the possibility of domination of the community by a priestly class. My impression is that at Zuñi the priesthood is more powerful as a group. The Hopis also regard one clan as first, but it seems to have little practical effect. All Pueblos are at great pains to make power, both civil and priestly, so diffuse that egalitarianism will prevail. Perhaps it would be safe to say that the Keres, who in theory are most democratic, have the simplest gods; but these are the least like an amalgam of beast-gods and ghostlike spirits, assumed from a totemic type society.

If the Hopis were more egalitarian than the Zuñis, as I think they were, they should have the simpler totemic type gods and the Zuñis the more complex and defined deities, which is the reverse of what we find today. It could of course be argued that the Hopi kachina cult, with its vast number of beings represented, does indicate such a phase. Why then did they go on to the highly articulated deities? In popular opinion the Hopis were the greatest traders among the Pueblos.

[20] White, *The Pueblo of Santo Domingo*, 72.

Their trade was certainly extensive; Coronado's men found them in what is now Kansas, and they went as far as the Pacific and the Gulf of Mexico, but theirs was not essentially a trading economy. Probably the Zuñis traded an equal amount of salt, hides, and shells, also by barter.

There are other observations which must be made. It is true that men have clothed objects with their fears and desires to make them simple spirits, and that these spirits have then been combined with beast-gods. These often become "true-gods." Again I must raise difficulties if this theory is applied to the Pueblo supernatural world. First of all, on the available evidence the Pueblos were not totemic. The greatest of their beast-gods, the Horned Water Serpent, is not in any sense totemic. It is very likely that he was borrowed from outside cultures as a full-grown personification of a force of nature. If we take the "true-god" thesis, that is, one who has an idol, a shrine or house, and a cult, we have this in the War Twins. There are excellent pictures of the idols of the Zuñi war gods in their shrines on Thunder Mountain. Since they and Horned Water Serpent are common to all Pueblos, and well beyond, it seems likely that they entered the Pueblo pantheon very early, even though their schematic place may be late.

The problem as it appears to me is this: composite mankind may have logical stages of development, but individual cultures, even in relatively isolated circumstances, do not follow through such a series. Secondly, the mere fact that any stage is logical is no warrant for its existence, much less its inevitability.

Two relatively minor points might be made here. Any archaic cult of ancestors among the Pueblos is pure surmise, and also contains a false implication. Even at present the kachinas represent the ancestors only in a general way, as a part of the collectivity of spirits. In some Río Grande pueblos they may not be connected with the dead at all. There are a few instances where the canes around the altar are said to represent the dead of a particular society, which in theory might represent ancestors of a particular clan, but that is never stated. There is the world of living mankind and the world of spirits; the dead obviously fit into the latter somewhere, but there is nothing like the deified heroes, nor the semi-divine ancestors, real or imagined, who are so common in Greek culture.

As a minor point, Radin's belief that the kachinas were a recent introduction is very doubtful. It is based on an early theory of Parsons, who was prone to see European influence even as the source of witchcraft. While the question is by no means settled, there is some evidence from pictographs, and better evidence from pre-Spanish murals, that masked figures were a part of Pueblo religion before any European contacts.[21]

Radin's other statement, which follows closely on that concerning the kachinas, is a more serious and definite error, to my mind. I hope that this book has served to dispel the thought that the Pueblos "had no conception or delineation of deities higher than that generally encountered in the normal totemistic cultures." It would be possible for a good scholar to read through the literature, particularly if he concentrated on Zuñi, and arrive at some such conclusion. The error stems from the fact that ethnologists have had little systematic interest in the pantheon, a condition which left the available information badly scattered, a state of knowledge which is then projected upon the Indians.

Something, finally, must be said about monotheism and the tendency to monotheism. Monolatry, or the worship of a single god, is found in some very simple cultures, but it is by no means universal, nor confined to them. Monotheism, or the tendency to monotheism, is the recognition of one supreme god, above all other spirits; such a deity is a creator and a careful supervisor of the affairs of mankind. Radin has two views on this subject. He expressed one in the passage previously quoted: "The spread of monotheism is far more definitely a reflection of certain facts of a general sociological order . . . ." which he does not define. He also believed that monotheism was a philosophical point of view produced by individual formulators not bound by social determinism: "It is the characteristic of such individuals, I contend, always to picture the world as a unified whole, always to postulate some First Cause. No evolution from animism to monotheism was ever necessary in their case. What was required were individuals of a certain psychological type. Alongside of them and

[21] Dockstader, *The Kachina and the White Man*, 31 ff.

vastly in the majority have always been found others with a temperament fundamentally distinct, to whom the world has never appeared as a unified whole and who have never evinced any marked curiosity as to its origins."[22]

If we take the three Pueblo religions which have been surveyed in this book, there is nothing to disprove the last statement. The Keres Thinking Woman is very close to a monotheistic divinity, in the sense of being a creator—she produced the world by thinking outward into space—and she is supreme. She is the Great Mother, the earth; her alter ego is Iyatiku, the Corn-Mother, or the same divine principle in a more visible aspect. The only other deity on the Keres horizon is Paiyatemu, a rather lightly conceived male fertility spirit; he is a necessary appendage, but in the divine scheme has a role similar to that of a prince consort, except that his attentions are addressed to mortal women and never to the goddess, who is sexless. The conception of the Keres gods sounds primitive or basic. I am not at all sure that it is. If it were, it would exemplify a strong tendency to monotheism (not monolatry) at a simple stage of man's approach to his gods.

At Zuñi the tendency toward monotheism is exemplified, not by Pautiwa, the chairman of the Council of the Gods, but by A'wonawil'ona. Bunzel denied the existence of this sexless deity and the concept may have been the creation of priest-philosophers, or limited to esoteric groups, but this divinity existed, to be sure, in the minds of a number of Zuñis. From the information that comes down to us, this Zuñi divinity is dressed in more concepts than is Thinking Woman.

Tendencies toward monotheism among the Hopis developed there in times of social stress, and in towns where the pressure was greatest. I think it might be safe to say that the nomination of Sho'tokunungwa for the role of supreme god, and the actual elevation of Masau'u to such a role, was the result of a conflict between two cultures which centered in the town of Old Oraibi. Katchongva can be thought of as a priest-formulator, but he is not speculating in an unhindered philosophical atmosphere. The Egyptian monotheist, Amenhotep,

[22] Radin, *Primitive Man as Philosopher*, 28.

was a powerful ruler; he had nothing to gain and everything to lose by insisting upon his theories. He was willing to lose it. Katchongva is not trying to impose a belief beyond his speaking range, he is trying to preserve a limited culture; and monotheism seems to him to be a suitable weapon for defense. It is easier to explain a great spirit than a whole pantheon and it poses like against like: the god of the Hopis versus the god of the bohanna.

Again it appears that three nearly identical groups of people, who live within walking distance of one another, have developed very different deities, at various times and for obviously different reasons. Among the three tribes there is also a notable lack of interchange of gods. Paiyatemu seems to be the only exception, beyond the Horned Water Serpent and the Little War Twins. Very few of the kachina spirits are shared. The Sun is of course shared, in a general way, but earth deities are not.

Before turning to Freud it may be useful to consider the word monotheism, since it is subject to different meanings. Freud and Buber, and the dictionary, use the word in the strict sense of but one god, an *only* god in Freud's words. When the word is used in this sense one must be careful. Radin speaks of the complete credal triumph of monotheism in Christianity, and of the subtle appeal of monotheism. The appeal of polytheism is equally great, and monotheism has not triumphed in Christianity, which, in comparison with Judaism, is a step away from it. The trinity has theological value, but in ethnological context I do not see how it differs from the Winnebago one in four, or one in sixteen.

"Tendency toward monotheism" seems like a more useful term. It implies a single, all-powerful, source, a creator who is not otiose, but attends to his or her creations, at least when stimulated by the worship of men. Such a deity does not necessarily exclude other divinities. The form is not universal, but it is old; the Sumerian *Ea*, god of the deep, is such a figure. Since it would be hard to find any older information, one may assume that historically the "tendency toward monotheism" may arise at any time, and that it may or may not be a philosophical speculation. The problem of the one and the many, which is so central to Greek philosophy, may not be as essential to others as it is to us who have been raised upon that particular theme.

Freud

Freud has such an important place in modern thought that one must begin with a warning. The theories considered here are not the basis for his medical practice, which is not under discussion, but are rather by-products from clinical experience and a humane interest in human affairs. The essays which concern us were written many years apart; the earliest, *"Totem and Taboo,"* is of greatest importance. The entire book is readily available, so Part III, which bears upon our questions, will be considered by itself. Toward the end of his life he wrote another relevent book, *Moses and Monotheism.* Its particular argument is not of concern here, but some of its sidelights are.

Atheism was a basic premise about which Freud had no doubt. I find it somewhat ironic that the man who believed that there were no gods also believed that if you thought there were, it would be preferable, that it exemplified a higher type of mentality to believe in only one. The temptation to an excursus at this point is great, but I will cleave to the subject, and will restate it here. It is: "What has been mankind's relationship with the supernatural world; is it determined by some external or internal necessary factor? What place does mankind's relationship with a spirit-world have in contemporary thought?"

As an atheist Freud was faced with one very important question. If there are neither gods nor spirits, why has mankind been constantly preoccupied with belief in a relationship of both the individual and the social group and various supernatural powers? Freud's answer was twofold. The first was based upon early ethnologists, such as Tyler, Lang, Wundt, and Frazer. As Freud arranged the material, it comes out something like this: man goes through an animistic phase, or "system" in which the nucleus of experience lies in a belief in human souls. This belief may have originated from the experience of dreams, or from the observation of death. The shadow, the voice, the face, and even the will of the dead may cling to the living. They thus may be thought to exist in a spirit world. Spirits, whether sprites or gods, may be thought to correspond to these independent souls in some way. Man transfers his feelings about "ghosts" to a concept of independent "souls" and in time to greater spirits. Most important to a consideration of animism is the concept that man transfers what he feels about "souls," by analogy, to plants, and animals, and often to non-living objects.

Thus far we are not in Freud's domain, but we have established his base camp. He makes the following observation: "Animism is a system of thought, it gives not only the explanation of a single phenomena, but makes it possible to comprehend the totality of the world from one point, as a continuity." Granting animism as one system of thought, two other systems follow in the natural development of mankind. The second is a religious system, and the third a scientific system.

Freud claims that animism, although a system, is not a speculative system, but a technique for controlling men, objects, natural phenomena, and the like. In this control sorcery manipulates men, and magic controls spirits.

The heart of his theory is based upon an analogy. The progress of mankind, from animism to scientific mastery of the world about him, is comparable to the psyche's growth from birth to maturity. He further believes, I think, that the growth of the psyche provided the motivation and the power which enabled men to complete a similar cycle in history. The basic picture is again drawn from the early ethnologists. Primitive man used imitative magic to control his environment and, as Tylor phrased it, in doing so he mistook "an ideal connection for a real one." Or again, "men mistook the order of their ideas for the order of nature, and hence imagined that the control which they have, or seem to have, over their thoughts, permitted them to have a corresponding control over things." The dynamism of magic is the wish of any man.

The infant is faced with a similar dilemma. The young child has few means of satisfying his wishes, except by fantasy or hallucinations. As he grows a little older, he is able to express his wishes with motor activity in play. Play is often a kind of imitative magic. Freud stresses the "excessive valuation of the wish," which is common to both the child and to primitive man. Each equates a psychic act with an objective result. Since there is no such link in the real world between a thought and a result, skepticism sets in. The poor results which derive from an important wish are attributed to lack of piety or a failure of faith or belief.

Freud finds the phenomena of overvaluing psychic acts common to children, primitive mankind, and to mentally disturbed adults in our own culture. Not all kinds of mental disturbance lead to such a situation. To the phenomena, whether in an infant, a primitive, or a patient, Freud gave the name "the omnipotence of thought." The phrase can best be understood if it is related to the arts, where it has an undisputed validity. What a man or woman writes, or paints, or composes, or carves, or weaves, has in the beginning only the subjective reality of the wish and its form in the mind. Nonetheless, such a wish can be successfully projected into the world outside of the individual thinker, and persist there as a reality.

Freud is thoroughly convinced that man's grasp of the world is developed by stages: "In the animistic stage man ascribes omnipotence to himself; in the religious he has ceded it to the gods, but without seriously giving it up, for he reserves to himself the right to control the gods by influencing them in some way or other in the interests of his wishes. In the scientific attitude toward life there is no longer any room for man's omnipotence."

From clinical work he postulates stages in the growth of each individual psyche. In the beginning there is auto-eroticism; the libido is directed toward its own body. In a second stage, narcissism, the impulse has as its object its own ego. Thereafter the psyche establishes relationships, and preferably interrelationships, with objects outside the individual body and ego. Freud would transfer this same scheme to the history of mankind. Man "personified his affects, populated the world with them and then rediscovered his inner psychic processes outside himself. At times such a mechanism offers psychic relief to the individual or to the group by spreading the burden abroad, objectively, and the idea by granting relief gains particular force."

When these ideas are arranged as likely stages, they become not only statements of possible fact, but ideals as well: "We may venture to compare the various evolutionary stages of man's conception of the universe with the stages of libidinous evolution of the individual. We find that the animistic phase corresponds in time as well as in content with narcissism, the religious phase corresponds to that stage of object finding which is characterized by dependence upon the parents, while the scientific stage has its full counterpart in the individual's state of maturity where, having renounced the pleasure principle and having adapted himself to reality, he seeks his object in the outer world."[23]

Since maturity is at best an elusive and transitory—one could probably say momentary—goal, Freud added a note or two to the scale: "We are therefore prepared to find that primitive man transferred the structural relations of his own psyche to the outer world, and on the other hand we may make the attempt to transfer back into the human soul what animism teaches about the nature of things."

I am under the impression that the outline Freud presented in "Totem and Taboo" was intended as a description of fact. In another work, *The Future of an Illusion,* he reviews the stages as an analogy only; but since it carries the evolution one step farther it is worth quoting at length.

"We know that the human child cannot well complete its development towards culture without passing through a more or less distinct phase of neurosis. This is because the child is unable to suppress by rational mental effort so many of those instinctual impulses which cannot later be turned to account, but has to check them by acts of repression, behind which there stands as a rule an anxiety motive. Most of these child neuroses are overcome spontaneously as one grows up . . . . In just the same way one might assume that in its development through the ages mankind as a whole experiences conditions that are analogous to the neuroses, and this for the same reasons, because in the ages of ignorance and intellectual weakness it achieved by purely affective means the instinctual renunciations, indispensable for man's communal existence. And the residue of these repression-like processes, which took place in antiquity, has long clung

[23] Sigmund Freud, "Totem and Taboo," in *The Basic Writings of Sigmund Freud,* 876–77.

on to civilization. Thus religion would be the universal obsessional neurosis of humanity. It, like the child's, originated in the Oedipus complex, the relation to the father. According to this conception, one might prophesy that the abandoning of religion must take place with the fateful inexorability of a process of growth, and that we are just now in the middle of this phase of development."[24]

In an inexorable scheme of human evolution, an only god preceeds the end of all religion. Freud had several theories about monotheism. One is sociological. With regard to Amenhotep (IV) he states: "Through the victorious sword . . . Egypt had become a great power . . . . This imperialism was reflected in religion as universality and monotheism."[25] Since this monotheism was such a brief interlude (of Sun worship) he is forced to another speculation: a latency period, or a time of incubation. The analogy is again with a patient. A man may come away from a shocking experience, such as a train wreck, with no apparent psychic disturbance. After a period of "incubation" strong symptoms of disturbance appear. After the shock of the violent suppression of Amenhotep's monotheism in Egypt it reappears with the monotheism of Moses.

There is no necessity in such a schemata. Freud held another view which, so far as I know, he did not apply to monotheism, but since we are so deep in the projection of fantasies into the world of reality, I may as well add it here. Clinically the process is called "system formation." In speaking of the structure of dreams, delusions, and the like he says, "An intellectual function in us demands the unification, coherence and comprehensibility of everything perceived and thought of, and does not hesitate to construct a false connection." He made this point in connection with animism and then fell into several pages of fascinating medical detail. I hope his spirit will forgive me for projecting into that chapter something which is not there, but certainly should be. If there is within us any innate intellectual, or psychic, function which demands unification of experience, objective or subjective, monotheism would be an inevitable result in man's experience with his gods.

[24] Sigmund Freud, *The Future of an Illusion*, 77–78.
[25] Sigmund Freud, *Moses and Monotheism*, 22.

Freud's well-known basic theory concerning gods revolves around the Oedipus complex: "Probably the mother deities were developed when the matriarchy was being limited, in order to compensate the dethroned mothers. The male gods appear at first as sons by the side of the great mothers; only later do they clearly assume the features of the father. These male gods of polytheism mirror the conditions of patriarchal times. They are numerous, they have to share their authority, and occasionally they obey a higher god. The next step, however, leads us to the topic that interests us here: the return of the one and only father deity whose power is unlimited."[26]

My most positive reaction to these theories is that Vienna must be a very poor place in which to study Indians, or any other "primitive" groups of mankind. Perhaps, somewhere, there is a tribe which lives in fear, and by magic only manipulates the world about it. If there are such people, they might represent the childhood of mankind. I am doubtful of the possibility, but will only consider the Pueblos.

Primitive man is not a child in any sense. The idea that he is has a lengthy history. During the 18th century, there was a theory of great popularity which pictured the primitive man as living in a kind of golden age of childlike simplicity and bliss. That vision died. During the next century Europeans referred to the natives they engaged as "boy." We are prone to use the same word in reference to the Chinese, whose civilization antedates ours by many centuries. In Freud, the feeling that primitive men represent the children of mankind is pretty well doctored up, but it is not essentially changed.

When Samuel Johnson wrote *Rasselas* he was trying to combat a running tide of opinion which held that childlike men were, if not superior, at least happier. Freud rather reverses that proposition. Primitive men were childish, or infantile, but if they were comparable to presently observable infants, they must have existed in a state of frustrated anxiety in which only their thoughts could produce effects in the external world.

There were men in the Southwest perhaps thirty thousand years ago. Likely they were simpler than their descendants, and they may

[26] *Ibid.,* 106.

represent the infancy of mankind, but since not even their skeletons can be found we can hardly surmise what their thoughts and emotions were. These will have to be calculated from present primitives, who are still animists. When one examines the Pueblos he finds that they are thoroughgoing realists. Their basic need is food, which they get chiefly by farming. In Cushing's *Zuñi Breadstuff* he describes the creation of a new field for floodwater farming, a process which takes two years. A brush dam is put up across a gully, and smaller dams are set to distribute, not the water, but the top soil that washes down. Then small barriers are built around the field to capture the wind-borne soil of dust storms. When the soil is deep and rich enough, it is planted, and irrigated by the flood waters. Under the conditions of place there could be no more scientific approach to the problem of farming. Our modern equipment, such as bulldozers and sub-soilers, would be a step backward. The Pueblo farmer was also able to develop special strains of corn and cotton which were adaptable to his needs.

It is true that these fields were also subject to magical rites and offerings. It is better when men and the spirits co-operate. Weather of course is not subject to scientific control by any society, and it thus provides an area in which emotions—always wishes if you are a farmer—have free play. The modern urbanite may be depressed by a rain, but a farmer will be either delighted or horrified, depending upon its relationship to his practical desire.

The magic involved in the case of the field is not very similar to the fantasy projection of the child. It is a realistic appraisal of all possibilities. I have done everything practical to ensure the success of the crop; I have accounted for my own psychic anxiety about it by placing boundary stones, and by making offerings of prayer-feathers to the spirits who represent unknown or doubtful possibilities. I have further satisfied all social obligations connected with the field, such as my right, or the clan's right, to own or to use it, and my duty to the aged priest by planting at least a part of the crop on the date he selects as proper and propitious.

Neither is the Pueblo Indian childlike in his relations with his fellow men, sorcery being a possible exception. My impression is that there are very few sorcerers who think of themselves as such. In conversation the Indian is roundabout in his speech, and may be as devious as any Byzantine ambassador in his presentation, but he is not living in a haze of unreality.

Freud held in favor of a highly normative system. One norm was the mature adult. In the animistic stage man ascribes omnipotence to himself; later he delegates this to the gods, or the adults near to him—"object finding"—after which the successful man, having adapted himself to reality, seeks his object in the outer world. Or in terms of society, after finding his gods, he still tries to manipulate them in the interests of his wishes. In the mature stages of the individual, or of society, the scientific attitude prevails, and "there is no longer any room for man's omnipotence."

Such thought gives rise to a second norm. In order to arrive at a communal society, the individuals who compose it must renounce to a great extent the basic "pleasure principle," and repress large areas of personal wishes. To repeat: in "the ages of ignorance and intellectual weakness it [mankind] achieved by purely affectual means the instinctual renunciations, indispensable for man's communal existence."

To me the analogy between man as the microcosm of society, or more importantly, society as the macrocosm of man, has doubtful value. Without denying various parts of the separate theories, the combination seems to cast shadows across one truth, and shed no light on the history of mankind. I am satisfied that the animistic phase postulated by Freud does not apply to the animistic Pueblos. I am certain that no society has yet reached a scientific attitude in his sense; thus we are left with an indefinite middle term, and we are the middle. As either individuals or as a society we objectify some things; we also take a scientific approach to some problems. So do the animistic Indians. If we discard the future as unknown, and find no solid evidence for a particular past, the picture changes. We have a present. It is composed of many responses to the world. Some of these are objectively useful, some are regressive in individual adaptation or in social arrangements, others seem to be independent of any necessary value. These are mixed in varying proportions in individuals and societies. In order to avoid prolonging a series of indefinite references, these elements may be called factors. Many of the same possibilities were available to primitive men, and they succeded and failed in a proportionate scale. The Zuñis did not invent the motorcar; they did practice surgery with the use of anesthetics. If an American or European town of four thousand should be isolated for a long period of time, without recourse to books, it would be interesting to see what the populace would contrive, individually and socially, in response to the multitudinus demands of the objective world. All men, as groups, have a common set of possibilities which may be realized in varying degrees.

Freud had another norm; in concluding *Civilization and Its Discontents* he wrote: "The fateful question of the human species seems to me to be whether and to what extent the cultural process developed in it will succeed in mastering the derangements of communal life caused by the human instinct of aggression and self-destruction. In this connection, perhaps the phase through which we are at this moment passing deserves special interest. Men have brought their powers of subduing the forces of nature to such a pitch that by using them they could now very easily exterminate one another to the last man. They know this—hence arises a great part of their current unrest, their dejection, their mood of apprehension."[27] The book was published in 1929.

By that standard the Pueblos have done exceedingly well, and should perhaps be thought of as the parents, rather than the children, of the race. The late Dutch scholar and student of civilization, Henri Frankfort, singles out the Zuñis when attacking Toynbee's theory of "arrested civilizations." "Why," he says, "should these chimaeras and a feverish desire for 'advancement' disturb the satisfaction of people who have attained the double integration of individual and society and of society and nature?"[28] He holds that a society should take time to reconnoiter its road. Perhaps the integration Frankfort spoke of is a little neater than it would appear on the mesas; but the Pueblo who prays to the spruce tree he cuts, worships a number of

[27] Sigmund Freud, *Civilization and Its Discontents*, 143–44.
[28] H. Frankfort, *The Birth of Civilization in the Near East*, 14.

gods with varying degrees of seriousness, and uses a purebred sire for his flock is, if not entirely integrated into his society and its world, at least in a position to have a shrewd grasp upon a number of man's possibilities.

Buber

The psychological and the economic or social interpretations of animism are in one way a rather late development, and at times depend upon reading back into early texts meanings which were not necessarily there. Philosophical or religio-philosophical speculations, which touch upon animism, polytheism, and monotheism, began very early in western culture. The father of Greek philosophy, Thales of Miletus (a town which would be in Turkey today), flourished at the beginning of the sixth century B. C. Very little of his thought survives in any form, but from fragments, and opinions of later writers, he had two theories of interest to this study. To begin with, he equated, or drew a strong parallel between, animism and what we now call pantheism. He also stated the question of the one and the many. How do they relate? By his contemporaries he was called an atheist, which meant that he denied the current polytheistic pantheon. His most famous phrase, which was quoted by both Aristotle and Plato, is that "All things are full of gods." According to scholars, it is said that he derived this view from the study of amber and the magnet.

"It has been thought odd that he should posit 'life' in all inanimate objects on the strength of the magnet, which was a unique manifestation; but if he treated amber and got the same manifestation, it may be that he thought that all objects had the same power if one knew how to evoke it; and that he therefore thought that the whole Cosmos was a living thing, nourished by the life-giving water of which it was composed, and that each particular object in it was likewise alive. He was called by some an atheist; but tradition shows him to be a pantheist, seeing the life-force, which he equated with the divine, in the Whole and in every part."[29]

Without any proof, I suspect that he was building his philosophy

[29] Kathleen Freeman, *Companion to the Pre-Socratic Philosophers*, 54.

282

upon the evidence of animists who could not have been far away—not as far as Zuñi is from Walpi. However that may be, he raised a question: "Is god one or many, and in what fashion is he one or many?" The question is not related to time or place. A Dakota Indian said: "*The sicun* is an immaterial god whose substance is never visible. It is the potency of mankind and the emitted potency of the gods. Considered relative to mankind, it is many, but apart from mankind it is one."

In either of these views there is a strain of realism; the experience is available to everyone, even if the answer is ambiguous. Possibly Thales used the magnet as a metaphor. In any case, animism provided a coherent view of the world, a value which both Freud and Buber recognize. The later history of Greek philosophy, as it struggled with the one and the many, is well known. The only point which needs to be made here is that it was, at least in Plato, a great step away from realism. In the tenth book of the *Republic* there is the following dialogue:

"God, whether from choice or from necessity, made one bed in nature and one only; two or more such ideal beds neither ever have been nor ever will be made by God.

"Why is that?

"Because even if he had made but two, a third would still appear behind them which both of them would have for their idea, and that would be the ideal bed and not the two others."

The text is of course very good, but I am not sure there is any advance in thinking. How many beds God made, if he made any, is entirely removed from the world of experience. If I may refer back to Freud—and since I aim to raise questions rather than answer them, I think it proper—is Plato's statement not a "system formation" such as people construct in dreams and delusions? Is it not logical only in the same sense and likely to lead to false connections?

The question of the one and the many was not settled in ancient philosophy, but toward its end any possible role for animism was ruled out. As Sallust, the friend of the Emperor Julian, phrased it: "To say that these objects are sacred to the Gods, like various herbs and stones and animals, is possible to sensible men, but to say that they

are gods is the notion of madmen." Our world, I believe, is not altogether populated by madmen, nor by sensible men. Neither group
has given any conclusive answer to the questions all can ask.

Martin Buber arrives last in the sequence of thinkers presented
here, not because I think he has a better answer, but because he has a
different one, which was again based upon the problems of animism.
Buber drew material from both psychiatry and ethnology, and has
in turn influenced each of these studies.

Although Buber has a specific goal which is not new—the vindica-
tion of an all-encompassing monotheism—he does not use Plato's
method of fiat, but builds it stone by stone from the ground. One
important aspect of Buber's realism may come from Kierkegaard,
who felt that paradox was a normal situation in life, religion, and
philosophy. Paradox leaves man at loose ends, and when these loose
ends are frayed, which is certain to be the case unless he resorts to
"system formation," the important item becomes a middle-term. In
the uncertain caverns of my being, and the even more confusing world
outside myself, I must find some kind of midway relationship between
the two which has either more certainty or more value.

Buber is able to accept animism. To him the essential reality is a
relationship, a mutual relationship, between, first, man and nature;
second, between man and man; and third, between man and gods—a
series which culminates in the Eternal Thou. His linguistically based
term "Thou" expresses the existence of mutuality, "I and Thou,"
no matter what the object may be, whether a stone, or God. The
alternative situation is "I and *It.*" The equation exists, but it is static.

If we consider the world of nature first, we find that while Buber
specifically rejects any such thing as a tree-spirit or dryad, he does
feel that there is such a power as Orenda or Mana (we may add
Ianyi to make it Pueblo). This Orenda gets its power from a long
continued "relationship" with the tree—the tree, I take it, is Buber's
symbol for all of nature—and at the same time it is the effective force
for stirring relationship. He feels, reasonably, that in establishing
such a situation primitive man has a great advantage over modern man.

The human psyche is just as important to Buber as it is to Freud;
without it there could be no relationship, and he carries that idea con-

sistently up to the Eternal Thou. God needs man, just as much as man needs God. In Pueblo terms, "The sun needs something to shine on." The role of the psyche differs greatly in the two thinkers. (Psyche is here used not in the sense of soul, nor essence of livingness, but as the totality of responses: rational, impulsive, creative, delusional, instinctive or what you will, that go to make up a human being.) For Freud there was one objective world, an *It* in Buber's terms. The correlative was not "object finding," but merely the projection of one's internal psyche, which is likely to be a dangerous process since it distorts objective reality. Buber feels that the psyche can reach a higher reality if it is half out of its nest and is looking both ways.

On the subject of art the two men are very close. Freud admitted the projection of such an art-forming wish as a reasonable kind of fantasy. In such a case there exists a relationship much like Buber's ideal *Thou*. Buber stands somewhere between Plato and Freud on the subject. "This is the Eternal Source of Art: a man is faced by a form which desires to be made through him into a work. This form is no offspring of his soul, but is an appearance which steps up to it and demands of it the effective power." In other words, the external world presents a challenge which the individual resolves by some creation—an artistic middle term.

However, even in art the presence of Orenda has some kind of independent strength. If the individual carries through the act of creation, "if he speaks the primary word out of his being to the form which appears, then the effective power streams out, and the work arises." What also arises, in my mind at least, are some philosophical questions. Is this position a statement of animism or pantheism? In a paraphrase of a preSocratic philosopher he states, "Yet it is in spirit that nature is timelessly enveloped." Again he says, "If I have both will and grace, that in considering the tree I become bound up in relation to it. The tree is no longer *it*." I am not sure that grace and Orenda are interchangeable. Grace, in the sense of mercy or forgiveness, is not a comparable idea; it involves a single, not necessarily only, god, with wishes comparable to those of mankind.

State of grace would be a closer parallel. At times Buber sounds like a pantheist, as in the following paraphrase from Thales: "There is no such thing as seeking God, for there is nothing in which He could not be found." The "He" has been added to Thales' fragment, "All things are full of gods." The pronoun indicates possibilities which are not the same as those of a surmised pure animism. A "He" is a separate being whose power differs from Orenda. The effect may be the same, but the relationship is with an independent personality. Buber is looking forward to the Eternal Thou. Between lies the rough ground of polytheism which must be accounted for.

Men have had a *Thou* relationship with many gods. While animism, in this system, is something of a virtue, polytheism is not. But it is a reality. If an intensity of relationship is the highest state of reality, the worship of many gods must be included, and one must admit to all the links in an unbroken chain of sequence in mankind's experience. Nothing can be lost, or in error, simply because of its place in history; history deals with men as it may. Buber was looking for a unifying principle.

Animism provides a unity. In Freud's words it "is a system of thought, it gives not only the explanation of a single phenomena, but makes it possible to comprehend the totality of the world from one point, as a continuity." Polytheism is not so attractive in that its historical role has been to divide; and perhaps even more importantly, polytheism is the enemy of all systems, it would seem. There is a bed behind the bed, in eternal form, whether you are Plato, Aquinas, or Buber or Freud. The question is, where do you find the unity?

Buber's answer to the problem of including polytheism—and in any evolutionary system leading toward a unity it must be included—follows. The place assigned by Buber is again a paraphrase of a Greek philosopher, this time Heraclitus. "Men have addressed their Eternal *Thou* with many names. In singing of Him who was thus named they always had the *Thou* in mind; the first myths were hymns of praise. Then the names took refuge in the language of *It;* men were more and more strongly moved to think of and to address their eternal *Thou* as an *It*. But all God's names are hallowed, for in them He is not merely spoken about, but spoken to."

In 500 B.C. Heraclitus said much the same thing: "God is day-night, winter-summer, war-peace, satiety-famine. But he changes like fire which, when it mingles with the smoke of incense, is named according to each man's pleasure." I quote the passage because I admire the severely simple view of the Greek philosopher, and because it raises a question. The gods of many names are one. If they are one, they or He include everything: famine as well as satiety.

The goal for Buber is centered not so much upon the affirmation of the Eternal Thou as it is upon a moment which we would call an epiphany, perhaps. "These moments are immortal, and most transitory of all; no content may be secured from them, but their power invades creation and the knowledge of man, beams of their power stream into the ordered world and dissolve it again and again. This happens in the history both of the individual and of the race."[30]

Buber modified, after forty years, his view that it is in spirit that the world of nature is enveloped, by adding in a postscript that God also has personality. Personality, to my mind, calls up the image of some kind of anthropomorphism and disturbs the logical structure of his earlier system.

I think the first difficulty of the system is that it is too cheerful. One does have a relationship based upon mutuality with certain trees and plants, with particular mountains, or with some tide-pools and, of course, with many animals. Such a relationship is an ideal. On the other hand Buber did not mention, perhaps because he was not a farmer, that one also has a mutuality with a dust or hail storm which has blasted the field he has tended. The relationship is no less intense, but it is one of hatred, which is not an ideal.

Likewise, it is difficult to love all gods. "But all God's names are hallowed" is a difficult proposition. It is hard to believe that those who addressed the Aztec god Tlaloc, to pick a god at random, were in reality addressing an Eternal Thou behind him. Perhaps they were, but if a system is to be built upon the thought, it must include the ambivalence of a mutual relationship with the objective world: a recognition of love and hate, or delight and fear, and an adjustment to the many blank spaces between the moments which are immortal.

The second problem concerns the distinction between physical

[30] Martin Buber, *I and Thou.*

objects and ideas as objects. With a tree, or a stone, or a mountain, or a mountain lion, there is little doubt—brushing Berkeley aside—about the other object involved in the relationship. With a spirit or god not joined to such an object, the situation is somewhat different. A few men have met anthropomorphic gods. One Hopi saw Masau'u, just around the bend in the road. A short while ago, as time flies, a Cambridge Don not only met Pan, but carried on a conversation with him in a mixture of Attic and modern Greek. For most men, however, gods make their appearance as ideas, even though they may be represented as idols, either on the page or in sculptured figures.

There are several problems which may become confused. The one just stated is very old. "Thunder and lightning are given facts; but can this be said of Zeus, the god who sends them? At all events, he does not belong to the realm of things that meet the senses."[31] That is a simple duality that was closed by Thales when he rejected the old pantheon and set in its place some kind of elaborated animism, or pantheism, which identified objective reality with divine force. In a moment I will present what seems to me to be the Pueblo attempt to close a similar gap.

A second difficulty arises from a duality in internal, or psychic, reality. According to Freud, man may have "personified his affects, populated the world with them and then rediscovered his inner phychic processes outside himself." While I don't deny this mechanism, it must be taken bite-size where it may have validity as a psychic reality. If the same mechanism is applied to "stages" of mankind, such as animism and the others discussed in this chapter, the proposition is something else. The statement assumes some sort of corporate "man," and while it is obvious that there is more unity than individuality among members of a culture, or of mankind, that should not be used to blur specific realities.

To be precise, Masau'u is not a projection of my inner psychic processes, except to the degree that I have altered him while writing his story. I first met him as one kind of objective, though ideational, reality, not of my own making except in that literary change. He is now a part of my objective and subjective world, but if I had to link

[31] W. Jaeger, *The Theology of the Early Greek Philosophers*, 19.

him to a continuous chain of human experience, I would be troubled. Like the Pueblo priest gathering spruce boughs, I find that the effective powers are likely to grow only on certain trees.

When similar thoughts trouble people they may use an idol, or some other type of symbol, to bring objective reality to the idea of a god and thus shorten the gap between the human and the divine. The Pueblos, like the Greeks, chose dramatic impersonation. The two realities are thus, at least for the time of the incarnation, reconciled vividly and agreeably for the onlooker, who may also be a participant. The kinetic, as well as visual, identification with the gods must have proved effective, since the "kachina cult" has not only not died out, as Fewkes confidently predicted it would, but has grown stronger in some areas. As time passes and the Pueblo culture, including those gods who represent it, are challenged more severely, it is possible that the comfort afforded by the objectivity of masked impersonations of the gods and spirits will become even more necessary.

At this point the reader may anticipate some sort of synthesis, but there will be none. In the beginning I promised that each reader could become an Ovid, and rewrite these myths of the gods in his own poetry. In concluding I also offer each reader the possibility of becoming an Aristotle, and of contriving his own synthesis.

I have added this last chapter with but one thought in mind. Pueblo religion is not simple, nor is it the quaint survival of an arrested civilization. It is but one response to the same baffling problems which have beset everyone who thinks, no matter in what age he lives, nor what his conclusions may be. I am sure that no one who has read the earlier chapters will doubt the complexity of the Pueblo pantheon, nor the vitality of Pueblo responses to the particular land from which they emerged and the challenges it has set.

I would like to close there, but I must repeat one idea concerning the opinion which holds that the Indians are childlike, that they speak in grunts which could not possibly convey a wish, much less an idea, and that they may as well be regarded somewhat like buffalo: since they are nearly extinct they should either be preserved in a cultural museum—whatever that means—or be put out of their misery by some kind of dispersal.

The buffalo, and now the wild horses of Nevada, do fit some such category; we will have to do something about them, without considering their opinions. If only the vulgar held the same view of the Pueblos, there would be no cause for complaint, but that is not so. Bandelier once wrote that the Pueblos "were but grown up children, with all the appetites and desires of an adult." I am not sure that the quotation is exact, since I don't want to find it again. It may even have some merit as a description of the human race—but not of all members of it.

Language is a barrier; if I do not understand, the other party speaks gibberish; if from politeness he modifies his speech to include English, he may, even though he is adequately trilingual, sound a little childish. After more than four centuries of Spanish and Anglo converse there is still no systematic dictionary or grammer for Pueblo languages.

Fortunately the Pueblos, like other Indians, are patient—which is not a childlike attribute, but one born of great experience, the passage of time, and a little knowledge, which makes do when necessary, when the future is uncertain. Some branches of Pueblo culture are undoubtedly in crisis today, but some always have been. Looking back, the Pueblos have two great assets: they are still there, which is a Herculean feat for any culture—and, they are still dancing.

TABLE FOR RELATING TOWN NAMES TO TRIBES AND LINGUISTIC GROUPS

I. Zuñi:

One town only: Halona (Ant Hill), in this book referred to simply as Zuñi, south of Highway 66 and west of the Continental Divide.

II. Keres: linguistically belongs to Uto-Áztecan group.
   Seven towns in two groups.
   Western Keres: two pueblos located about halfway between Albuquerque and Zuñi:
      1. Acoma
      2. Laguna, established in 1700 with mixed population
   Río Grande Keres:
      3. Santa Ana, at confluence of Jémez and Río Grande
      4. Sía, a few miles further up the Jémez River
      5. Santo Domingo, San Felipe, Cochití; on Río Grande midway between Santa Fé and Albuquerque

III. Hopi:
   Towns on or near three separate Mesas in northeastern Arizona:
   A. First Mesa (or East):
      1. Hano or Tewa, an intrusive group of Tewa stock
      2. Sichomovi
      3. Walpi (These three towns appear as one.)
   B. Second Mesa (or Middle):
      1. Shongopovi
      2. Mishongnovi
      3. Shipaulovi
   C. Third Mesa (West)
      1. Old Oraibi
      2. New Oraibi, called Kyakotsmovi
      3. Hotevilla, conservative offshoot of Oraibi
      4. Bakavi, another, smaller offshoot
      5. Upper Moencopi, Lower Moencopi; some distance from the Mesas. Lower Moencopi is a Traditionalist village.

   The above three tribes are the only ones studied in this book, but to avoid confusion I list the three other Pueblo tribes, since the names of many of the towns are familiar and the reader may wish to place them.

IV. Tewa:

Six villages on the upper Río Grande above Santa Fé:
1. San Juan
2. Santa Clara
3. San Ildefonso
4. Tesuque
5. Nambé, Pojoaque; virtually extinct
6. Hano, on Hopi First Mesa

V. Tiwa:

1. Taos, Picurís; both in far northern New Mexico
2. Isleta, Sandía; near Albuquerque. The North and South groups speak dialects which are not mutually understandable.

VI. Towa:

1. Jémez; single surviving town, up Jémez River from Sía.
The Towa once included the large and famous Pecos.

BIBLIOGRAPHY

THE FOLLOWING BIBLIOGRAPHY includes only titles referred to in the text; it is not a survey of literature on the Pueblos. Parsons and Titiev cite many other titles, as do most of the books listed below. However, they leave out literary works such as *Masked Gods: Navaho and Pueblo Ceremonialism* by Frank Waters (Albuquerque, University of New Mexico Press, 1950), and Edmund Wilson's account of Zuñi in *Red, Black, Blond and Olive*, a study of four civilizations (New York, Oxford University Press, 1956). There also exists, at least concerning the Hopis, an indeterminate amount of ephemera—handbills and short tracts by, about, or directed to the Indians. Some day these will be of great value in tracing the course of interaction between ideas and cultures.

For those interested in the Pueblo natural environment, the State Bureau of Mines and Mineral Resources, Socorro, New Mexico, has an excellent list of maps and geological studies. These include vegetation, geology, and topography. They also list and sell United States Geological Survey and Bureau of Mines maps, some of which are large scale. There are quadrangles for the Río Grande Pueblo area, for the Western Keres area (not complete for Acoma), but none for Zuñi. The same institution also publishes an excellent popular series, of which Roy W. Foster's *Southern Zuñi Mountains* (Socorro, 1958) is particularly relevant.

Arizona is not so lucky. Their Bureau of Mines, at the University of Arizona, has a colorful geologic map of Navaho and Apache counties, which covers most of the Hopi area. On Plateau geology there is an old but readable work, *Mount Taylor and the Zuñi Plateau* by C. E. Dutton (United States Geological Survey, Washington, 1895). Climate and the history of climate are treated in J. T. Hack's

The Changing Physical Environment of the Hopi Indians of Arizona (The Museum, Cambridge, 1942).

Periodicals and Special Publications

Aberle, S. D. *The Pueblo Indians of New Mexico, Their Land, Economy and Civil Organization.* American Anthropological Association Memoirs, Vol. LXX. Menasha, 1948.

Bailey, Vernon. *Life Zones and Crop Zones of New Mexico.* North American Fauna, No. 35. Washington, 1913.

Bandelier, Adolph F. "An Outline of the Documentary History of the Zuñi Tribe." *Journal of American Ethnology and Archaeology,* Vol. III. Boston, Houghton, Mifflin Co., 1892.

Benedict, Ruth. *The Concept of the Guardian Spirit in North America.* American Anthropological Association Memoirs, Vol. XXIX. Menasha, 1923.

Boas, Franz. *Keresan Texts.* American Ethnological Society Publications, Vol. VIII, Part I. New York, 1928.

Colton, Harold S. "Hopi Deities." *Plateau,* XX, No. 1. Reprinted in *Hopi Customs, Folklore and Ceremonies,* Reprint Series No. 4. Flagstaff, Museum of Northern Arizona, 1954.

Cushing, Frank H. *Zuñi Breadstuff.* Indian Notes and Monographs, Vol. VIII. New York, Museum of the American Indian, Heye Foundation, 1920.

————. "Origin Myth from Oraibi." *Journal of American Folk-Lore,* Vol. XXXVI, No. 139. Lancaster, American Folk-Lore Society, 1923.

Disbrow, Alan E., and Stoll, Walter C. *Geology of the Cerrillos Area, Santa Fé County, New Mexico.* State Bureau of Mines and Mineral Resources, Bulletin 48. Socorro, 1957.

Dockstader, Frederick J. *The Kachina and the White Man.* Cranbrook Institute of Science Bulletin 35. Bloomfield Hills, 1954.

Dumarest, Nöel. *Notes on Cochití, New Mexico.* American Anthropological Association Memoirs, Vol. VI, No. 3. Lancaster, 1919.

Ellis, F. H. "The Woman's Page: Laguna Pueblo." *El Palacio,* Vol. LXVI, No. 1. Santa Fé, 1959.

Fewkes, Jesse W. "The Butterfly in Hopi Myth and Ritual." *American Anthropologist,* Vol. XII, No. 4. Washington, 1910.

————. "Minor Hopi Festivals." *American Anthropologist*, Vol. IV, No. 3. New York, 1902.

————. "The Snake Ceremonials at Walpi." *A Journal of American Ethnology and Archaeology*. Vol. IV. New York, 1894.

Goldfrank, Esther S. *The Social and Ceremonial Organization of Cochiti.* American Anthropological Association Memoirs, Vol. XXXIII. Menasha, 1927.

Judd, N. M. *The Material Culture of Pueblo Bonito.* Smithsonian Miscellaneous Collections, Vol. CXXIV. Washington, 1954.

Kirk, R. F. *Introduction to Zuñi Fetishism.* Papers of the School of American Museum of Natural History, Vol. XVIII, Part II. New York, 1917.

Kroeber, Alfred L. *Zuñi Kin and Clan.* Anthropological Papers of the American Museum of Natural History, Vol. XVIII, Part II. New York, 1917.

Lambert, Marjorie F. *Paa-ko.* The School of American Research, Monograph 19. Santa Fé, 1954.

Nequatewa, E. "Dr. Fewkes and Masauwu." *Hopi Customs, Folklore and Ceremonies.* Museum of Northern Arizona Reprint Series, No. 4. Flagstaff, 1954.

————. *Truth of a Hopi and Other Clan Stories of Shungopovi.* Museum of Northern Arizona Bulletin No. 8. Flagstaff, 1936.

Newman, S. *A Practical Zuñi Orthography.* Papers of the Peabody Museum of American Archaeology and Ethnology, Vol. XLIII, No. 1. Cambridge, 1954.

Parsons, E. C. *Hopi and Zuñi Ceremonialism.* American Anthropological Association Memoirs, Vol. XXXIX. Menasha, 1933.

————. *Notes on Zuñi.* American Anthropological Association Memoirs, Vol. IV, No. 3, Part I; No. 4, Part II. Lancaster, 1917.

————. "The Origin Myth of Zuñi." *Journal of American Folk-Lore,* Vol. XXXVI. No. 139. Lancaster, American Folk-Lore Society, 1923.

————. *A Pueblo Indian Journal, 1920–21.* American Anthropological Association Memoirs, Vol. XXXII. Menasha, 1925.

————. *The Scalp Ceremonial of Zuñi.* American Anthropological Association Memoirs, Vol. XXXI. Menasha, 1924.

————. *Tewa Tales.* American Folk-Lore Society Memoirs, Vol. XIX. New York, Stechert & Co., 1926.

Parsons, E. C., and Beals, R. L. "The Sacred Clowns of the Pueblo and Mayo-Yaqui Indians." *American Anthropologist*, Vol. XXXVI. Menasha, 1934.

Pepper, George H. *Pueblo Bonito*. Anthropological Papers of the American Museum of Natural History, Vol. XXVII. New York, 1920.

Reiter, Paul. *The Jémez Pueblo of Unshagi, New Mexico*. Monographs of the University of New Mexico and the School of American Research, No. 5. Santa Fé, 1938.

Scholes, F. V. "Documents for the History of New Mexico Missions of the Seventeenth Century." *New Mexico Historical Review*, Vol. IV, No. 1. Santa Fé, 1929.

Simmons, L. W., ed. "Southwest Issue." *American Anthropologist*, Vol. LVI, No. 4, Part I. Menasha, 1954.

Stephen, A. M. "Hopi Indians of Arizona." *The Masterkey*, Vol. XIII, No. 6; Vol. XIV, Nos. 1, 3, 4, 6. Los Angeles, Southwest Museum, 1939–40.

―――. "Hopi Tales." *Journal of American Folk-Lore*, Vol. XLII, No. 163. New York, American Folk-Lore Society, 1929.

Titiev, M. *Old Oraibi, a Study of the Hopi Indians of Third Mesa*. Papers of the Peabody Museum of American Archaeology and Ethnology, Vol. XXII, No. 1. Cambridge, 1944.

Voth, H. R. *The Oraibi Soyal Ceremony*. Field Columbian Museum Pub. 61, Vol. III, No. 2. Chicago, 1901. (Anthropological Series).

―――. *The Oraibi Summer Snake Ceremony*. Field Columbian Museum Pub. 83. Vol. III, No. 4. Chicago, 1903. (Anthropological Series).

―――. *The Traditions of the Hopi*. Field Columbian Museum Pub. 96, Vol. VIII. Chicago, 1905. (Anthropological Series).

Wallis, W. D. "Folk Tales from Shumopovi, Second Mesa." *Journal of American Folk-Lore*, Vol. XLIX, No. 191–92. Lancaster, American Folk-Lore Society, 1936.

White, Leslie A. *The Pueblo of Santa Ana, New Mexico*. American Anthropological Association Memoirs, Vol. LX. Menasha, 1942.

―――. *The Pueblo of Santo Domingo, New Mexico*. American Anthropological Association Memoirs, Vol. XLIII. Menasha, 1935.

―――. *The Pueblo of San Felipe*. American Anthropological Association Memoirs, Vol. XXXVIII. Menasha, 1932.

Whiting, A. F. *Ethnobotony of the Hopi*. Museum of Northern Arizona Bulletin No. 15. Flagstaff, 1950.

Government Documents

Benedict, Ruth. *Tales of the Cochiti Indians.* B.A.E. *Bulletin No. 98.* Washington, 1931.

Bunzel, Ruth L. "Introduction to Zuñi Ceremonialism." B.A.E. *Forty-seventh Annual Report,* 1929–30. Washington, 1932.

———. "Zuñi Katcinas." *Ibid.*

———. "Zuñi Origin Myths." *Ibid.*

Cushing, Frank H. "Outlines of Zuñi Creation Myths," B.A.E. *Thirteenth Annual Report,* 1891–92. Washington, 1896.

———. "Zuñi Ritual Poetry." *Ibid.*

Fewkes, Jesse W. "Designs on Prehistoric Hopi Pottery." B.A.E. *Thirty-third Annual Report,* 1911–12. Washington, 1919.

———. "Hopi Katcinas." B.A.E. *Twenty-first Annual Report,* 1899–1900. Washington, 1903.

Henderson, Junius, and Harrington, J. P. *Ethnozoology of the Tewa Indians. Bulletin No. 56.* Washington, 1914.

Hopi Hearings. U.S. Department of the Interior. Bureau of Indian Affairs, Hopi Agency, Keans Canyon, Arizona, 1955.

Stevenson, M. C. "Ethnobotany of the Zuñi Indians." B.A.E. *Thirtieth Annual Report,* 1908–1909. Washington, 1915.

———. "The Sia." B.A.E. *Eleventh Annual Report,* 1889–90. Washington, 1894.

———. "The Zuñi Indians." B.A.E. *Twenty-third Annual Report,* 1901–1902. Washington, 1904.

Stirling, M. W. *Origin Myth of Acoma and Other Records.* B.A.E. *Bulletin No. 135.* Washington, 1942.

Swanton, John R. *The Indian Tribes of North America.* B.A.E. *Bulletin No. 145.* Washington, 1953.

White, Leslie A. "The Acoma Indians." B.A.E. *Forty-seventh Annual Report,* 1929–30. Washington, 1932.

Books

Bancroft, Hubert H. *History of Arizona and New Mexico, 1530–1880.* San Francisco, The History Co., 1889.

Beaglehole, Ernest. *Notes on Hopi Economic Life.* New Haven, Yale University Press, 1937. (Yale University Publications in Anthropology, No. 15.)

Benedict, Ruth. *Zuñi Mythology*. 2 vols. New York, Columbia University Press, 1935.

Bowra, C. M. *The Greek Experience*. Cleveland, World Publishing Company, 1957.

Brown, Norman O. *Hermes the Thief: The Evolution of a Myth*. Madison, University of Wisconsin Press, 1947.

Buber, Martin. *I and Thou*. New York, Scribners, 1958.

Colton, Harold S. *Hopi Kachina Dolls, with a Key to Their Identification*. Albuquerque, University of New Mexico Press, 1949.

Collison-Morley, Lacy. *Greek and Roman Ghost Stories*. Oxford, Blackwell, 1912.

Cumont, Franz. *Oriental Religions in Roman Paganism*. New York, Dover Publications, 1956.

Cushing, Frank H. *Zuñi Folk Tales*. New York, G. P. Putnam's Sons, 1901.

Dodd, E. R. *Euripides Bacchae*. Oxford, The Clarendon Press, 1960.

Farnell, Lewis Richard. *The Cults of the Greek States*, Vol. V. Oxford, The Clarendon Press, 1898, 1909.

Fergusson, Erna. *Dancing Gods*. New York, Knopt, 1931.

Frankfort, H. *The Birth of Civilization in the Near East*. Garden City, Doubleday, 1950.

Frazer, J. G. *The Worship of Nature*, Vol. I. London, Macmillan, 1926.

———. *The Fear of the Dead in Primitive Religion*. 3 vols. London, Macmillan, 1933–36.

Freeman, Kathleen. *Companion to the Pre-Socratic Philosophers*. Oxford, Blackwells, 1959.

Freud, Sigmund. "Totem and Taboo." *The Basic Writings of Sigmund Freud*. Ed. by A. A. Brill. New York, The Modern Library, 1938.

———. *Civilization and Its Discontents*. London, Hogarth, 1946.

———. *Moses and Monotheism*. New York, Knopf, 1955. (Vintage Books.)

———. *The Future of an Illusion*. Garden City, Doubleday, 1957.

Graves, Robert. *The Greek Myths*. 2 vols. Baltimore, Penquin Books, 1955.

Gunn, John M. *Schat-Chen: History, Traditions and Narratives of the Queres Indians of Laguna and Acoma*. Albuquerque, Albright and Anderson, 1917.

Guthrie, William K. C. *In the Beginning*. London, Methuen, 1957.

———. *Orpheus and Greek Religion*. London, Methuen, 1935.

Hermequaftewa, Andrew. *The Hopi Way of Life Is the Way of Peace.* Tape recorded by Thomas Noble, Shungopavi, n.d.

Hodge, F. W. *Spanish Explorers in the Southern United States.* New York, Charles Scribner's Sons. 1907.

Jaeger, W. *The Theology of the Early Greek Philosophers.* Oxford, The Clarendon Press, 1947.

Kittredge, G. L. *Witchcraft in Old and New England.* New York, Russell and Russell, 1956.

Lumis, C. F. *Pueblo Indian Folk-Stories.* New York, The Century Company, 1920.

Murray, G. *Five Stages of Greek Religion.* Garden City, Doubleday, 1955.

Nilsson, Martin P. *A History of Greek Religion.* Oxford, The Clarendon Press, 1956.

Northrop, S. A. *Minerals of New Mexico.* Albuquerque, University of New Mexico Press, 1959.

Parsons, E. C. *The Pueblo of Jémez.* Andover, the Phillips Academy, 1925.

———. *Pueblo Indian Religion.* 2 vols. Chicago, University of Chicago Press, 1939.

Pausanias. *Description of Greece.* London and Cambridge, The Loeb Classical Library, 1949.

Radin, Paul. *Monotheism Among Primitive Peoples.* Basel, Switzerland, Ethnological Museum, 1954.

———. *Primitive Man as Philosopher.* New York, Dover Publications, 1957.

———. *Primitive Religion.* New York, Dover Publications, 1957.

———. *The Trickster.* New York, The Philosophical Library, 1956.

Rose, H. J. *Handbook of Greek Mythology.* New York, Dutton, 1959.

———. *Religion in Greece and Rome.* New York, Harper, 1959.

Stephen, A. M. *Hopi Journal.* Edited by E. C. Parsons. 2 vols. New York, Columbia University Press, 1936. (Columbia University Contributions to Anthropology, Vol. XXIII).

Stubbs, Stanley A. *Bird's-Eye View of the Pueblos.* Norman, University of Oklahoma Press, 1950.

Talayesva, Don. *Sun Chief: The Autobiography of a Hopi Indian.* Ed. by L. W. Simmons. New Haven, Yale University Press, 1942.

Vaillant, G. C. *The Aztecs of Mexico.* Harmondsworth, Penquin Books, 1950.

Watson, Don. *Indians of the Mesa Verde.* Mesa Verde National Park, Mesa Verde Museum Association, 1955.

Yamada, G. *The Great Resistance, a Hopi Anthology.* New York, n.d. No publisher is given for this religious tract.

INDEX

Acoma: founded in classic age, xiv; scientific farming, 38; vessel broken on graves, 55–56; sky city, 104; pantheon, 117

Agaves: *see* Kwan men

Agriculture: 161, 164, 279

Ahaiyuta (Zuñi War Twins): 214

Al, or Horn Society: *see* Two Horn Society

Alosaka: 19, 101, 125f.; *see also* Muingwu

Altar: 122, 155, 180

Ancestor(s): worship, 74; cult of, 269

Animal(s): prey, 176; rending and eating, 204–205; becomes a god, 222; rebirth of, 256

Animism: 174, 250ff.; three views of, 264ff.; system of thought, 274, 286

Animistic stage: 275

Antelope Society: 229

Apaches: 211–12

Apollonian culture: 204

Apoyan Ta'chu (Zuñi Father Sky): 87

Arrow poisoning: 228

Arrow Youth: 188

A'shiwannis (Zuñi priests of the six directions): 169

Awatobi: 12–13, 19, 211

Awitelin Tsita (Zuñi Mother Earth): 87

A'wonawil'ona (Zuñi creator god): 81, 85ff., 123, 271

Aztecs: 172, 184

Badger: and emergence, 106–107; clan, 150

Balolookong: *see* Horned Water Serpent

Banyacya, Thomas: 47–48

Battle of the Seasons: 145, 166–68, 227

Bear: claws, 43; curer, 126, 260; guards, 186

Bear clan: 20, 27, 125

Beast gods: 221

Beetle: 237; dead become, 72ff.; war character, 73

Biological order: 107
Bisexual gods: 81
Blood: of rabbits, 20; drunk by fetish, 255
Bow Priests: 114, 212, 228
Breath: 9, 155, 159, 254–55
Bull-roarer: 101
Bureau of Indian Affairs: 37
Burial: in houses, 13; flexed, 53, 56

Cacique (town chief): 106
Cactus clan: 229
Calendar: 156f., 161ff.; Hopi, 162; table, 162–63; horizon, 164
Castañeda: 183, 259; and Pueblo culture, xiii; and population, xv; and cremation, 56
Chama'hia (Hopi stone people): 252–53
Chief of all: 99
Childbirth Water Woman: sometimes identified with Sand Altar Woman, 82; and Tih'kuyi, 133
Cliff dwellers: 66, 72
Cliff Palace, Mesa Verde: xv
Cloud blowers: 75
Cloud-people: 14, 57, 77
Clowns: 74, 131, 194ff.; and incest, 200; anal and oral aspects, 204; dance directors, 206; and war, 207
Comanches: xvi, 212
Continence: 54, 158, 191, 201
Corn: clan, 112; dance, 146
Corn Maidens: 145–48, 150, 166
Corn-Mother: 121
Corn (Thunder) Mountain: 113, 158, 185, 193
Cosmos, cyclical: 3–4
Cotton mask, on dead: 53
Council of the Gods: 58, 79, 199
Creation: stories, 63; by song, 92; pattern, 93–94
Creators: 14, 81ff.
Cremation: 56f.
Crook of life: 126, 130, 156
Crutsi (Keresan ordinary people): 257
Curing: 153, 177
Cuwimi Kai (Santa Ana turquoise house): 184

Dawn Lake: 178
Day of Purification: 41, 43

Dead: 64, 67, 154, 257; return, 15; "cooked," 50; draw living, 51; fear of, 52; go to Grand Canyon, 58; bear burdens, 60; and crops, 74–75; as clouds, 76; and snakes, 225

Dead towns, in New Mexico and Arizona: 65

Demeter: 19, 84, 116, 121

Devil: 4, 10, 47, 258

Dionysos: 146, 204, 222, 257

Directions: chiefs of, 78, 166; Muingwu's address to, 130; system of, 169ff.; source of power, 176–77

Dual year: 165

Eagle: 106; youth, 67ff.

Earth: circular, 89; scum on water, 89; soft and spongy, 104; Mother, 123, 131, 176

Effigy: bundle represents Masau'u, 33; of Horned Water Serpent, 246, 248

El Moro, New Mexico: 182

Emergence: 5, 44, 103ff.; at Cochití, 106; Hopi, 107; and gestation, 109

Eototo (Masau'u): 19

Farfan, Capt. Marcos: 186

Fasts: 158

Feathers, used to invoke gods and dead: 76

Fetishes: 123, 183, 227, 255; Corn-Mother, 51; curing, 124; animal, 176; snake, 223

Fire: and sun, 4, 21; courage puts out, 9; Masau'u taught use of, 15; and life, 21; Masau'u afraid of, 23; drill, 21, 88; pit, 72

Firebrand-youth: *see* Shulawitsi

Flint shaman: 106

Flood: 108ff., 193, 245; flash at Sía, 109; punishment and sacrifice, 110

Flute ceremony: 83, 126

Gainat (Keresan special people): 257

Galaxy fraternity (curing society): 203

Game animals: 189, 255

Gatoya (Hopi snake monster): 241

Germinator: 16, 19, 125, 131; *see also* Alosaka and Muingwu

Grand Canyon, Arizona: 83, 187, 240

Great Fire fraternity: 160, 178

Great Spirit: 36

Greek: religion, ix, 25; earth, 89

Hades: 4, 19, 58

Hahai Wuhti (Hopi mother of kachinas and Water Serpent): 246

Halona (Zuñi ant place): 95, 115

Hard Beings Woman: *see* Huruing Wuhti

Hawikuh (early Zuñi town): 210, 243

Hawk priest: 154

Heart: of cactus, 120; of Yellow Woman, 189

Herma: representing Hermes, 10; representing Masau'u, 26–27

Hermequaftewa, Andrew: on Spider Woman, 18; on Purification Day, 46; on Hopi land, 180

Hermes: 21, 25f., 31

Hopis: travel, 25; isolation, 38; winter, 129; Sun Trail, 231; traders, 268

Hopi Hearings: 37, 97, 138

Horned Water Serpent: 101, 110f., 221ff., 244ff.; causes flood, 109; and ghost, 110; god of waters, 225, 234; and Coyote, 245

House of the Dead: 54, 71

Huruing Wuhti: 37, 82ff., 132, 240ff.; as spider, 91; double goddess, 92; sea goddess, 93

Hu'waka (Serpent of the Heavens): 239

Ianyi (Keresan "mana," power, or blessing): 124, 252, 284

Iarriko (corn-ear fetish, represents Iyatiku): 55, 123, 258

Initiation: 248

Isleta: and Traditionalists, 90; dual year, 165

Itiwana (Zuñi center): 112, 146, 169

Itiwonna (corn-ripe): 164

Iyatiku (Keresan Corn-Mother): 55, 94, 105, 116, 121ff., 123, 254; judges her children, 58; brings up sun, 140; and Koshari, 144

Jémez: River, 109; clowns, 207; Mountains, 252

Kachina(s): 49; rain bringers, 65; real, 77; attack Acoma, 78; from Hopi word "*kachi*," "spirit father," 79; at Laguna, 105; dolls, 128; masks, 175; home in San Francisco Mountains, 181; not pantheon-oriented at Hopi, 268; not recent, 270; few pan-Pueblo, 272; cult, 289

Kachina names: Masau'u, 23–24; Salimobia, 62, 160–61, 248: blue, guardian spirit, 74; Bloody Hand Print, 77–78; Hototo, 130; Ne'paiyetemu (Newekwe Youth), 146; Ahul, 150–51; Ahulani, 150–51; Tawa (Sun), 151; Chakwena (Ku'yapalitsa), 188; Bitsitsi (associated with Paiyatemu), 203; Ahe'a (nurse of Water Serpent), 249

Katchongva, Dan: Hopi Traditionalist leader, 39; leader of Sun clan, 138; priest formulator, 271

Keres: towns, xix, of Río Grande, 38; priests attend dead, 52; dead go north, 57; deities, 116; year, 161

Keresan sisters, mothers of mankind: 90, 94, 104, 116, 118ff., 142

Kiaklo (Zuñi myth-bearing supernatural): 61; visits Lake of the Dead, 63; seduces sister, 199

Kivas (ceremonial chambers): secret rites in, 16; of gods; or Huruing Wuhti, 83

Knife-Wing: 178, 258

Kohkang Wuhti (Spider Grandmother): 95ff.

Ko'ko (*Kaka*—Zuñi gods and kachinas): 61, 64, 78, 161

Kolowisi (Zuñi Water Serpent): 113, 245, 247–49

Kopishtaiya (Keresan collectivity of spirits): 85, 144, 153

Kosharis (Keresan clowns): 143, 194

Ko'thluwala'wa (Zuñi lake, abode of the dead): 58, 148, 161

Koyemshis (Zuñi clowns): 198

Ku'yapalitsa (Zuñi virgin huntress, goddess of game): 188

Kwan men (Agaves): 59, 79, 101; One Horn Society, 14; conduct dead, 14; and tribal initiation, 15; bell-ringers, 16; visit graveyard, 17; kindle fires, 21; and path to sun, 36–37; and Talayesva, 72

Lady of the Eastern Ocean: 92

Laguna: 119

Lake of the Dead (Listening Spring): 58, 63

Land of Spirits: 64

Life Pattern of Hopis: 41, 97

Lightning: 101f., 167; and fertility, 33, 235–36; and Alosaka, 127; stone, 183; War Twins make canyons with, 216; and snakes, 223; as a water snake, 235

Lion: 176, 221

Little Colorado River: 43, 58, 243

Lomavaya, Lawrence: 47

Lunations: 161

Magical power: 69–70, 210

Manzano Mountains, New Mexico: 187

Masau'u (Skeleton Man): 94, 121, 128, 222, 260, 288; spelling, xix; god of boundaries, 4; god of war, 4, 35, 219; trickster, 4, 29ff.; god of death, 8, 12; and Hermes, 14–15, 27; *Wuya* of Kwan chief, 15; Great Spirit, 16; god of fire, 17, 21; god of fertility, 18; distinguished from Germinator, 20; at planting and harvest, 22; god of travelers, 25; not Navaho, 28; and Hopi lands, 29; wears clothes backward, 61; and Muingwu, 131

Masewa (Keresan War Twin): 106, 206, 214

Maski (graveyard, Masau'u's kiva): 12

Masks, and gods: 257

Matcito (first Hopi chief): 42

Matrilineal principle: 39, 133

Matsailema (Zuñi younger War Twin): 214

Ma'we (Zuñi Salt Woman): 185f.

Mayans: 184

Mesa Verde, Colorado: xiv, 183, 187

Migrations: 115

Mi'li (Zuñi fetish): 123

Miochin (spirit of Summer): 168

Mogollon: culture, xiv; Baldy, 181

Molawia ceremony (return of Corn Maidens): 145f

Monongye, David: 16

Monotheism: 270, 272

Montezuma, return of: 45

Moon: 90, 129, 136, 162; sent to the Sun, 84; Mother, 85; and calendar, 161; "dangerous," 162; and Yellow Woman, 188–89

Morityema (spirit of Spring): 175

Morning Star: 102, 136, 155, 159

Motsni (a shrike, helps at emergence): 6, 177

Mountain of Turquoises: 66, 69

Mount Chalchihuitl, New Mexico: 184f.

Mount Taylor, New Mexico: 181, 189

Muingwu, or Germinator: 93–94, 125ff., 173, 179; earth god, 8; created by Hard Beings Woman, 82; patron of Two Horns, 101; figurine, 126; god of Nadir, 128; impersonator, 130; see also Alosaka

Muski (underground): 12

Mustard clan: 150

Mythologic age: 8

Naotsete (Keresan sister): 90, 116

Nature, power of: 261

Navahos: xvi, 25, 66, 119, 212

Netted gourd: 127, 131

Newekwe (Galaxy fraternity of nondivine clowns): 202

Newekwe Youth (patron of Zuñi clown society): 146f.

New Fire: 157f., 162

Niman ceremony (farewell to kachinas): 128

North Priest: 227

Obscenity: 196

O'mauuh (Hopi cloud): 79

One Horn men: see Kwan men

Öng Wuhti (Hopi Salt Woman): 190

Oraibi: near point of emergence, 7; lands, 27; domain, 43; good dead in, 59

Oshatsh (Keresan sun): 78

Oyoyewi (Keresan younger War Twin): 214

Paiyatemu (Sun Youth): 142ff.; stone image of, 55; masks of, 78; hidden, 140; patron of clown society, 143, 194; as a group, 144; his evil sisters, 147–48; order of, 158; god of dew, 193; sent away, 197; a father of War Twins, 215

Palatkwapi (ancient Hopi town): 110

Palulukonti (Hopi fertility ceremony): 245

Pamurti rite: 150

Pantheon, at Zuñi: 78–79

Parrot clan: 190

Patki clan: 100, 112

Pautiwa (chief of Council of the Gods): 62, 148–50, 158, 249; belongs to Sun clan, 149; coming of, 160

Pecos: and Comanches, 211; destruction of, 232

Pekwin (Zuñi Sun priest): 114, 146, 157, 160

Perea, Fray Estevan de: 228

Phallic: trickster, 197; Hopi clowns, 201

Pilakho (wood from Shipapu): 21

Pinnanne (Zuñi breath or life): 254

Piros: xvii, 211

Planting stick: 54

Polytheism: 278

Powaka (witch): 49

Powamu ceremony: 126, 129–31

Prayer: feathers, 6, 23; sticks, 173

Pueblo(s): land grants and population, xvii; linguistic units, xix; lived underground, 4–5; cosmos, 79; pantheon, 137; warcraft, 209ff.; non-totemic, 233, 269; non-pantheistic, 251

Pueblo Bonito: 183, 226; not a temple, xi; population, xv; and herma, 26; and crooks, 127

Pueblo Revolt: xvi, 13, 120, 184, 211f.

Purification: 54, 153

Purifier: 44

Purtuwishta (lightning people): 240

Queranna (Keresan clown society): 144, 205

Quetzalcoátl: 244

Rabbits: 22, 24, 153, 254

Radin, Paul: 264ff.

Rattlesnake: and women, 233; and curing, 243

Resurrection: 147

Rite, planting: 33

Road: 139; to Maski, 15; closed for return of dead, 16; of meal, 55

Running, good for crops: 22

Sacred: lakes, 59; terrace, 180

Sacrifice: of chief's children, 111; human, 113

Salimobias (spirit warriors of the six directions): 62, 160–61, 248

Salt Old Woman: 146, 185, 214, 252

Sand Altar Woman, Tuwa'boñtumsi: 100; sister of Germinator, 19; goddess of crops, 82; mother of mankind, 94; lost earth-mother?, 133

San Felipe: 252

Santa Ana Tamaya): 206; war chief, 106; cardinal points of, 172; spruce-gathering, 252

Santa Fé, New Mexico: 183, 212

Santo Domingo: dance, xi; images with dead, 55; kachinas, 78; land grant, 184; robbery, 185

Scalp dance: 219

Scott, Simon: 37

Seed: of all kinds, 104; gatherers, 122

Shakak (spirit of Winter): 166–68, 222

Shalako (Zuñi ceremony): xviii, 194

Shipapu: 21, 91, 103, 105; place of emergence, 7; dead go to, 51; under lake, 58; at Laguna, 109; plank drum represents, 128

Shiwannas (Keresan dead as rain-makers): 57

Shi'wanni: Zuñi Rain priest, 63, 85; creator of stars, 94

Shi'wano'kia: Zuñi priestess of fecundity, 85; creator of Earth Mother, 94

Shongopovi, folk tales from: 27

Sho'tokunungwa (Hopi lightning, star and war god): 98ff., 219

Shro-tu-na-ko (memory or instinct, sister of Thinking Woman): 91

Shrui'sthia (Keresan spirit of Fall): 175

Shulawitsi (firebrand-youth): 25, 150

Sía: size, xv; creation story, 106; mythology, 121

Sichomo (Flower Mound, in underworld): 128, 173

Sikyatki (Hopi ruin): 19, 226

Si'wulutsiwa (Zuñi father of clowns): 199

Smoke: ritual, 75; planting, 155

Snake(s): clan, 25; on stone tablet, 42; legend, 83; Youth, 83; curer, 223, 243; dances, 224, 236; and Greek gods, 224; images, 226; jar, 227; and underworld, 229; guardian spirit, 231; medicine, 237; Virgin, 238; Sía society, 239; myth, 240ff.; Maiden, 241

Sorcery: 279

Soyal ceremony (Hopi winter solstice): 42, 154–56

Soyohims (short Hopi ceremonies): 151

Spaniards: 96, 212

Spider Grandmother: 35, 95ff., 132, 240, 260; keeper of the fire, 18; and Thinking Woman, 91; mother of all, 132; and War Twins, 213

Spruce: 251

Stone(s): Hopi boundary, 26–27, 253; sacred tablet, 40, 42–43; addressed, 177; lion, 237; power of, 253

Strife, origin of: 96

Sun: 90, 136ff.; clan, 40, 160; destroys world, 41; father, 51, 85, 87; Trail, 58; and Hard Beings Woman, 83, 93; flowers, 108; always existed at Zuñi, 137; infant presented to, 139; made by Uretsete, 140; anthropomorphic at Sía, 141; god of seasons, 144, 152, 162; House, 153; priest, 155; and war, 161; sends game, 222

Supernatural power: 256

Supreme Being: 100

Sus'sistinako (Sía Thinking Woman): 82, 89ff., 104; *see also* Thinking Woman

Taboos: 29, 232

T'aiowa (Hopi counterpart of Paiyatemu): 142

Talaschomo (hill where Hard Beings Woman lived): 82

Talayesva, Don: carries offering to Masau'u, 8–9; buries uncle, 52–53; dream of land of dead, 70ff.; and Spider Grandmother, 98; and snake, 230

Taos, New Mexico: 173

Tawaki (Sun house): 156

Thinking Woman, Sus'sistinako: 82, 116, 134, 260; sex of, 90; reason personified, 90–91; sits on Iyatiku's right shoulder, 91; and monotheism, 271

THli'akwa (Turquoise Man): 185–86

Thunder Mountain: *see* Corn Mountain

Tih'kuyi (mother of game): 133

Tiponi: 75, 126; Hopi fetish of office, 41; mother of people, 131

Ti'yo (Snake Youth): 240

Tokonaka (may be Masau'u): 101

To'mapa (shrine on west side of Corn Mountain): 158

Tompiro: 211

Totemism: 178

Tower, in underworld: 109

Traditionalists: 35, 38, 90, 97

Trickster: 196ff.; culture hero, 34; scatters fruit, 198

Tsi'ty'icots'a (Keresan Salt Woman): 190

Turquoise: 183ff.; mixed with corn meal, 55; and Hard Beings Woman, 83; Hill, 184; Mountain, 185, 192

Tuwa'boñtumsi: *see* Sand Altar Woman

Twin Mountain: 185, 193

Two Horn Society: 16, 19

Underworld: 49ff.; infernal, 9; home of Iyatiku, 58; two forms, 59, 104; Hopi, 70; Laguna, 105; unpleasant, 107; Zuñi, 108 and sky, 127

Universe: 88
Utsete: *see* Keresan sisters
U'wannami (rain-makers): 57

Village Chief, of Hopis: 219
Virgin of the earth: 125

Wafer bread: 54
Walpi: ceremony for return of the dead, 16; Masau'u closes spring, 25
War chiefs: 102, 142
War Twins: 97, 103, 142, 181, 185, 209ff., 214; at Oraibi, 36; use lightning, 101; Oyoyewa, 106; Pookong, Hopi (elder), 154, 214; rain-makers, 158; hunting, 209; and Sun, 209, 217f.; children of Sun and Yellow Woman, 213; Balonga, Hopi (younger), 214; adventures, 215ff.; as War Captains, 219
We'nima (Zuñi name for lake): 63
Wenimats (home of the kachinas): 57, 59
Whirlwind Old Man: 107
White House: 57, 115, 166
Wimi: (Hopi ways): 38
Winter solstice: 151ff.; Acoma, 152–54; Zuñi, 156–61
Witches: 226, 258–59; Two-Hearts, 40, 70; Powaka, 49
Woodpecker Boy: 106
Wren: 95
Wuwuchim ceremony: 15, 164
Wuya (clan ancient): 15

Yahoya (youth created by Hard Beings Woman): 93
Yaya (mother): 124
Yellow Woman, Kochinako: 78, 166, 188–89
Yepnane (Zuñi substance of flesh): 87

Zeus: 81, 128
Zuñi(s): scientific farming, 38; view of unborn, 50; River, 58; pair of creators, 94; water-strider, 95; had tails, 107; modern, 170; Salt Lake, 185ff.

of which *Pueblo Gods and Myths* is the seventy-first volume, was inaugurated in 1932 by the University of Oklahoma Press, and has as its purpose the reconstruction of American Indian civilization by presenting aboriginal, historical, and contemporary Indian life. The following list is complete as of the date of publication of this volume:

1. Alfred Barnaby Thomas. *Forgotten Frontiers:* A Study of the Spanish Indian Policy of Don Juan Bautista de Anza, Governor of New Mexico, 1777–1787. Out of print.
2. Grant Foreman. *Indian Removal:* The Emigration of the Five Civilized Tribes of Indians.
3. John Joseph Mathews. *Wah'Kon-Tah:* The Osage and the White Man's Road. Out of print.
4. Grant Foreman. *Advancing the Frontier, 1830–1860.* Out of print.
5. John Homer Seger. *Early Days among the Cheyenne and Arapahoe Indians.* Edited by Stanley Vestal.
6. Angie Debo. *The Rise and Fall of the Choctaw Republic.*
7. Stanley Vestal (ed.). *New Sources of Indian History, 1850–1891.* Out of print.
8. Grant Foreman. *The Five Civilized Tribes.* Out of print.
9. Alfred Barnaby Thomas. *After Coronado:* Spanish Exploration Northeast of New Mexico, 1696–1727. Out of print.
10. Frank G. Speck. *Naskapi:* The Savage Hunters of the Labrador Peninsula. Out of print.
11. Elaine Goodale Eastman. *Pratt:* The Red Man's Moses. Out of print.
12. Althea Bass. *Cherokee Messenger:* A Life of Samuel Austin Worcester. Out of print.
13. Thomas Wildcat Alford. *Civilization.* As told to Florence Drake. Out of print.
14. Grant Foreman. *Indians and Pioneers:* The Story of the American Southwest before 1830. Out of print.
15. George E. Hyde. *Red Cloud's Folk:* A History of the Oglala Sioux Indians.
16. Grant Foreman. *Sequoyah.*
17. Morris L. Wardell. *A Political History of the Cherokee Nation, 1838–1907.* Out of print.
18. John Walton Caughey. *McGillivray of the Creeks.*

19. Edward Everett Dale and Gaston Litton. *Cherokee Cavaliers:* Forty Years of Cherokee History as Told in the Correspondence of the Ridge-Watie-Boudinot Family. Out of print.
20. Ralph Henry Gabriel. *Elias Boudinot, Cherokee, and His America.*
21. Karl N. Llewellyn and E. Adamson Hoebel. *The Cheyenne Way:* Conflicts and Case Law in Primitive Jurisprudence.
22. Angie Debo. *The Road to Disappearance.* Out of print.
23. Oliver La Farge and others. *The Changing Indian.* Out of print.
24. Carolyn Thomas Foreman. *Indians Abroad.* Out of print.
25. John Adair. *The Navajo and Pueblo Silversmiths.*
26. Alice Marriott. *The Ten Grandmothers.*
27. Alice Marriott. *María:* The Potter of San Ildefonso.
28. Edward Everett Dale. *The Indians of the Southwest:* A Century of Development under the United States. Out of print.
29. Adrián Recinos. *Popol Vuh:* The Sacred Book of the Ancient Quiché Maya. English version by Delia Goetz and Sylvanus G. Morley from the translation of Adrián Recinos.
30. Walter Collins O'Kane. *Sun in the Sky.*
31. Stanley A. Stubbs. *Bird's-Eye View of the Pueblos.*
32. Katharine C. Turner. *Red Men Calling on the Great White Father.*
33. Muriel H. Wright. *A Guide to the Indian Tribes of Oklahoma.*
34. Ernest Wallace and E. Adamson Hoebel. *The Comanches:* Lords of the South Plains.
35. Walter Collins O'Kane. *The Hopis:* Portrait of a Desert People. Out of print.
36. Joseph Epes Brown. *The Sacred Pipe:* Black Elk's Account of the Seven Rites of the Oglala Sioux. Out of print.
37. Adrián Recinos and Delia Goetz. *The Annals of the Cakchiquels.* Translated from the Cakchiquel Maya, with *Title of the Lords of Totonicapán,* translated from the Quiché text into Spanish by Dionisio José Chonay, English version by Delia Goetz.
38. R. S. Cotterill. *The Southern Indians:* The Story of the Civilized Tribes before Removal.
39. J. Eric S. Thompson. *The Rise and Fall of Maya Civilization.*
40. Robert Emmitt. *The Last War Trail:* The Utes and the Settlement of Colorado.
41. Frank Gilbert Roe. *The Indian and the Horse.*
42. Francis Haines. *The Nez Percés:* Tribesmen of the Columbia Plateau. Out of print.

43. Ruth M. Underhill. *The Navajos.*
44. George Bird Grinnell. *The Fighting Cheyennes.*
45. George E. Hyde. *A Sioux Chronicle.*
46. Stanley Vestal. *Sitting Bull:* Champion of the Sioux, A Biography.
47. Edwin C. McReynolds. *The Seminoles.*
48. William T. Hagan. *The Sac and Fox Indians.*
49. John C. Ewers. *The Blackfeet:* Raiders on the Northwestern Plains.
50. Alfonso Caso. *The Aztecs: People of the Sun.* Translated by Lowell Dunham.
51. C. L. Sonnichsen. *The Mescalero Apaches.*
52. Keith A. Murray. *The Modocs and Their War.*
53. Victor W. von Hagen (ed.).*The Incas of Pedro de Cieza de León.* Translated by Harriet de Onis.
54. George E. Hyde. *Indians of the High Plains:* From the Prehistoric Period to the Coming of Europeans.
55. *George Catlin. Episodes from "Life among the Indians" and "Last Rambles."* Edited by Marvin C. Ross.
56. J. Eric S. Thompson. *Maya Hieroglyphic Writing:* An Introduction.
57. George E. Hyde. *Spotted Tail's Folk:* A History of the Brulé Sioux.
58. James Larpenteur Long. *The Assiniboines:* From the Accounts of the Old Ones Told to First Boy (James Larpenteur Long). Edited and with an introduction by Michael Stephen Kennedy.
59. Edwin Thompson Denig. *Five Indian Tribes of the Upper Missouri.* Edited and with an introduction by John C. Ewers.
60. John Joseph Mathews. *The Osages:* Children of the Middle Waters.
61. Mary Elizabeth Young. *Redskins, Ruffleshirts, and Rednecks:* Indian Allotments in Alabama and Mississippi, 1830–1860.
62. J. Eric S. Thompson. *A Catalog of Maya Hieroglyphs.*
63. Mildred P. Mayhall. *The Kiowas.*
64. George E. Hyde. *Indians of the Woodlands:* From Prehistoric Times to 1725.
65. Grace Steele Woodward. *The Cherokees.*
66. Donald J. Berthrong. *The Southern Cheyennes.*
67. Miguel León-Portilla. *Aztec Thought and Culture:* A Study of the Ancient Nahuatl Mind.
68. T. D. Allen. *Navahos Have Five Fingers.*
69. Burr Cartwright Brundage. *Empire of the Inca.*
70. A. M. Gibson. *The Kickapoos:* Lords of the Middle Border.
71. Hamilton A. Tyler. *Pueblo Gods and Myths.*